Reading
WOMEN
Writing

A series edited by Shari Benstock and Celeste Schenck

Reading Gertrude Stein
by Lisa Ruddick

READING
Gertrude Stein

BODY, TEXT, GNOSIS

Lisa Ruddick

Cornell University Press

ITHACA AND LONDON

Copyright © 1990 by Cornell University

All rights reserved. Except for brief quotations in a review, this book, or parts thereof, must not be reproduced in any form without permission in writing from the publisher. For information, address Cornell University Press, 124 Roberts Place, Ithaca, New York 14850.

First published 1990 by Cornell University Press.

International Standard Book Number 0–8014–2364–3
Library of Congress Catalog Card Number 89-46133
Printed in the United States of America
Librarians: Library of Congress cataloging information appears on the last page of the book.

♾ The paper used in this publication meets the minimum requirements of the American National Standard for Permanence of Paper for Printed Library Materials Z39.48–1984.

For Cass

Contents

Foreword

As the editors of *Reading Women Writing*, we are committed to furthering international feminist debate. To that end, we seek books that rigorously explore how differences of class, race, ethnic background, nationality, religious preference, and sexual choice inform women's writing. Books sensitive to the ways women's writings are classified, evaluated, read, and taught are central to the series. Of particular interest to us are feminist criticism of non-canonical texts (including film, popular culture, and new and as yet unnamed genres); confrontations of first-world theory with beyond-the-first-world texts; and books on colonial and postcolonial writing that generate their own theoretical positions. Dedicated primarily although not exclusively to the examination of literature by women, *Reading Women Writing* highlights differing, even contradictory, theoretical positions on texts read in cultural context.

Lisa Ruddick's *Reading Gertrude Stein: Body, Text, Gnosis*, the third volume in the series, examines the cultural and psychosocial contexts of Stein's pre–World War I writing—"Melanctha," *The Making of Americans, G.M.P.*, and *Tender Buttons*. Ruddick defines these works as "serial acts of self-definition" in which Stein redefined her relation to intellectual precursors and discovered within herself unconscious processes through which to channel her most radical linguistic experiments. *Reading Gertrude Stein* revises our notion of Stein's relation to her former teacher William James, a man who represented nineteenth-century beliefs in progress, science, and "character"; it also introduces the heretofore unrecognized relation of Stein's writing to Freud's work. Stein did not come to Freud through his writings or through self-analysis. Instead, she discovered the psychic principles he theorized through her own stylistic experiments: that is, she came to Freud through writing. Recognizing the violence of historically determined sexual difference at the level of feeling, Stein separated herself, artistically and emotionally, from two "fathers"—William James, her intellectual precursor, and Daniel Stein, the family patriarch.

In *The Making of Americans* Stein contests the hierarchy of social arrangements under patriarchy. In the stylistic and thematic work of "repetition" in this text, Stein reveals (and emotionally conquers) the violence inherent in the gender categories of "male" and "female." The technique of repetition, the first and most artistically powerful of Stein's discoveries, leads her away from nineteenth-century family structures and cultural values toward modernism. She moves away from William James toward Sigmund Freud, whose work she begins to revise. Stein breaks out of the categories to which James's thought had assigned her and "denaturalizes" Freudian gender arrangements through experimental language. This first, radical shift in Stein's thought and writing practice gives birth to another: her work moves in "feminist" directions, evident in the "opaque style" of *G.M.P.* and *Tender Buttons,* which, Ruddick notes, "release[s] a new female identification." In *G.M.P.,* she moves "south to the mother," staging a subversive attack on the word-world of patriarchy, exploding its false forms and discovering a "mother tongue" that gives voice to feelings of joy and power. Her "emotional experiment," the rejection of heterosexuality, and her "artistic experiment," the release from genre categories, are wedded to each other.

Tender Buttons, arguably Stein's most successful experimental text, follows from these discoveries. Beyond the feminist and linguistic orientations of this text, Ruddick points to a third element—gnosticism. Stein radically revises the Bible, "unlocking within its patriarchal symbols a suppressed, woman-affirming story." She defines herself *against* Western ontotheology, but weaves together strands of its history to produce her own gnostic text. *Tender Buttons* develops two antithetical impulses, according to Ruddick: the polysemous play of language and the cryptic code of a "buried, alternative truth."

Reading Gertrude Stein resituates Stein in relation to her intellectual precursors, to the history of psychoanalysis and theories of psychosexuality, and to her modernist contemporaries. The question of Stein's modernism becomes in Ruddick's text the question of Stein's feminism: "Onto the drama of Stein's self-situation within twentieth-century thought is grafted another drama, that of the private emotional crises that her intellectual evolution simultaneously reflected and prompted." She was moved toward a gnostic feminism that unveiled the psychosexual violence of social organization, especially its history of violation, and engendered forms of "post-sacrificial" thought, denaturalizing patriarchal dualisms. Ruddick discovers a central paradox of Stein's writing: its language of disorientation and disruption orients the reader ethically and morally according to feminist-modernist principles.

S.B.
C.S.

Acknowledgments

I am grateful to the American Council of Learned Societies and to Harvard University for support in the research and writing of this book. A leave of absence from the University of Chicago in 1986–87 provided eighteen uninterrupted months for writing, and a term at the Mary Ingraham Bunting Institute in 1987 gave me the opportunity to present part of the manuscript to and exchange ideas with a group of scholars within and beyond my field, from whom I learned a great deal.

An earlier version of the first section of Chapter 1 appeared in *Modern Fiction Studies* 28 (1982–83), copyright © 1983 by the Purdue Research Foundation, West Lafayette, Indiana 47907. Permission has been granted by the Department of English and American Language and Literature, Harvard University, to reprint in Chapter 1 material that appeared in *Modernism Reconsidered*, Harvard English Studies 6 (Cambridge, Mass.: Harvard University Press, 1983). Material in Chapter 3 appeared earlier in *Critical Essays on Gertrude Stein*, edited by Michael J. Hoffman (Boston: G. K. Hall, 1986). For permission to quote from Gertrude Stein's notebooks I am grateful to the Estate of Gertrude Stein and to the Yale Collection of American Literature, Beinecke Library, Yale University.

Many friends and colleagues have had an influence on the shape and scope of this book, and I am happy to record my appreciation here. For comments on individual chapters I thank Elizabeth Abel, Lauren Berlant, Wayne Booth, Paul Goldstein, Wendy Griswold, Lorraine Helms, Robert Kiely, Cristanne Miller, Janel Mueller,

Michael Murrin, Cornelia Nixon, Joel Porte, Bruce Redford, Brenda Silver, Janet Silver, Jeffrey Stern, Catharine Stimpson, and Robert von Hallberg. Shari Benstock's reading of a draft of the book furnished invaluable suggestions. I am grateful to Celeste Schenck for her comments on a paper that would become Chapter 4 and, most important, for her heartening confidence in this project from an early stage. Marianne DeKoven generously shared her expertise on Stein; her searching chapter-by-chapter commentary spared me some mistakes and provided the subtle prompting I needed to clarify and broaden the theoretical dimensions of my argument. Beth Ash read versions of two chapters and helped me to think my way toward the book on sacrifice that I hope will evolve from this one. I thank Elizabeth Helsinger for her painstaking and illuminating comments on several chapters and for conversations that time and again helped me to piece together the larger meanings of my interpretations of Stein's texts.

My parents, Dorothy Ruddick and Bruce Ruddick, and my sisters, Abby Ruddick and Margie Ruddick, read parts of the book in draft; I am grateful for their responses (expert in various ways) and for their unstinting support. I am also grateful to Dr. Brenda Solomon for assistance and encouragement with the psychoanalytic materials. For conversations that enlightened and cheered me I thank Laurie Wohl. My graduate students at the University of Chicago were wonderful readers of Stein; throughout, the book benefits from their insights, large and small. I also thank Marianne Eismann for research assistance and for indispensable help, with Solveig Robinson, in preparing the final manuscript.

Although my subject in the pages that follow is a master of play, the long work of writing the book sometimes threatened to turn into a leaden affair. I was fortunate to have four friends whose commitment to the idea of this project kept my enthusiasm and confidence alive. Ronald Thomas read versions of each chapter and gave me suggestions that greatly improved the manuscript; more than that, his steady friendship as we both toiled over our evolving books made the labor of writing less lonely. William Veeder, who supported the project from its earliest, sketchiest stages, read the whole manuscript (more than once) with a unique combination of analytic rigor and intellectual gusto; many of his brilliant hunches found their way into my argument, sometimes changing the look of an entire chapter. I thank Robert Ferguson for his detailed and imaginative readings of draft after draft, for his revelatory yet practical ideas about how the book as a whole might be shaped, and for something he contributed to my work that is harder to define: he discerned a stronger voice behind the voice in which I was writing the book, and he prodded me (no easy task) to bring it forward. The completed manuscript bears the marks of his encouragement everywhere.

Finally, no one has done more to sustain my faith in this book than my husband, Cass Sunstein. I vividly remember the day thirteen years ago when he typed my undergraduate thesis as I struggled to write the final pages; it seemed to me a miraculous act of friendship at the time, but neither of us had any way of knowing then what genuine miracles of loving support the coming years would show him capable of. He commented on every draft of this book, helping me to bring into relief whatever seemed unusual or especially innovative in my argument; at the same time, he buoyed me with his conviction that there was a difference between the book that often seemed an intolerably taxing member of our household and the other book, composed of words that meant something to both of us. His spiritual and intellectual companionship turned a project that would otherwise have been a mere obsession for me into a source of shared pleasure and discovery.

LISA RUDDICK

Chicago, Illinois

Reading Gertrude Stein

Introduction

This book is about the self-creation of Gertrude Stein. Stein produced much of her finest writing before the First World War; her works from *Three Lives* to *Tender Buttons* have a creative momentum that her later works, for all their experimental interest, rarely achieve. In this book, I identify the sources of that momentum. The texts to which I attend—"Melanctha," *The Making of Americans, G.M.P.*, and *Tender Buttons*—were serial acts of self-definition.

Stein never situated herself within the Anglo-American literary tradition, as most other modernists of her stature did. But her works before World War I quietly struggle with a series of intellectual precursors. The precursors changed as Stein's thinking and her artistic self-conception became increasingly radical. Initially, she defined herself against William James, an important early influence who looms over her first distinguished fiction as an inspiration and as a burden. "Melanctha," the subject of Chapter 1, is the work in which Stein borrowed most closely from James but also began to express her restlessness with him. By the time of *The Making of Americans*, she waged war on James, openly in her notebooks and covertly in the novel, as I show in Chapter 2.

James had come to represent to her everything she now questioned about the nineteenth century, and as she went about "killing the nineteenth century" through a modernist literary practice, she pulverized the ideals that had once drawn her to James but now repelled her—specifically, the nineteenth-century faith in progress, in science, and in "character." In *The Making of Americans*, what explodes nineteenth-century beliefs and values is what Stein calls "repetition," a force within herself and her prose that she identifies with unconscious process. As she reflected on this aspect of her work, her thinking swerved away from James and toward Freud, whose idea of the unconscious confirmed the value of what was happening in her artistic practice. A claim of Chapter 2—that Freud, to whose ideas Stein was exposed through her brother Leo, is a presence in the background of *The Making of Americans*—may come as a surprise, since Stein is generally thought not to have been interested in psychoanalysis. But in *The Making of Americans*, she borrows from Freud a set of concepts involving conscious and unconscious processes. Her turn from James to modernism and "repetition" has the quality of a turn from James to Freud.

Chapter 3 is about the texts of 1911–1912, in which Stein first used the hermetic style brought to fruition in *Tender Buttons*: "Eat ting, eating a grand old man said roof and never never re soluble burst."[1] Something happened in her work the moment she developed this style: her thinking moved in a feminist direction (although I use the word *feminist* with qualifications). In fact, the new style made the shift to feminist themes possible. Throughout her career, Stein's stylistic experimentation was not so much the vehi-cle for new ideas as the thing that made new ideas thinkable for her. She had seen from her own artistic evolution as she worked on *The Making of Americans* how insufficient William James's theories were becoming for her; and now, when she developed the opaque style, that style itself helped to release a new female identification.

Although at this juncture Stein did not consciously define herself against a precursor, her evolving feminism distanced her from Freud. The very gender relations that Freud explains but simultaneously naturalizes, Stein now denaturalizes, showing how the categories "male" and "female" are violently made. Now, Stein battles not just the nineteenth century but, more broadly, the social arrangements that fall under the term "patriarchy." She is not only

---

[1]Gertrude Stein, *Tender Buttons* (New York: Claire Marie, 1914), p. 56, hereafter cited in the text, abbreviated *TB*. I use this rather than the more widely available reprinting of *Tender Buttons* in the *Selected Writings of Gertrude Stein*, ed. Carl Van Vechten (New York: Random House, 1945), because the latter contains numerous typographical errors.

a modernist but also a "spy" in the alien territory of male dominance.[2] At the same time, she voices new feelings of joy and
power, for to see patriarchy as an imposition rather than as the
natural state of things is to begin to define a world beyond it. Stein
thinks of herself as slipping through a crack in patriarchy, "mov-
[ing] South" to find a zone within which the "fathers are dead."[3]

Finally, as an extension of her feminist thinking, Stein develops
in this phase a set of sophisticated ideas about the play of drive in
language. She thinks of herself as uncovering a mother tongue; in
uncanny anticipation of the ideas of Hélène Cixous, Luce Irigaray,
and particularly Julia Kristeva, she comes to see woman or mother
as an axis within language.

Out of this period of intense, subversive thinking came *Tender
Buttons*, Stein's most successful experimental text and indeed the
most exciting work of her career, whose explosiveness has not
been recognized despite a great deal of critical attention. What I
identify in *Tender Buttons*, in addition to the feminist and linguistic
orientation it shares with the preceding texts, is gnosticism. This
work, which has been treated for the most part as stylistically
important but resistant to sustained interpretation, is far more intellectually cohesive than has been supposed. In the midst of its
linguistic play lies a series of substantive thoughts that point in the
direction of a gnostic feminism. Now Stein's precursor text is the
Bible: she contests and corrects that text, unlocking within its patriarchal symbols a suppressed, woman-affirming story. In so
doing, she defines herself artistically against Western ontotheology
in a way that has parallels in certain alternative strands of historical
Christianity itself, notably in the gnosticism of the early Christian
era and in medieval mysticism. Yet Stein's gnostic vision has no
clear source; it is her own brilliant creation, the expression of a
spirituality that had been lurking deep beneath the surface of her
earlier works.

With each chapter of this book, the sources of Stein's creativity
become more mysterious. In the first chapter, the stamp of William
James on "Melanctha" will be quite evident. With *The Making of*

[2]"I spy" (*TB* 52).
[3]Gertrude Stein, *G.M.P.*, in *Matisse Picasso and Gertrude Stein with Two Shorter
Stories* (Barton, Vt.: Something Else Press, 1972), pp. 275, 274.

Americans, Freud, by contrast, is a friendly intellectual presence rather than an influence. He did not so much supply Stein with ideas as confirm certain beliefs she was developing independently. In the third phase, as Stein's thinking evolves in a feminist direction, the link to Freud becomes a matter of similarity rather than of further conscious glances in his direction. The feminism Stein now develops, moreover, is uniquely hers. In its simultaneous focus on the family triangle and the operations of language, it resonates with the work of recent feminist and psychoanalytic theorists, rather than with theories of her own day. Finally, the gnosticism that emerges in *Tender Buttons* is Stein's own wild "excreat[ion]" (*TB* 58), something that uncouples her from her contemporaries altogether.

This book tells two stories at once. Onto the drama of Stein's self-situation within twentieth-century thought is grafted another drama, that of the private emotional crises that her intellectual evolution simultaneously reflected and prompted. In the same texts in which Stein was defining herself as a modernist, she was doing a kind of emotional work that intersected in concrete ways with her intellectual struggles.

Her initial attraction to William James, as well as her ultimate rejection of his ideas, was a matter not just of her intellectual but also of her emotional orientation. As James's student in college, Stein was drawn to his theories because they gave her a way of rethinking a conflict she perceived in herself, between sexual desire and sexual self-loathing. James's psychology views the tension between promiscuous and conservative mental habits—specifically, "habits of attention"—as an essential feature of a healthy mental life. Stein easily projected her sexual conflict onto what in James were issues of attention, and thereby found a way to see her conflict itself as creative rather than paralyzing. As we will see, her mapping of sexual issues onto James's psychology helped to produce "Melanctha," where she refigures herself as Jeff Campbell, a character who adjusts creatively both to sexual conflict and to conflicting tendencies in his attention.

But there were parts of Stein that Jeff (and William James) did not express, and she channeled these into her characterization of the heroine, Melanctha. The play in "Melanctha" between Jamesian values and still-inchoate alternatives anticipates the squaring off of

Jamesian "pragmatism" and "repetition" in Stein's next important work, *The Making of Americans*. While writing *The Making of Americans*, she underwent an emotional upheaval. James had given her a set of values that served her for a time, but those values had had the effect of making her safe from her sexuality. As she began to accept and define herself sexually, in the years 1908–1911 (when she was forming a couple with Alice Toklas), she entered into a silent quarrel with James. The Jamesian Stein, as reflected in the characterization of Jeff Campbell, had been in important respects a self-alienated Stein; in fact, the self-ideal that Stein drew from James was ultimately repressive. As she worked on *The Making of Americans* and evolved the idea of repetition, which was her weapon against Jamesian pragmatism, she was also developing a sense of herself as an embodied and erotic person. As I suggest in the course of interpreting *The Making of Americans*, the intellectual and the psychosexual issues were fused in such a way that Stein could not have developed along one of these axes without simultaneously moving along the other.

As she worked free of James's powerful influence, Stein was privately working free of the oppressive influence of her (deceased) father. Daniel Stein—along with his son and surrogate, Leo—occupies the place in Stein's psychosexual struggle that William James occupies in her intellectual struggle. *The Making of Americans* is a work of patricide, along both fronts. As Stein came to unleash repetition—an earthy, sensual energy—in herself, she imagined herself murdering the various "fathers" who seemed to stand in the way of all her sexual and artistic powers: Daniel Stein, Leo Stein, William James, and the bourgeois patriarchs she had left behind in America.

The Making of Americans released at once Stein's erotic feelings, her patricidal rage, and her experimental daring. As her literary style became, in her own view, happily "dirty," repetitive, and therefore anti-Jamesian, she also became able to affirm what she had formerly thought of as the dirty part of herself, her lesbian sexuality. She detached herself from a repressive father and, in the same movement, from bourgeois, classical fiction. *The Making of Americans* begins as a bourgeois narrative but ends as an avant-garde experiment, unique in its time. Its newness both evolved from and made possible Stein's private struggle; by the end of the novel, she had gathered the courage to write off her father. At the same time, paradoxically, she became able for the first time to ground herself in him, accepting from him certain powers that she thought essential for her art.

Hidden behind the battle between father and daughter in *The Making of Americans* is a mother, at whom Stein does not want to look. Although Stein includes a portrait of her mother in *The Making of Americans*, it bespeaks a repression on her own part. Like the other maternal figures in her early fiction, the character she bases on Amelia Stein in *The Making of Americans* is powerless, wan, and negligible. But in the year after finishing that novel, Stein took a new emotional risk and began to ground herself in her mother, recovering an archaic memory of a time in her life when her mother had been a powerful presence. Her maternal (and preoedipal) memories, which were not entirely conscious but which suffused her imagination, released both stylistic play and feminine themes in her work. Thus, while Stein's work in this next period is in some sense woman-affirming, its "feminism" is shot through with unconscious process.

Again a psychosexual issue existed alongside the intellectual and aesthetic issues. As I suggest in Chapter 3, the meaning to Stein of her rich and playful new style is incest: she pictures herself returning to the mother's body through an experimental prose. She is still imaginatively a patricide. But the father whom she fantasizes killing is now the father of the Oedipus complex, who tabooed the mother's body. Stein's relationship with Alice Toklas gave her the security to begin to explore these threatening maternal themes. She allowed her infantile memories of the mother to seep simultaneously into her erotic life with Toklas and into her prose.

With *Tender Buttons*, there was no new emotional shift. Rather, *Tender Buttons* is the work of genius for which the emotional work of the preceding years prepared Stein. Patricide, the paternal inheritance, and mother-love are all present in *Tender Buttons*, but reworked in such a way as to create a text whose ideas are compellingly original. In *Tender Buttons*, Stein takes us into the deep background of the world of the fathers, exploring its machinery but also the alternative possibility of a "left hop," a sinister leap to an anti-patriarchal wisdom (55).

Like Stein's work, my own critical methods have a psycho-analytic and (differently) a gnostic dimension. In recent years, Stein studies have been tremendously enriched by the insights of poststructuralism. The work, particularly, of the French theorists of female *différence*—Kristeva, Cixous, and Irigaray—has seemed specially relevant to a consideration of Stein's various experimental styles. Since the appearance in 1983 of Marianne DeKoven's book *A Different Language*, which draws on this body of theory, Stein's interpreters have had a much more nuanced sense of the nature of Stein's polysemy than was possible in the years before poststructuralism. My own understanding of what Stein was about as an artist owes a great deal to the insights of poststructuralism, as will be apparent in the readings that follow.

Nonetheless, I also depend on a second and quite different theoretical vocabulary, which cuts across the poststructuralist vocabulary in ways that some readers may find strange and even controversial. I am interested not just in Stein's stylistic experimentation but also in her themes, and as I move to her texts in the hermetic style, in the second half of the book, the entire idea of examining "themes" becomes fraught with controversy. There has been a great deal of debate recently as to how to approach Stein's most experimental texts. Some readers have been tempted to try to decode these works, while others, by far the majority, have insisted that any pursuit of continuous meanings amounts to a betrayal of the polyvalence of the texts. DeKoven embodies this latter position, in its poststructuralist articulation: "There is no reason to struggle to interpret or unify either the whole of *Tender Buttons* or any part of it, not only because there is no consistent pattern of meaning, but because we violate the spirit of the work in trying to find one. Like the rest of the [writing in this style], *Tender Buttons* functions anti-patriarchally: as presymbolic *jouissance* and as irreducibly multiple, fragmented, open-ended articulation of lexical meaning."[4]

Quite simply, I believe that a text can be polysemous and still have themes, or "patterns of meaning." There is no question that Stein opens up what is sometimes called *jouissance*, or the play of

[4]Marianne DeKoven, *A Different Language: Gertrude Stein's Experimental Writing* (Madison: University of Wisconsin Press, 1983), p. 76.

the signifier. But the fact that a person's language is mobile and polysemous does not mean that the person cannot at the same time be thinking "about" various things, in ways that can be traced and interpreted. Dreams, for example, are polysemous; a word or other symbol in a dream is likely to mean many things at once. Yet a careful investigation of the dream will reveal its special motifs and preoccupations, its themes. One way of describing how my approach to interpretation differs from those that exalt Stein's indeterminacy is that those approaches have more in common with poststructuralism, and mine (in spite of an overlap) with classical psychoanalysis. My disagreement with the proponents of indeterminacy is not about the fact of Stein's polysemy but simply about the taboo on sustained interpretation that in their view goes along with it.

Thus, I maintain that Stein's *G.M.P.*, though it by no means has a plot, does have discernible contours. About halfway through this work, Stein breaks into her new, hermetic style; I find in this new material what amounts to a series of dream motifs, involving a child's loss, and then a poet's recovery, of the mother's body. The text is indeed full of wordplay that has no particular connection to these motifs, wordplay that is daring and important in itself; my interpretation has no pretension to comprehensiveness, nor in fact do I think that *G.M.P.* is a unified text in the way that, say, "Melanctha" is. Still, I believe that in order to get at some of the implications of the wordplay itself, one must understand its meanings for Stein—meanings that one comes at by piecing together the mother-dream itself, since Stein conceives of her polysemy as reviving the maternal axis of language.

In such a text, Stein is not only dreaming but also thinking—figuring out something, for example, about mothers, fathers, and the operations of language. I identify in *G.M.P.* not only unconscious process but also a series of highly suggestive *ideas* (another prohibited word, from the poststructuralist perspective). Whereas many of Stein's sentences seem to ask to be understood primarily as linguistic experiments, a reader who comes upon the words, "fathers are dead," may well start asking what is going on. Might the death of fathers mean something, in the context of the rest of the work? Is Stein somehow angry at fathers? I believe that it is inevitable, and perfectly valid, to ask such questions (which is not to say that one will always be able to answer them). Stein is engaged not just in an anti-patriarchal linguistic practice but also in anti-patriarchal thinking, and it would be a mistake to lose sight of her ideas in the name of indeterminacy.

In the final chapter of this book, the dialogue within my discourse between "polysemy" and "ideas" becomes extreme, for I think that in *Tender Buttons* Stein quite knowingly stimulates two opposite impulses in the reader at once: first, the impulse to yield to the (here, quite ornate and wonderful) play of her language and, second, the impulse to decipher that language as if it were some sort of a code. The first of these tendencies has been well represented in recent criticism of *Tender Buttons*. My reading, on the other hand, while respecting the polysemous nature of *Tender Buttons*, suggests that this text is at the same time *cryptic*. I hear in Stein's words not just formal play but also, often in the same words, a variety of witty, subversive, and veiled messages. I hope to make *Tender Buttons* audible not just as wordplay but also as speech.

The author of *Tender Buttons* is a gnostic reader, who unlocks within the master text of Western culture a buried, alternative truth. At the same time, she is a gnostic writer, who half hides her own subversive thinking, yet in such a way that readers who devote themselves to her text can learn to follow her. This is not to suggest the presence in *Tender Buttons* of a code, within which each word has a single meaning to be uncovered. Instead, there is a wild mumbling, which each reader will interpret somewhat differently. But Stein does want to provoke her readers to try to reconstruct meanings. At the same time that her polysemy makes monologistic interpretation impossible, her text encourages another sort of interpretation, an act of gnostic speculation in itself.

Thus one can encounter in two different ways, simultaneously, a poem like "Cream," which reads: "In a plank, in a play sole, in a heated red left tree there is shut in specs with salt be where. This makes an eddy. Necessary" (54). "Cream" is a rich poem on the level of experimentation; following this axis, one sees a lexical play with words suggesting wood (plank, tree) and water (salt, eddy), as well as a series of puns ("sole" as fish or as shoe bottom; "be where" as "beware"; "in specs" as "inspects"). A stylistic analysis of the poem would show, among other things, where meanings coalesce into momentary continuities and where they disperse again under the force of soundplay and polyvalence. On the other hand, the same poem is susceptible to interpretation. In Chapter 4 I read the poem in terms of Stein's thinking about a "shut in specs" concealed "in a plank"—a shut-in speculation, or wisdom, concealed "in a plank," or in the theological symbol of the cross. At various points in *Tender Buttons*, Stein as a gnostic reader reinterprets the cross, uncovering its alternative, woman-centered meanings, its hidden wisdom. Hence, "be where," or beware.

Both Stein's stylistic play and her gnostic process are in some sense anti-patriarchal. The stylistic play represents an assault on what Stein herself (like many current theorists) conceives of as phallic language; it frees up the normally suppressed, and somehow feminine, multiplicity of the signifier. Stein's gnosticism, on the other hand, recreates from the Bible a subversive message about and for women, which Stein then passes along in a secretive style that the sympathetic reader can learn to unpack. But these two textual processes, polyvalent play and gnosticism, are virtual opposites. The one unsettles all codes; the other virtually creates a code.

This is a paradox but not a problem. It seems to me that *Finnegans Wake*, for example, also mobilizes the play of the signifier, yet repays the efforts of readers who wish to find paths through the text. Criticism that interprets Joyce's book, even relying on paraphrase, enriches rather than reduces our understanding of the text, so long as there is no claim that the paraphrase captures the single meaning of a word or a passage. *Tender Buttons* sensitizes its readers in two directions at once; with every sentence, we have a choice whether to focus on the play or to listen for meanings, or indeed to oscillate between the two responses. This doubleness is what makes the text provocative. *Tender Buttons* sets the reader in motion in a way that neither a simply playful word-surface nor a straightforward feminist polemic could do.

A final word about my critical vocabulary: as is evident from the foregoing synopsis, this book, along its biographical axis, is concerned with moments of self-discovery and integration in Stein's psychic life. That I think such integration possible implicates me in a concept of the unitary self that sits uneasily with the idea of the decentered subject familiar from poststructuralism. How can it make sense to speak in terms of Stein's evolution as a person, when within her texts, as I simultaneously argue, her experimental practice shatters the unitary "person" through polysemy, mobility, everything that comes under the term *jouissance?*

I think that in order to experiment seriously with a textuality that challenges Western metaphysics, a poet—perhaps particularly a woman poet—must have a cohesive sense of self. One thing the following chapters show is how much courage Stein had to summon for each new literary experiment. Each time she made a fresh assault on the grounded subject, or the grounded logos, she had (paradoxically) to ground herself somewhere. Her experimentation was anti-patriarchal, to be sure, but precisely because she knew as much, she had to work to strengthen and define herself, so that her own father—not the "paternal logos" but the actual, remembered Daniel Stein—would not destructively haunt her. I do not think that this fact in itself would surprise a poststructuralist. But the poststructuralist would call this evolving self a fiction, whereas I think that to treat it thus would be to devalue, and even to misunderstand, Stein's (or any other artist's) personal growth. Thus I attempt, throughout the book, to integrate some of the insights of poststructuralism with what I can only call a humanist understanding of the artistic process.

1

"Melanctha":
The Costs of Mind-Wandering

Gertrude Stein thought of herself as having spent her life escaping from the nineteenth century into which she had been born. This chapter is about the ambivalent beginnings of that escape. With the story "Melanctha," Stein made her first leap into modernist modes of representation; she herself described the story (immodestly but plausibly) as "the first definite step away from the nineteenth century and into the twentieth century in literature."[1] Yet the text looks backward at the same time.

"Melanctha" carries on a private conversation with William James, Stein's college mentor and the central figure in the early drama of her self-definition as a modernist. Along one of its axes, Stein's story reads as a tribute to James's psychological theories— theories that despite their well-known continuities with modernist aesthetics are nineteenth-century in their ethics. Yet at the margins of the story, other material shows Stein already beginning to define herself against James.

The love plot of "Melanctha" borrows heavily from James's psychology; indeed, Stein's debt to James is much deeper than has been supposed. But like all intellectual precursors, James was a burden as well as an inspiration, and as early as "Melanctha" Stein began struggling to free herself from him. James's psychology had appealed to her in college for its heartening vision of moral and

[1]Gertrude Stein, *The Autobiography of Alice B. Toklas* (New York: Harcourt, Brace, 1933), p. 66.

practical success, which helped her to overcome some of her own self-doubts and inhibitions; in "Melanctha," this ideology of success permeates her characterization of Jeff Campbell, who in fact is her idealized self-portrait through the lens of James. But Jeff and his success plot are already too limiting for Stein, and details at the fringes of the story signal alien ethical and artistic commitments that will soon move into the foreground as Stein wages war more consciously on her teacher.

Among the themes in "Melanctha" that stand in tension with the Jamesian plot of mental success is the notion of a wisdom superior to instrumental thinking, a wisdom grounded in the body. Technically, the story violates James's values by indulging in a kind of aimless play; more than that, it transcribes irrational process, forming itself according to a principle of motivated repetition that is continuous not with James's ideas but with the psychoanalytic view of mental life that will soon dislodge James's presence in Stein's work. Finally, "Melanctha" has a latent feminism, which places on trial the individualistic and (in Stein's mind) ultimately male value system absorbed from James, which she still honors in the characterization of Jeff Campbell.

The two lovers in the story, Melanctha and Jeff, are the products of Stein's imaginative self-splitting. As she experimented artistically with the different ethical systems that attracted her, she bifurcated herself into a manly Jamesian example and a mysterious woman who became a magnet for her conflicts. Melanctha is the locus of ambiguity in the story. As the focus of this chapter shifts, toward and then away from James, the character Melanctha assumes the appearance, first, of a mere failure in the evolutionary struggle, then of a priestess of the body, and finally of a victim of patriarchal relations.

"Melanctha" and the Psychology of William James

It is a commonplace of Stein criticism that her stylistic experimentation owes something to James's psychological theories, to which she was exposed in college. Michael J. Hoffman, Donald Sutherland, Richard Bridgman, Wendy Steiner, and others have traced features of Stein's various literary styles to James's idea of the "stream of consciousness."[2] But the content as well as the style of Stein's early fiction bears the heavy imprint of James.[3] Once his stamp on this work is evident, James is recognizable as Stein's one intellectual father, the person who contributed most to her first expressions of artistic power but who then became part of the nineteenth century that she had to escape. Her aggression against him would finally become conscious in the period of *The Making of Americans*, but even in "Melanctha," where she is closest to his thinking, she embraces his ideas in one zone of her text but besieges them in another.

Stein met William James in 1893, when she took his introductory philosophy course at Harvard. James shared the lecturing with two other professors; he led the unit on psychology, assigning a newly condensed version of his *Principles of Psychology*. Before graduating, Stein enrolled in seven more psychology courses, two of them taught by James. Later she went to medical school at James's urging, with a view toward a career in psychology. Although she ultimately dropped out of medical school, Stein and her mentor remained irregularly in touch even after her expatriation. She entertained him in Paris, and in 1910, shortly before his death, James warmly acknowledged the copy of *Three Lives* she had sent him.[4]

[2]See Michael J. Hoffman, *The Development of Abstractionism in the Writings of Gertrude Stein* (Philadelphia: University of Pennsylvania Press, 1965), pp. 52, 86–87, 213; Hoffman, "Gertrude Stein and William James," *Personalist* 47 (1966): 226–33; Donald Sutherland, *Gertrude Stein: A Biography of Her Work* (New Haven: Yale University Press, 1951), pp. 6–8; Ronald Levinson, "Gertrude Stein, William James, and Grammar," *American Journal of Psychology* 54 (1941): 124–28; Richard Bridgman, *Gertrude Stein in Pieces* (New York: Oxford University Press, 1970), pp. 102, 133–34; Carl Van Vechten, "How to Read Gertrude Stein," in Linda Simon, ed., *Gertrude Stein: A Composite Portrait* (New York: Avon, 1974), p. 51; Edith Sitwell, from *Taken Care Of*, anthologized in Simon, p. 111; Wendy Steiner, *Exact Resemblance to Exact Resemblance: The Literary Portraiture of Gertrude Stein* (New Haven: Yale University Press, 1978), p. 46; Jayne Walker, *The Making of a Modernist: Gertrude Stein from "Three Lives" to "Tender Buttons"* (Amherst: University of Massachusetts Press, 1984), pp. 14–15.

[3]Bridgman (p. 75) moves beyond the stylistic features to note something Jamesian in the "crude opposites" portrayed in *The Making of Americans*; Hoffman associates with James what he takes to be a practice in Stein of "character definition by verbalization" (*Development of Abstractionism*, p. 51); and Steiner convincingly compares James's concept of identity and Stein's manner of approaching the subjects of her literary portraits (pp. 29–30).

[4]See Donald Gallup, ed., *The Flowers of Friendship: Letters Written to Gertrude Stein* (New York: Knopf, 1953), p. 50; Bridgman, p. 22.

Many years later, Stein referred to an intellectual debt to James, describing him as "the important person in [her] Radcliffe life" and one of "the strongest scientific influences that I had."[5] James's science pervades her early writing. "Melanctha," in particular, is so close, in its characterizations, to James's theory of the mind as to approach psychological allegory.

This story, generally recognized as Stein's first work of distinction, is set off from her previous literary endeavors (including, incidentally, the two other stories in *Three Lives*) by a psychological deepening, a sensitivity to the mixed tones of life. "Melanctha" reworks material from *Q.E.D.*, the very early novelette in which Stein had given a minimally disguised account of her first love affair, with May Bookstaver.[6] *Q.E.D.*, however, lacks texture; it describes the romance in a baldly schematic way. The two main characters have few features beyond those that figure in a controlling opposition: Helen, the seducer, is passionate and daring, while Adele, the character modeled on Stein, is sexually inhibited and devoted to bourgeois values. The two women argue and cause each other pain, but do not otherwise affect each other. The story ends in a situation of romantic "dead-lock."[7]

When Stein went back to this material in 1905 and reworked it as "Melanctha," she turned it into a meditation on conflicting ways of knowing. What happened was that twelve years after studying psychology in college, she began to use that training for her creative work. In "Melanctha," a fusion suddenly took place between her artistic practice and her early studies with William James.

The lovers of "Melanctha" are opposed not simply in their sexual attitudes, like the couple in *Q.E.D.*, but also in their manner of focusing on the world. The battle of wills Stein had depicted in *Q.E.D.* becomes, in the characters of Melanctha Herbert and Jeff Campbell, a battle of rival modes of perception. Thus reconceived, the characters are in a position to learn from each other. The new perceptual issues, which are traceable to James, receive a delicate treatment; they enter the story not as a theoretical debate between

---

[5]Stein, *The Autobiography of Alice B. Toklas*, p. 96; Stein, *Wars I Have Seen* (New York: Random House, 1945), p. 63.

[6]See Leon Katz, Introduction to *Fernhurst, Q.E.D., and Other Early Writings by Gertrude Stein* (New York: Liveright, 1971), pp. xi–xvii.

[7]*Q.E.D.*, in *Fernhurst*, p. 133.

the lovers but as a half-articulated source of strain and attraction between them.

Stein commented, many years later, on what she had learned as a psychology student at Harvard:

> I became more interested in psychology, and one of the things I did was testing reactions of the average college student. . . . [S]oon I found . . . that I was enormously interested in the types of their characters. . . . I expressed [my] results as follows:
> In these descriptions it will be readily observed that *habits of attention are reflexes of the complete character of the individual.*[8]

The experimental outcomes reflect what she had learned in James's course. In the text for that course, James had written that "what is called our 'experience' is almost entirely determined by our habits of attention."[9]

What are "habits of attention"? James describes immediate experience as presenting a barrage of sensory impressions, teeming and confused. If a person is to accomplish anything beyond "star[ing] vacantly" (P 223) at this array of phenomena—indeed, if he or she is to begin the business of survival—selections must be made. Our practical nature compels us to remain inattentive to all but those objects that bear upon our individual needs. As a result, he says, "we actually *ignore* most of the things before us" (P 37). "We are all seeing flies, moths, and beetles by the thousand," for example, but for most of us, for all "save an entomologist," these things are "non-existent" (P 39). They fail to enter our experience. Our ability to bring into focus only those objects that suit our practical needs, and to ignore the rest, James calls "selective attention"—or "habits of attention" (P 37, 39).

---

[8]Stein, "The Gradual Making of The Making of Americans," in *Lectures in America* (New York: Random House, 1935), pp. 137–38 (emphasis added). Hugo Münsterberg directed the experimental work described here, but there is little evidence that he was an influence; Stein had learned her psychology from James. See *The Autobiography of Alice B. Toklas*, in which Stein gives Münsterberg a brief mention but continues: "The important person in Gertrude Stein's Radcliffe life was William James" (p. 96).

[9]William James, *Psychology: The Briefer Course*, ed. Gordon Allport (New York: Harper and Row, 1961), p. 39, hereafter abbreviated as *P*, and cited in the text.

Some individuals, James speculates, are more fixed in their perceptual habits than others; adults, for example, are more likely than children to approach the world with inflexible patterns of attention. "In mature age," writes James, "we have generally selected those stimuli which are connected with one or more so-called permanent interests, and our attention has grown irresponsive to the rest." "Childhood," on the other hand, "has few organized interests by which to meet new impressions and decide whether they are worthy of notice or not" (P 88). The result is an extreme "sensitiveness" in youth "to immediately exciting sensorial stimuli"—particularly to stimuli of "a directly exciting quality," "intense, voluminous, or sudden"—and to "strange things, moving things, . . . etc." (P 88). The child is captivated by sensory impressions not because they serve as "means to a remote end"— not because they bear upon some personal interest—but because they are "exciting or interesting *per se*" (P 90).

Here we begin to see filaments of connection with "Melanctha." Stein describes her heroine as "always wanting new things just to get excited."[10] In James's phrase, Melanctha likes what is "exciting or interesting *per se*." This habit of attention distinguishes her from her lover, Jeff Campbell, whose perceptions are formed by specific needs. Jeff "wanted to work so that he could understand what troubled people, and not to just have excitements" (116). As happens with the adults James describes, his contact with the world always forms itself about a practical end. Jeff—who believes in "always know[ing] . . . what you wanted" from experience (117)— stands as a model for the selective mind that elevates to notice only those objects that bear upon well-formulated goals. A question endlessly debated by Jeff and Melanctha is whether life is to consist of "excitements" cultivated for their own sake or whether it should be directed toward broader ends.

For James, the attraction to what is "exciting . . . *per se*" typifies childhood. But he adds that this "sensitiveness to immediately exciting sensorial stimuli," although usually outgrown, "is never overcome in some people, whose work, to the end of life, gets

[10]Stein, "Melanctha," in *Three Lives* (New York: Random House, 1936), p. 119, hereafter cited in the text.

done in the interstices of their mind-wandering" (P 88, 89). For these people, perceptual life continues to consist of immediate, aimless sensation; "so-called permanent interests" fail to become prominent and screen out the welter of impressions.

This description fits the case of Stein's Melanctha. James uses the term *mind-wandering*, or *wandering attention* (P 95), to describe such a receptiveness to sensation—and *wandering* is also Stein's word for her heroine. The references in "Melanctha" to the heroine's many "wanderings" have rightly been considered part of a sustained euphemism for sex, but one might as easily reverse the emphasis and say that sex itself stands in the story as a metaphor for a certain type of mental activity. Melanctha's promiscuity is part of an experiential promiscuity, an inability or unwillingness to approach the world selectively. Her sexual wanderings are part of a "wandering attention" that takes in experience without mediation.

The earlier novelette, *Q.E.D.*, used little indirection or euphemism. Although scenes involving anything more intimate than a "passionate embrace" were decorously skipped, it was clear what the words describing the lovers' experiences meant; there was none of the vagueness that seems to pervade "Melanctha." The "wanderings" that happen to occur in *Q.E.D.* are the quite literal wanderings of two young women through New York in search of a trysting place.[11] But in "Melanctha," sexual wanderings become "wanderings after wisdom," after "world knowledge," after "real experience" (97). "And so Melanctha wandered on the edge of wisdom," searching for "something realler" (101, 108). If this is euphemism, it is euphemism of an elaborate sort that brings to mind issues of wisdom, knowledge, and experience, as well as the romantic events described.

Melanctha and Jeff represent mental poles. James describes the apparatus of selective attention, which in Stein's story Jeff exercises and Melanctha does not, as strengthened by words and concepts, to which we "grow more and more enslaved" with the years (P 195). Objects that fail to conform to our semantic "pigeonholes" are "simply not taken account of at all."[12] These words and stock

11See *Q.E.D.*, in *Fernhurst*, pp. 75–80.
12James, "The Hidden Self," in *A William James Reader*, ed. Gay Wilson Allen (Boston: Houghton Mifflin, 1971), p. 93; see, too, P 192, 195.

concepts, besides determining what objects we will select for notice, distort our perceptions of those objects that we do observe. For "whilst part of what we perceive comes through our senses from the object before us, another part (*and it may be the larger part*) always comes out of our own mind" (*P* 196).

For most people, that is, sensation is modified by ideas. We rarely perceive a datum in its "sensational nudity" (*P* 181); what James calls preperception almost always obscures the object with anterior associations. This issue enters "Melanctha" in the form of an opposition between "thinking" and "feeling." Melanctha charges Jeff with an inability to feel because of his incessant thinking. "Don't you ever stop with your thinking long enough ever to have any feeling Jeff Campbell," she asks—and he answers, "No" (132). Because she herself takes in impressions without adapting them to conventional ideas or labels, every experience is new for her (119). She has what James in a fanciful moment labels genius—"the faculty of perceiving in an unhabitual way" (*P* 195).

James says that "thinking in words" is the most deeply ingrained method of distilling impressions (*P* 213). Stein's character Jeff tends (at first) to "think . . . in words" (155). Maybe this propensity has some connection to his "talking . . . all the time" (134). Melanctha, for her part, "never talked much" (134). "When you get to really feeling," she senses, "you won't be so ready then always with your talking" (135). Jeff, moreover, knows how to "remember right," whereas Melanctha "never could remember right"—the subject of a long squabble between the two (178, 100). Memory is another euphemism, this time for romantic fidelity. "No man can ever really hold you," Jeff tells Melanctha, "because . . . you never can remember" (191). But here again the sexual theme is conflated with the perceptual. Memory is part of the machinery of preperception. James writes that the associations a particular experience arouses in a person will naturally depend on his or her memories—and the more memories involved, the less fresh the experience itself will be (*P* 143, 193). Thus Melanctha's pathological forgetfulness is of a piece with her mind-wandering. Jeff charges her with "never remembering anything only what you just then are feeling in you" (182).

It is customary to view "Melanctha" as a story of two people who reach a romantic standoff because their natures are hopelessly "antithetical."[13] Yet there is something positive in the bond between the lovers, in spite of—or just because of—their characterological opposition. Melanctha and Jeff are not only contrasting character types but also personifications of warring principles that exist *in every mind*. According to James, every mind synthesizes the tendency to impose stock categories and the instinct for new and alien impressions. "There is an everlasting struggle in every mind between the tendency to keep unchanged, and the tendency to renovate, its ideas. Our education is a ceaseless compromise between the conservative and the progressive factors," or between the attachment to fixed categories and the "progressive" reaching after unfamiliar impressions (P 194).

The two faculties coexist in an "everlasting struggle." The relationship of the lovers in "Melanctha" is itself described as a struggle: "It was a struggle, sure to be going on always between them," and "a struggle that was as sure always to be going on between them, as their minds and hearts always were to have different ways of working" (153). The dynamic of struggle and compromise that unites the divergent energies of the mind as James describes it is a prototype for the complex pairings, partings, and mental adjustments of the lovers of "Melanctha."

The conservative and the progressive elements described by James are mutually dependent. The difficulty of being exclusively "conservative" has already been suggested. To the mind hardened in its conceptual patterns, much of the world is simply lost. The progressive factor, the impulse to seek out fresh impressions, brings such a mind back into contact with the tang of things as they are.

Some such need for novel perceptions attracts Jeff Campbell to Melanctha. He sees her as a "teacher" who can instruct him in "new feeling" and "wisdom" (125, 158, 205). He needs a kind of mental renovation: his conservatism requires the aid of the progressive tendency if it is to recover a sharp sensational focus. But Melanctha has needs, too, which draw her to Jeff, for as James says, "if we lost our stock of labels, we should be intellectually lost

13Bridgman, pp. 53, 56.

in the midst of the world" (*P* 103). Among other things, our very bodies depend upon our having stable mental categories for food, shelter, danger, and help (*P* 103).

Unselective perception may be exciting, but it is also impractical and ultimately life-threatening. James conceives of the issue in evolutionary terms: "Its own body . . . MUST be [a] supremely interesting [object] for each human mind. . . . I might conceivably be as much fascinated . . . by the care of my neighbor's body as by the care of my own. . . . The only check to such exuberant non-egoistic interests is natural selection, which would weed out such as were very harmful to the individual" (*P* 61–62). Melanctha has just these "exuberant non-egoistic interests." Not knowing what she wants, lacking selfish pursuits of any sort, she "wander[s] on the edge of wisdom" (101) without attending to her personal safety. She has a "reckless" quality—an extension of the perceptual recklessness that induces her to seek new experiences at any cost (208).

In uncanny repetition of James's formulation, the nonegoistic Melanctha is as much interested in "the care of [her] neighbor's body" as in "the care of [her] own." The only work she ever seems to do is to tend the ill, the confined, and the newborn. She stands in sharp contrast to her "selfish" friend Rose Johnson (214), who pursues her own advantage while neglecting others—the ailing Melanctha, whom she turns away at the end of the story, and her own infant, who dies because she forgets about him. In Rose one finds a projection, in caricature, of the features that receive a more complex treatment when they appear in the character of Jeff.

"Selfishness" is James's own term for the selection we exercise in the interest of survival (*P* 61). Rose (although in Darwinian terms her obliviousness to her offspring is problematic) is at once the supremely self-centered character of "Melanctha" and the consummate mental conservative, who knows "what she want[s]" from experience, who "never found any way to get excited," and who speaks in the voice of "strong common sense," which never proceeds beyond bland prejudgments and stock ideas (201, 207, 199). Melanctha, then, would profit from some of the conservatism or selfishness that marks Rose and, to a lesser extent, Jeff. Her perceptual life, stimulating as it is, is dangerous. She achieves knowledge through a series of close escapes, and she is only "in her nature" when "deep in trouble" (92).

Melanctha is drawn to Jeff—and finally to Rose—precisely because these characters lead lives of "solid safety" (210). "Melanctha Herbert never had any strength alone ever to feel safe inside her" (233), so she clings to those whose mental stability complements the fluidity of her own mind. "And Melanctha Herbert clung to Rose in the hope that Rose could save her. Melanctha felt the power of Rose's selfish . . . nature. . . . She always felt a solid safety in her" (210).

In the persons of Melanctha and Jeff, opposing mental tendencies draw together from mutual need. The "struggle" in which the two engage is necessary for both; it is a version of the struggle that must take place between the conservative and the progressive factors in each mind if cognition is to proceed with suppleness. And finally, it is a struggle that subtly changes the lovers. This point is missed by the reading that finds in the relationship two people "in a standoff."[14]

Jeff slowly gets the perceptual renovation he expects from Melanctha. His ability to accept change is one thing that distinguishes him from the drastically limited Rose Johnson. At first he "held off" (109); as happens when any sort of habit is changed, "the material" (to use a description of James's) opposes "a certain resistance to the modifying cause" (P 2). Jeff is for some time "too scared" (in Melanctha's view) "to really feel things" (123); he recoils from the rush of alien sensation, which, in James's phrase, is a "threatening violator or burster of our well-known series of concepts" (P 195). But he is not so fixed as to remain completely a conservative mind. Gradually he begins "to feel a little." He ceases to be "sure . . . just what he wanted"; he stops thinking "in words"; he begins to "wander"; and before long he can "lose all himself in a strong feeling" (116, 129, 155, 149, 154). His transformation is complete when "at last he had stopped thinking"—"he knew very well now at last, he was really feeling" (144).

Then he commits himself to a long phase of "wandering" with

[14]Bridgman, p. 53.

Melanctha, which gives him a new perspective on the phenomena of the immediate universe:

> Jeff always loved in this way to wander. Jeff always loved to watch everything as it was growing, and he loved all the colors in the trees and on the ground, and the little, new, bright colored bugs he found in the moist ground and in the grass he loved to lie on and in which he was always so busy searching. Jeff loved everything that moved and that was still, and that had color, and beauty, and real being. (149)

It is a change for Jeff, who was initially repelled by "new things" altogether (119), to be interested in such sharp, individual minutiae as "little, new, bright colored bugs." This is purposeless and un-selective attention at its height. The little "bugs" that now appeal to Jeff may even be Stein's way of remembering one of James's own illustrations: "We are all seeing flies, moths, and beetles by the thousand, but to whom, save an entomologist, do they say any-thing distinct?" (P 39). To Jeff, now that selective attention has relaxed, such trivial and unserviceable objects do enter con-sciousness in their particularity. Bugs are elevated to importance as vessels of "real being."

"You see Melanctha," Jeff remarks, "I got a new feeling now, you been teaching to me, . . . and I see perhaps what really loving is like, like really having everything together, new things, little pieces all different, like I always before been thinking was bad to be having" (158). "Little pieces all different": the uniqueness of each object comes into focus as the generalizations and preconceptions fade. As Stein was later fond of remarking, "what is strange is this": every phenomenon, if perceived naïvely, appears in its dis-tinctness from all other phenomena.[15] Stein shares James's own fondness for "that quality *sui generis* which each moment of imme-diate experience possesses for itself."[16]

---

[15]Quoted in Robert Bartlett Haas, ed., *A Primer for the Gradual Understanding of Gertrude Stein* (Los Angeles: Black Sparrow Press, 1971), p. 150.

[16]Ralph Barton Perry, *In the Spirit of William James* (New Haven: Yale University Press, 1938), p. 80.

In the two sentences describing Jeff's wandering phase, the word *and* appears nine times.[17] Such a passage, in which *and* links a variety of perceptions in what seems a single moment, reflects Stein's technique of parataxis, whereby multiple phenomena are shown "all . . . equally and simultaneously existing in perceptual fact."[18] Again, attention is a submerged issue. James comments that, as a result of selective attention, "accentuation and emphasis" are ubiquitous in perception (*P* 37). It is virtually impossible for the normal adult to attend uniformly to a number of simultaneous impressions. Only God or a hopeless sluggard can survey all parts of the universe "at once and without emphasis" (*P* 223). But in Jeff, as "little pieces all different" come before consciousness connected by the equalizing *and*, this condition of dispersed attention prevails. He is learning from Melanctha how not to select.

"The sodden quiet began to break up in him" (195). But Jeff proceeds carefully, in cycles of direct feeling followed by recuperation and quiet. He "held off" (109) at the right moments. These phrases describe the risks of love, but the pain Jeff experiences is also that of incoming "wisdom" (205), of new experience, what James calls the "threatening violator or burster of our well-known series of concepts" (*P* 195). Every unfamiliar impression tears a bit at the fabric of the mind.

Jeff's periods of suffering are followed by healing and reflection. In these periods he assimilates new knowledge. "Now Jeff was strong inside him. Now with all the pain there was peace in him. . . . Now Jeff Campbell had real wisdom in him, and it did not make him bitter when it hurt him, for Jeff knew now all through him that he was really strong to bear it" (204–5). Finally, his new insights contribute to his instrumental goals as a doctor: "Jeff always had strong in him the meaning of all the new kind of beauty Melanctha Herbert once had shown him, and always more and more it helped him with his working for himself and for all the colored people" (207). He returns to "regular" living (193) in the realm of convention

[17]See Stein's "Poetry and Grammar," in *Lectures in America*, p. 213; Levinson, p. 126.

[18]Donald Sutherland, "Gertrude Stein and the Twentieth Century," in Haas, ed., *A Primer*, p. 149.

and practical interests, but with a formulation of the world enriched by contact with direct experience.

This, for James, is the pattern of all learning, the end toward which the tension in every mind between "the conservative and the progressive factors" draws (*P* 195). Jeff is a model of mental growth, conceived in Jamesian terms. His encounter with Melanctha, far from "destroy[ing] his life,"[19] preserves him from intellectual death by forcing a fusion between competing tendencies in his own mind.

Jeff as Stein's Self-Portrait

One way to bring out William James's importance for Stein is to place Jeff, her purest Jamesian creation, against his prototypes in her earlier writings. In Jeff, Stein was able to envision a character who resolved and benefited from internal struggle. For her earlier characters, however, self-division had assured impotence. These characters were paralyzed by the tension between promiscuous and conservative impulses. In the portrait of Jeff Campbell, Stein reconceived this self-division in positive terms, terms that had been suggested to her a decade before by James.

Her very early, painfully divided characters are often versions of herself, and they suggest why James's ideas might have appealed to her in the first place. Stein's attraction to James in college had much to do with his giving her a language to apply to conflicts she perceived in herself. Her obliquely autobiographical college essays, known now as the "Radcliffe Themes," shed light on her emotional life during the period in which she encountered James.[20] These pieces dwell on the figure of a young woman in whom a strongly sensual nature competes with a need for self-mastery.

"In the Red Deeps," for example, is a self-portrait of a girl frightened by her own sadomasochistic fantasy life. She recalls a period

---

[19]Rosalind S. Miller, *Gertrude Stein: Form and Intelligibility* (New York: Exposition Press, 1949), p. 31.

[20]The "Radcliffe Themes," written for a composition course in Stein's junior year, are anthologized in Miller. Hereafter they are cited in the text. I use "The Temptation" to refer both to the piece of that name and to its earlier, untitled version.

during childhood when she experimented with various sorts of self-inflicted pain and fantasized about tortures she might devise for others. But she has an attack of conscience, characterized by a "haunting fear of loss of self-control" (108). The sexual component of the forbidden impulses is underscored by the title, borrowed from the chapter in *The Mill on the Floss* about romantic secrecy and guilt.

"The Temptation" again sets illicit pleasures against self-reproach. The heroine, an indistinct surrogate for Stein, is in church one day when a strange man leans heavily against her. She enjoys the "sensuous impressions," but again has a "quick revulsion," and asks herself, "Have you no sense of shame?" Yet still "she did not move." The conflict leaves her immobilized; she vaguely indulges herself, but only passively (154–55). Later her lapse stigmatizes her; her companions, who have seen everything, upbraid her, and she becomes "one apart" (151).

When the characters Stein writes about in these college compositions are not oppressed by conscious fears of impropriety, they have vague inhibitions that are no less paralyzing. Stein writes a theme about a boy who is both frightened and interested when a pretty girl asks him to help her across a brook. Once again, "he . . . could not move" (146). Finally he accommodates her, only to flee in alarm. These characters never pass beyond the faintest stimulation; they prefer loneliness to the risk of losing control.

Although none of the characters in these early pieces is a lesbian, Stein's emerging sexual orientation must have exacerbated her sense of being "one apart," or (as a kind of self-punishing translation) secretly too sexual. Whether or not she yet defined herself as a lesbian, the pressures she was feeling, in some preliminary way, were those of the closet. Her characters in these essays do not dare to let anyone in on their sexual feelings. Stein's own romantic experience in college was limited to a mildly flirtatious friendship with her psychology teammate Leon Solomons—a friendship that, as she recalled in a later notebook, was "Platonic because neither care [*sic*] to do more."[21] The relationship was close and pleasant,

[21]P. 17 of notebook 11 in the *Making of Americans* notebooks, Gertrude Stein Collection, Yale Collection of American Literature (hereafter YCAL). Hereafter references to these notebooks will appear as *NB*, followed by the number or letter of

but to the extent that it bordered on flirtation it ironically made her feel asexual and freakish.[22] In the meantime, as her college compositions intimate, she experienced intense longings and loneliness.

Stein's preoccupation during her late teens with conflicts such as those in the "Themes" helps to account for her interest in James's psychology, and explains why of all her professors she singled James out for a sort of hero-worship.[23] James too sees a duality in human nature, one that traps a person between eagerness and self-control. But in his view, the self-division signifies not deviance but mental health. Every mind, by his account, has a promiscuous and a repressive element. In normal perceptual life, part of us is welcoming and indiscriminate, but another part excludes data from awareness. These are the two impulses that Stein later plays against each other in Jeff Campbell.

James's theories doubtless helped to alleviate Stein's guilt about what seemed threatening appetites and, at the same time, suggested a means of forgiving herself her inhibitions. The mind James describes naturally has its thirsty or revolutionary dimension, a menace but also a source of life: we would stagnate if we lost the taste for raw sensation. Stein evidently welcomed the parallel. The unruly libidos of the Radcliffe heroines are refigured in "Melanctha" as a form of perceptual openness: Melanctha Herbert is at once sexually and perceptually promiscuous, and she helps Jeff by introducing him to "excitements" both romantic and more broadly experiential. Stein later validates her inhibitions too, by associating them with selective attention. Jeff is romantically cautious and also incapable of focusing his senses on "new things"; these qualities make him attractive to the heroine of the story. Indeed, the very struggle between yielding and self-control that

---

the notebook in question, and (for convenience) the page number in Leon Katz's useful transcription of the notebooks. For example, *NB* A.12. In rare instances in which a notebook transcribed by Katz was unavailable in the original, I have relied on Katz's transcription.

[22]See Bridgman's discussion (p. 29) of Stein's composition "A Modern Sonnet to His Mistress's Eyebrows," which he sees as hinting at "the idea of an amorous attachment" but also as joking about the idea.

[23]See "Radcliffe Themes," p. 146.

immobilizes the characters of the "Radcliffe Themes" comes, with an infusion of James's psychology, to seem a creative part of consciousness.

One way to think of Jeff is as Stein's self-idealization through the filter of James. He is, after all, a version of Adele in *Q.E.D.*, who herself was a virtually unaltered Stein. But he is a transformed Adele, robust and successful. Adele, incidentally—or Stein, in the intermediate phase of *Q.E.D.*—had fallen in love but still experienced all the internal pressures of her earlier personae in the "Radcliffe Themes." Like the Radcliffe heroines, Adele-Stein is torn between her sexual curiosity and her inhibitions; the tension freezes her, making her an "unresponsive" lover (66). Ideologically, too, Adele feels caught, as her author did, between the lesbianism that marks her as "queer" and a bourgeois ideology that makes her wish to "avoid excitements" and become "the mother of children."[24]

But in Jeff Campbell, Stein transforms the tension in herself between sexual needs and conservative values into a source of strength. Jeff's competing impulses make him a more sensitive person and a better doctor. His one excursion into forbidden "excitements" only helps him to know himself better and to do more for others. James's ideas helped Stein to create an idealized self, conceived in terms of psychic vigor.

On the other hand, "Melanctha" also contains an image of failure to thrive. The heroine of the story does not fare so well as her lover. She never achieves mental balance, and she dies. In portraying Melanctha, Stein slips outside the Jamesian framework and the self-idealization attached to it.

Melanctha and the Wisdom of the Body

Melanctha herself, by William James's standards, is weak. One way to account for her presence—were we to remain within the limits of the Jamesian paradigm—would be to see her as an example of the high costs, in Darwinian terms, of mind-wandering.

---

[24]*Q.E.D.*, in *Fernhurst*, pp. 77, 56, 59. I take the word "queer," applied to Adele, to refer to her lesbianism.

Melanctha is not ultimately changed by her affair with Jeff. Whereas he assimilates the new mode of perception Melanctha has given him, she fails to be impressed by his "solidity," his conceptual grip on the world. She tries to adapt to him for a time, but ends by reverting to her former "excited," "reckless," wandering ways (219, 208).

Rose Johnson, who might have served as a replacement, then rejects her, and the desertion "almost killed her" (233). This might seem an extreme reaction, but in Rose, Melanctha has lost her last point of contact with the "solid safety" of the conservative temperament (210, 233). "Melanctha needed Rose always to let her cling to her. . . . Rose always was so simple, solid, decent, for her. And now Rose had cast her from her. Melanctha was lost, and all the world went whirling in a mad weary dance around her" (233). Melanctha is "lost": as James said, without mental conservatism, "we should be intellectually lost in the midst of the world" (P 103). Melanctha loses touch with the "solid" tendency, and "all the world went whirling in a mad weary dance around her." This is a fair description of what would happen to a mind severed from all perceptual habit and banished to the flux of unfamiliar sensation. Melanctha virtually drowns in the continuum of the world.

Her physiological death, some paragraphs later, seems to follow as a matter of course. Critics have seen in the stories of *Three Lives*, each of which ends with a heroine's death, shades of naturalism. This reading assumes a special force in light of the Jamesian or Darwinian psychological drama of "Melanctha." In Stein's heroine one observes a character unfit for the world who is weeded out by a brand of natural selection. In James's psychology the person who has no mechanism of selective attention is ill suited for the business of self-preservation. The survival of the fittest militates against those "exuberant non-egoistic" individuals who, careless of their own personal safety, diffuse their attention equably over experience. But Melanctha has persisted in wandering on the perilous "edge of wisdom" (101), suppressing personal interests in the name of "excitement." In the end, "tired with being all the time so much excited" (161), she succumbs to the social and bodily suicide that, as James makes plain, would be the outcome of any life of wholly unselfish or unselective perception (P 60–61).

The case of Melanctha, if one reads it, then, in the light of James, is an admonition. Yet Melanctha's failure by James's standards could lead one as easily to question James's values as to take a critical view of the heroine. I have sketched a reading of Melanctha's story as a negative example, but it could just as well be thought of as a protest against the entire notion of mental success represented by Jeff. For in the moral universe of "Melanctha," self-preservation is not clearly the highest good. Part of the story pulls away from the psychological framework supplied by William James and from the Darwinian gospel of success attached to it.

"Melanctha" is Stein's most deeply Jamesian text, but it comes belatedly, at a point when its author is just beginning to strain against James. Within a few years her notebooks show her explicitly defining herself against him. In "Melanctha," her early ambivalence creates a kind of ethical polyphony. The story hovers somewhere between the ideas and views Stein shared with James and quite different, still indistinct values that would soon propel her in new directions.

James's psychology is shot through with Darwinism; the important thing, in his view, is to thrive. Stein's attachment to this perspective is evident in her sympathetic portrait of Jeff Campbell, the good doctor who does his work and moves ahead professionally. But Melanctha, who has no instinct for survival, is of course portrayed at least as sympathetically herself. She receives a much more positive treatment than her antecedent in *Q.E.D.*, the thoughtless seducer Helen. In the move from *Q.E.D.* to "Melanctha," the moral center of the story has shifted toward the promiscuous member of the couple, whose model was not Stein herself but her former lover May Bookstaver.

Melanctha, far from being merely an object of pitying diagnosis, has qualities that elevate her above a mere survivor like Rose. Her imperfect instinct for self-preservation is the cost of her superior "wisdom," which the story sets against instrumental knowledge as embodied by Jeff and as preached by James. Against the background of James's theories, the word *wisdom* in "Melanctha" can be thought of as referring to the heroine's reckless immersion in the senses, but the word has a spiritual resonance as well. Jeff seems to be pointing to a mysterious power in Melanctha when he speaks of a "new feeling" she has given him, "just like a new religion to me" (158). The world she opens up for him is a world of "real being" (149). This spiritual quality of hers is never explained, but it pushes her beyond the ethical boundaries defined by James's *Psychology* and, for that matter, by James's own more spiritually oriented writings.[25] Part of Stein's story is about a "way to know" that has no bearing on practical life but is more elevated than mere sensory abundance.

At the risk of trying to define precisely something the text leaves vague and suggestive, I want to approach Melanctha's wisdom by setting it alongside some other details in her story, which seem to have nothing to do with the framework of Jamesian psychology. Stein's heroine has a special intimacy with the mysteries of the body. Melanctha is close to the upheavals of birth, death, and puberty. She watches over her dying mother; this seems to be the most important thing she has ever done for or with her mother. She tends Rose Johnson as Rose gives birth, acting as a sort of midwife, even to the extent of moving Rose away from her husband for the last part of the pregnancy. ("When Rose had become strong again [after the delivery and the baby's death] she went back to her house with Sam" [225]). Melanctha's story is bounded by her own puberty, the time in her twelfth year when she is "just beginning as a woman" (91), and by her death.

These details—the death of the mother, the birth of the baby, Melanctha's puberty, and her death—were superimposed on the original plot of *Q.E.D.*, and they signal changes in Stein's thinking. The details involving birth and death—which, along with the setting in the black community, were inspired by Stein's clinical experiences at Johns Hopkins Medical School[26]—bear no obvious relation to the primary story of the romance with Jeff Campbell, and they give the narrative of "Melanctha" a wandering quality. Although they are never digested into the main plot, the narrative pulls back to these events, often out of sequence. The story begins,

[25]James does not associate spirituality with sexuality. See, for example, "A Suggestion about Mysticism" and "A Pluralistic Mystic," in *Essays in Philosophy*, in *Works of William James*, ed. Frederick Burkhardt, Fredson Bowers, and Ignas Skrupskelis (Cambridge: Harvard University Press, 1978).

[26]See *The Autobiography of Alice B. Toklas*, p. 100.

for example, not where one would expect it to begin but with the delivery of Rose's baby, which, we will later find out, actually *follows* the entire love affair of Melanctha and Jeff: "Rose Johnson made it very hard to bring her baby to its birth. Melanctha Herbert who was Rose Johnson's friend, did everything that any woman could" (85). I associate Melanctha's hazily defined wisdom with her quality of presiding at moments of bodily change or upheaval. The text makes no such connection explicitly, but these fragmentary data embedded in "Melanctha" will begin to form a more cohesive picture in Stein's later work.

Within a few years Stein will depart from James altogether by grounding her idea of consciousness in what might be called the rhythms of the body. She will develop a notion of wisdom as a kind of thought that knows its ties to the body. As her spirituality comes to the surface, an emphasis on bodily experience, as sacred and taboo, marks the difference from James's own brand of spirituality. To quote from the dense text of *Tender Buttons,* the most extraordinary thing Stein wrote in the teens, "*out of an eye* comes research" (11, emphasis added); knowledge emanates *from* the eye, like tears. Or (to use a more opaque passage) spiritual knowing or "in-sight" is continuous with anatomical functions like giving milk or suckling: "MILK. Climb up in sight climb in the whole utter" (47). *Tender Buttons* stages bodily upheavals great and small, from eating to giving birth and dying. An early hint of these preoccupations appears in the liminal Melanctha, stationed at the crises of the body.

Significantly, William James's psychology would not account in an interesting way for Melanctha's intimacy with the body. Compared to a near contemporary like Freud, James seems to keep the body out of focus, except in its role as a machine absorbing data and maintaining itself in existence. Nor would Melanctha's sexuality be something James would illuminate. Melanctha's involvements in birth, death, and sensual experience give her a kind of wisdom distinct from James's instrumental knowledge. To describe the notion of bodily consciousness that develops in Stein's subsequent work, it will be necessary to use a vocabulary closer to psychoanalysis than to the theories of James.

Stein's notebooks and subsequent works suggest to me that in her characterization of the embodied Melanctha, she was depicting something she saw in herself, for all her simultaneous identification with (and self-projection in) the more controlled and rational Jeff Campbell. In one of the notebooks for *The Making of Americans*, Stein identified a side of herself she called "the Rabelaisian, nigger abandonment, Vollard [the art dealer], daddy side" (*NB* DB.47). That she associates her bodily gusto, or everything Rabelaisian in herself, with something she calls "nigger abandonment" suggests that the extreme racism she expresses in "Melanctha"—for example, in depicting blacks as carefree and promiscuous—served (among other things) her own need to distance a part of herself about which she was ambivalent. She had her own sensuous side, which she projected in racial terms perhaps so she could simultaneously idealize and depreciate it; and by playing to the racism of her audience, she partially disguised the dimension of self-exploration in the story.

The Style of "Melanctha": Stein's Resistance to James

The various themes that point away from James are disconnected and half-hidden; one might hardly notice them if it were not for their intimations of the direction Stein's work was soon to take. But the formal techniques of the story are a step ahead of its themes. Here a tension with James's thinking becomes obvious.

Stein divides her manner of narration between two "ways of knowing." One is linear and progressive; the other is circular and rhythmic, and has something in common with the wandering quality of Melanctha's mind. Although in its overt ethics, "Melanctha" does not decide between Jeff's and Melanctha's forms of knowledge, structurally the story succumbs to wandering. The experimental style signals a departure from the values Stein had learned from James, which her story still enshrined (thematically) in the portrait of Jeff Campbell.

Like the other stories of *Three Lives*, "Melanctha" has an obtuse narrator, one who cannot quite get a grasp on the material. The narrator seems to wish to point the story in particular directions, but keeps losing the thread. The character Jeff Campbell is instrumentally oriented; because he has practical interests, he knows where to focus his attention, knows what he wants. To the extent that it makes sense to compare a narrator's and a character's ways of thinking, the narrator of the story, by contrast, lacks a guiding conception of what he or she wants. William James would not approve of such a person or of such a way of putting a narrative together.

An "instrumental" narrator—to sustain for a moment this some-what artificial analogy—would have pronounced emphases and an ability to tell how particular details bore on the story as a whole. Of course, all stories slip past their tellers in one way or another, but a story may be narrated in a more or less single-minded way. Stein's narrator fails to build up a theme. Periodically, he or she seems to try to form the narrative as an answer to a single question: why did Melanctha fail in life? "Why was this unmoral, promiscuous, shift-less Rose married, and that's not so common either, to a good man of the negroes, while Melanctha with her white blood and attrac-tion and her desire for a right position had not yet been really married" (86). Yet the question, although repeated in various forms, never receives an answer. The narrator gives the impression of being accustomed to generalizing, often (as here) on the basis of racist stereotypes, but of becoming unhinged by the case of Melanctha: "But why did the subtle, intelligent, attractive, half white girl Melanctha Herbert, with her sweetness and her power and her wisdom, demean herself to do for and to flatter and to be scolded, by this lazy, stupid, ordinary, selfish black girl. This was a queer thing in Melanctha Herbert" (200).

Each time, the question why Melanctha's life has the shape it does is no sooner asked than it becomes diffused, for among other things, the heroine eludes the racist formulas through which the narrator tries to make sense of her case. The narration, as it actu-ally evolves, lacks linear causality—an absence that Marianne De-Koven associates with a form of literary impressionism.[27] The nar-rative structure depends neither on an internal logic directed at accounting for Melanctha nor, in the absence of this, on the simple

[27]See DeKoven, pp. 32–33. See also DeKoven's insightful discussion (pp. 30–32) of the obtuse narrative voice of *Three Lives*.

sequence of events in fictional time. For it begins almost at its chronological end, with the birth of Rose's baby, then slips all the way back to Melanctha's twelfth year. From there it makes its way up to her affair with Jeff Campbell, whereupon the focus unaccountably intensifies. No attempt is made to suggest what relation this material bears to the rest of Melanctha's life.

The narrator's formal sense is rather like that of the heroine, who "did not know how to tell a story wholly" (100). In fact, the lack of linearity becomes most pronounced in the portions of the narrative devoted exclusively to Melanctha. It is as if the mind-wandering heroine caused wandering disturbances in the way her own story is told. Jeff's story, considered in isolation, not only focuses on an instance of mental progress but also has itself a progressive form. In his case, the facts do appear in their proper temporal sequence. By the end, moreover, we can give a fair account of what his experiences have meant: we know that his affair has hurt him but has deepened him personally and professionally. Only Melanctha's experience comes to us in a confused order, and fails to build toward a conclusion. It ends with a nonconclusion; surprisingly, she gets sick, seems to get better, and dies. William James would have a terminology to apply to this confusion, but as a moral matter he would have no patience with a story that succumbed to this kind of shapelessness.

Another form of wandering that Stein's narrator shares with the heroine is a reluctance or inability to tag some data as more important than others—a collapse of emphasis. The earlier version of "Melanctha," *Q.E.D.*, moved firmly and easily to its crises. By comparison, all the stories of *Three Lives* curiously fail to advance or to build to a pitch. The dramatic outlines are flattened. The obtuse narrators resist (or are incapable of) theatrical moments, beginnings, and summations, failing to take proper hold even of genuine crises. The deaths of the heroines are reduced to casual data: "They sent [Melanctha] where she would be taken care of, a home for poor consumptives, and there Melanctha stayed until she died" (236). "While [the baby] was coming, Lena had grown very pale and sicker. When it was all over Lena had died, too, and nobody knew just how it had happened to her" (279).

A parallel absence of emphasis *within* sentences in "Melanctha" often creates a look of confusion. The narrator has, for example, three or four strong impressions of Rose Johnson, which have nothing in particular to do with one another. Rose is good-looking; she is dark-skinned; she is moody; she is selfish. Rather than subordinate any one of these thoughts to another, the narrator lists them all together: "Rose Johnson was a real black, tall, well built, sullen, stupid, childlike, good looking negress" (85).

Both the absence of linearity and the lack of emphasis are part of what a genuine Jamesian disciple would denounce as a failure of selective attention. The narrators of *Three Lives* lack clear "interests" that would keep them on a single track. Yet, as we already know, James does make a place for aimlessness. He suggests the importance of relaxing one's emphases from time to time; in this respect it is possible to see a continuity between his ideas and Stein's characterization of the reckless Melanctha. For this reason too one *might* think of the unfocused style and structure of "Melanctha" as continuous with Stein's early interest in *The Principles of Psychology*.

Such a view would run as follows. James claims that we coarsen experience by our emphases and designs; each act of selection has its cost in lost perceptual abundance. Stein, in embracing aimlessness, undoes selective attention; she makes a copious record of existence without exalting special objects to dominance. She gives a sense of the quality our perceptions have before we limit and rearrange them to suit our customary interests.

Although the stories of *Three Lives* are not so indiscriminate in focus as to constitute what we would now call stream-of-consciousness narratives, they do approach what James himself meant by the term he coined. James's chapter on "The Stream of Thought" (retitled "The Stream of Consciousness" for the abridged *Psychology*) is a reply to associationist psychology, which pictured sensations and ideas as discrete links in a chain. James claims that it is artificial to think of consciousness as atomized; our psychic life looks like a clean succession of thoughts only when we limit our account of it to those mental states that we inwardly name and fix our attention on. Between these sharp focuses, there is a "free water of consciousness," an indistinct mass of associations and connections that occupies us between one halting place and the next and suffuses even our clearest perceptions (*P* 32). We notice these in disinterested moments, when selective attention is relaxed. Consciousness "is nothing jointed; it flows" (*P* 26). Each thought casts ripples before and after, and we always have at least a "dawning sense of whither it is to lead" (*P* 33).

These ideas, then, might with some justice be viewed as containing a prophecy of Gertrude Stein's style. If Stein seems to let her focus wander, it is because she has no thought of moving forward as if life fell in segments. She strains against habits of attention that select and divide, and (by her own later account) against literary habits that parcel experience into "a beginning and a middle and an end."[28] I mean to say something more precise than that Stein's style resonates with James in the same way that all experimental modern narrative does. The special sense of "stream of consciousness" is retained here; the repetitive style of "Melanctha" replaces the expected peaks or halting places with a continuous flow of fading and beckoning—or overlapping—thoughts.

In *Q.E.D.* ideas were expressed singly: "'You are wrong, you are hideously wrong!' Adele burst out furiously."[29] "Melanctha" shows how a thought like this can dissolve into a succession of thoughts, each suffused with echoes from the last: "'Oh Jeff dear,' said Melanctha, '*I sure was wrong* to act so to you. *It's awful hard* for me ever to say it to you, *I have been wrong* in my acting to you, but I certainly was bad this time Jeff to you. *It do certainly come hard to me* to say it Jeff, but *I certainly was wrong* to go away from you the way I did it'" (202, emphases added). In spite of the repetitive content, no two of these phrases are identical. As in all the repetitive paragraphs of *Three Lives*, each pulse of thinking brings a configuration not quite the image of what preceded it. For as James notes, when one dips into the stream of mental life one finds perpetual difference. Habitually we think of a particular object or sensation as identical each time we encounter it; the task of attention is to recognize. But a liberated or innocent eye sees that the mass of peripheral thoughts endlessly changes, conspiring with an unstable context to produce a different constellation of experience each time an object is encountered.

[28]Stein, *The Geographical History of America* (New York: Random House, 1936), p. 218.

[29]*Q.E.D.*, in *Fernhurst*, p. 131.

"When the identical fact recurs, we *must* think of it in a fresh manner, see it under a somewhat different angle, apprehend it in different relations from those in which it last appeared" (*P* 23). For Stein to allow herself *exact* repetitions would be to falsify the small mutations of consciousness.

Others have speculated in similar ways about possible connections between Stein's technique and James's idea of the stream of consciousness.[30] Yet—to return to my larger point—whatever Stein's style might owe to James, she deviates from his values. It is a mistake to think of James's thoughts on the stream of consciousness as offering an implicit model for a diffuse or wandering literary style. That is to confuse his descriptive and his prescriptive aims.

James's chapter on the stream of thought is meant to describe an overlooked dimension of mental experience, not to champion it; he urges a theoretical attention to the fluid periphery of consciousness, not immersion in it at the expense of one's rational grip on things. The last thing he would recommend (in a text or in life) would be to suspend habits of conception in favor of the flux of momentary impressions. No writer who had read the *Psychology* with unmixed sympathy would be led by it to a style like Stein's. In James's scheme of things, wandering is the meanest possible use of the mind. It is a species of rest—something that occupies us between one focus and the next, or overcomes us in moments of fatigue. Whoever declines to rise from it is the moral equivalent of an infant or a brute. From the vantage point of James's psychology, Melanctha's mind is deficient because it does nothing but drift.

James himself, significantly, was repelled by "wandering" literature, as we know from his letters and elsewhere. "Literature," he writes, "has no character when full of slack and wandering and superfluity. Neither does life. *Character* everywhere demands the stern and sacrificial mood as one of its factors. *The price must be paid.*"[31] The crises and essential moments of consciousness fall

[30]See, for example, Hoffman, "Gertrude Stein and William James," pp. 226–33; Sutherland, pp. 6–8; and Bridgman, p. 102.

[31]William James, "Is Life Worth Living?" Quoted in Ralph Barton Perry, *The Thought and Character of William James*, 2 vols. (Boston: Little, Brown, 1935), 2:271.

precisely where aimlessness terminates and attention finds its object. These are the instants that produce all action. "Attention and effort" are indeed "two names for the same psychic fact" (P 16). Nor is there any value in a life that never finds its focus in volition and action—in the "manly concrete deed" (P 15). James's ethics is opposed to an art that never seems to announce its point. Thus, if we think of Stein's style as affected by her exposure to his theories, we must recognize that she has altered the focus by emphasizing a part of consciousness that he views as secondary and, when exercised exclusively, debased.

This gap is part of a tension between James's Victorianism and Stein's modernism. Our association of the idea of the stream of consciousness both with James's psychology and with techniques of modern fiction might contribute to a mistaken image of him as a sort of prophet of modernism. But James as the advocate of the "manly deed" is closer to Carlyle and Emerson, whom he revered, than to most of the artists we associate with modernism. James stands after all between two periods; aesthetically, therefore, he may present the appearance of either a strategist for the modernism Stein embodies or a member of the very generation she was distancing herself from when she wrote that she spent her life escaping from the nineteenth century.

He was both: Stein used James to hurtle herself into a modernist practice that was more modern than James. As an instance of this paradox, James's psychology indirectly contributed to a breakdown of moral contours in Stein's fiction. We saw that in the process of assimilating James, Stein found a way beyond the paralyzing self-scrutiny of the "Radcliffe Themes." In those compositions, and in Q.E.D., she struggled tediously with her own moralism, unable to write about her sexual yearnings without revulsion. Her first work using James's thought, on the other hand, shifts the focus to less charged perceptual themes, freeing her to consider various types of experience without so much displaced self-reproach. In Three Lives, Mrs. Lehntman and Melanctha Herbert are sexual wanderers, but their lack of self-restraint largely escapes judgment because it is a symptom of their indiscriminate attention.

The paradox is that James himself was an unembarrassed moralist, who would not have approved of being used in this way. Stein applied his ideas in a skewed form, with the effect of making her work relativistic, far more relativistic than James.

The collapse of ethical definition, one result of her use of James, of course contributes to the modern quality of *Three Lives*. "Melanctha," unlike the earlier *Q.E.D.*, is unmistakably a product of the twentieth century, in no small measure because of the dim-sighted, innocent narrator who fails to bring things to an ethical focus. *Q.E.D.*, written before Stein's Jamesian period (though after her studies with him), has a strident ethics: it is about lapses from innocence and problems of conduct. Even its title promises some sort of proof or absolute certainty. *Three Lives* (with its non-judgmental, descriptive title) offers us conformists and troublemakers but does not finally decide that one form of existence is finer than another.

It would not be too paradoxical to say that Stein, the moment she began to use James for her art, became more purely psychological than he. James's account of experience never isolates issues of perception from ethical questions. Even in the largely descriptive *Psychology*, he does not hesitate to advance certain values. His popular chapter "Habit," for example, is vocally prescriptive. It offers this sort of "practical maxim": "*Keep the faculty of effort alive in you by a little gratuitous exercise every day.* That is, be systematically ascetic or heroic in little unnecessary points" (*P* 16).

Not surprisingly, James's own tastes in literature favored works with implicit moral applications.[32] It is understandable (if ironic, for all the same reasons) that when Stein sent him a copy of *Three Lives*, in certain respects her purest Jamesian narrative, he lost interest after forty pages or so.[33] Stein's ethical blankness is the result of careful experimentation. The "Radcliffe Themes," her earliest preserved pieces, had been charged with ideals—among them, James's ideals of effort and heroism. A brief tribute to James himself captures her characteristic tone in these college years: "Is life worth living? Yes, a thousand times yes when the world still holds such spirits as Prof. James. . . . He stands firmly, nobly for

---

[32]See Perry, *Thought and Character* 2:259–60.

[33]Gallup, p. 50. James warmly acknowledges receipt of *Three Lives* but admits having put it down after a brief sitting.

the dignity of man. His faith is . . . that . . . of a strong man willing to fight, to suffer and endure" (146).

This is Gertrude Stein in a vein unfamiliar to most of us. She is
trying out, at this point, whatever postures come to hand. *Three
Lives* is the first sign of dislocation; here, moral absolutes give way
to the more impartial norms of psychology, and Stein abandons
questions of virtue and vice to ask whether a character is interesting or perceptually alive. Hence, she shifts the sympathetic center
of the story from the scrupulous Adele of *Q.E.D.* (who becomes Jeff
Campbell) toward the less moralistic, and more exciting, Melanctha Herbert.

The style and structure of "Melanctha," then, record a troubled
debt to James. James uses the term *mind-wandering* to disparage a
relaxed attention. Stein's story, on the other hand, is an unabashed
experiment in a kind of mind-wandering; it unsettles expectations
of linearity, dramatic emphasis, and moral definition.

Unconscious Pressures on the Narrative

What I want finally to suggest is that "Melanctha," in spite of its
lack of linearity, does have a wholeness that transcends the term
mind-wandering. The story coheres, in ways that demand another
sort of vocabulary than James's. Although it seems aimless from
one perspective, the story in its way is motivated—not by what
James would call "interests" on the part of the author or narrator
but by unconscious process.

"Melanctha" has a shape, which it gets not from logic or chronology, as *Q.E.D.* did, but from a tissue of associations resembling
what psychoanalysis terms primary process. I have described the
narrator's unfocused quality as a function of a relaxed attention.
According to James, a lapse of selective attention has the effect of
letting *any* impression or association enter consciousness. But
though this formulation might describe Dorothy Richardson's rendition (often) of the associative process, it does not square with
Stein's "Melanctha." Her narrator puts together events and images
that are symbolically cognate.

What secretly preoccupies the narrator of "Melanctha" is a pair
of events that keeps repeating itself: a woman fails to mother; a

man harms a woman sexually. The two events that ultimately destroy Melanctha are her expulsion by Rose Johnson, on whom she has depended for protection, and her sexual exploitation by Jem Richards. This sequence is anticipated by the two episodes that open the story, similar instances of failed mothering and sexualized male aggression. The first sentences describe Rose Johnson's unwillingness to give birth and her subsequent failure to keep her baby alive: "Rose Johnson made it very hard to bring her baby to its birth. . . . Rose Johnson was careless and negligent and selfish, and when Melanctha had to leave for a few days, the baby died" (85). Then the narrator's mind digresses to Melanctha's twelfth year, when she became the object of inappropriate attention from a coachman and consequently of quasi-sexual violence from her father. "Now when her father began fiercely to assail her, she did not really know what it was that he was so furious to force from her" (95).

The opening details—the death of the baby and the sexual attentions in Melanctha's twelfth year—appear to be digressions, but they fix a motif for the rest of the story. The narrator places these details alongside the subsequent betrayals by Rose and Jem, but without announcing a logical connection. Perhaps the repetitions unconsciously supply an answer to the question, why did Melanctha fail? Women, that is, did not give her maternal protection; men (with the important exception of Jeff) abused her. This generalization fits not only the two opening details and the final brutalities of Rose and Jem but also the events of Melanctha's very early life, presided over by a weak, unprotective mother and a rough, possessive father.

But the pattern, if it exists in the back of the narrator's mind, never coalesces into a generalization. Instead of explicitly condemning those who repeatedly fail Melanctha, the narrator expresses a vague pity for her that seems almost to locate the blame with her: "poor Melanctha could only find new ways to be in trouble" (93). The only sign of an impulse to extend blame to others is the repeated deviation of the narrator's mind from the expected chronology to characters and events that repeat the betrayal. What superficially looks like mind-wandering is a mix of obsessive reiteration and displacement.

Anger is deflected once more in the account of Melanctha's

death. Again, those who should be caring for her fail to do so; the narrator, however, rather than make a charge of negligence, gives a bland juxtaposition of facts. "They sent her where she would be taken care of, a home for poor consumptives, and there Melanctha stayed until she died" (236). The sentence would be emotionally intelligible if it read, "*but* there she died." The narrator doubly muffles the death, by consigning it to an adverbial clause: "until she died."

Suppressed anger, then, is a possible cause for the narrator's associative manner. In any case, the affect that might have accompanied the account of Melanctha's ruin is displaced into a series of analogies. The telling of the story is at once eerily repetitive and superficially cold. Thus the story, though aimless compared to something like *Q.E.D.*, is shaped by an unconscious logic—a logic of displacement. If the text seems modern in its wandering style, it also seems so in its associative logic. Nineteenth-century fiction, of course, often has a dream logic, but subordinated to another logic. *Jane Eyre*, for example, is arguably itself about a series of failed or lost mothers and male aggressors, but that narrative follows not the paths of the narrator's associations but (with rare exceptions) the sequence of events in time. Although Jane Eyre as a narrator has anger she wishes to control, we do not often sense the tug of repressed feelings on the *direction* of her story. By way of contrast, "Melanctha," like much other experimental fiction of the modern period, foregrounds primary process as a shaping principle.

William James sees each person's conceptual framework as besieged by a disorganized mass of impressions and associations, not by a rival, unconscious logic. Stein's story has what we might call an irrational form, a phrase James would have considered an oxymoron. It was, of course, Freud who at just this time was giving such a phrase meaning—to the mystification, incidentally, of William James, who wrote of his younger colleague in Vienna, "I can make nothing in my own case with his dream theories, and obviously 'symbolism' is a dangerous method."[34]

Stein is not (yet) articulating an *idea* of the unconscious, but her

---

[34]*The Letters of William James*, ed. Henry James, 2 vols. (Boston: Atlantic Monthly Press, 1920), 2:327–28. In spite of his methodological doubts, however, James admired Freud's efforts and thought that something useful would come of them. See Perry, *Thought and Character* 2:122.

formal experiment in "Melanctha" points away from the concept of the stream of consciousness as articulated by William James. The story is structured according to a principle of motivated repetition, a logic of the unconscious. Motivated repetition, as we will see, is just what will overrun and finally destroy sequential narrative in Stein's next major work, *The Making of Americans*.

The unconscious patterning of "Melanctha" owes nothing to Freud. Stein knew (or would soon know) quite a bit about Freud, but like some of her fellow modernists—I think particularly of Joyce, Woolf, and Faulkner—she made "discoveries" in fiction that suggestively paralleled Freud's theoretical discoveries without being due to them. Like these other novelists, she would come to view with ambivalent interest Freud's excavation of what seemed a similar psychic turf. Her writing, however, develops the look of unconscious process unusually early. Of the three writers I have named, only Joyce had by this time begun to do significant work, and beside Stein's story his *Dubliners*, however innovative in its symbolism and its forms of indirection, looks conventionally linear.

What was happening intellectually to Stein to stimulate or assist in the formal experiments of "Melanctha"? I think her shift toward something like primary process was—oddly—a secondary consequence of her involvement with modern art. The innovations of "Melanctha" reflect the intellectual atmosphere of Stein's first years amid the Parisian avant-garde. She had expatriated in 1903 and was living with her brother Leo, who himself was deeply involved in the business of "expounding L'Art Moderne."[35] A point that emerges clearly from the excellent and abundant scholarship on Stein's relationship to postimpressionist and cubist art is the importance of Cézanne to her first literary experiments.[36] Stein herself said in a famous interview that Cézanne (whose portrait of his wife she continually scrutinized while working on *Three Lives*) gave her a "new feeling about composition," for he did not subor-

[35]Letter of Leo Stein to Mabel Weeks, quoted in James R. Mellow, *Charmed Circle: Gertrude Stein and Company* (New York: Avon, 1974), p. 84.

[36]See Marjorie Perloff, "Poetry as Word-System: The Art of Gertrude Stein," in *The Poetics of Indeterminacy* (Princeton: Princeton University Press, 1981), p. 91; Walker, esp. pp. 1–13.

dinate the elements on his canvas to a "central idea." Instead, she said, he "conceived the idea that in composition one thing was as important as another thing. Each part is as important as the whole, and that impressed me enormously."[37]

We have seen a kind of prose transliteration of this dispersal of emphasis in the wandering style of "Melanctha"—the story to which Stein herself pointed as exemplifying the strategies she had evolved under Cézanne's influence.[38] So what art historians call Cézanne's "flatness"[39] furnishes not only an analogue but also an important inspiration for the kinds of stylistic flatness to be observed in "Melanctha."

Something else comes out in Stein's story: a kind of motivated repetition suggestive of veiled and displaced preoccupations. This second innovation is original to Stein; nothing in her artistic or literary environment prepares us for it. How did it evolve? As Stein, under the stimulus of Cézanne, began to develop a wandering style, the relaxation of emphasis freed up material from her own unconscious. The repetitive brooding that goes on in the margins of her story is her own brooding.

My reason for suggesting as much is that the pair of events that covertly structures her story (failed mothering and male sexual bullying) will recur in her subsequent work and then will resolve itself in various directions. In *The Making of Americans,* Stein revives the disappointing parents of "Melanctha," this time (as we will see) consciously making them portraits of her own mother and father. But there she comes to terms with the figure of her father, unleashing her now explicit rage and at the same time stealing back some good things from him. In *G.M.P.* and *Tender Buttons,* she goes on to revise and redeem the figure of the weak and remote mother.

I am saying that these texts performed psychological work, of a sort not unlike that which Virginia Woolf said *To the Lighthouse* performed for her.[40] "Melanctha" contains the faintest beginning

---

[37]Robert Bartlett Haas, "Gertrude Stein Talking: A Transatlantic Interview," in Haas, ed., *A Primer,* p. 15.

[38]Ibid.

[39]See Richard Shiff, "Seeing Cézanne," *Critical Inquiry* 4 (1978): 781.

[40]See Virginia Woolf, *A Writer's Diary,* ed. Leonard Woolf (London: Hogarth Press, 1969), pp. 101–2, 136.

of that work, as Stein raises parental specters to give them a preliminary inspection. But her anger and disappointment are still expressing themselves in various displacements.

The Feminism of "Melanctha"

I have been describing the narrative of "Melanctha" as driven by an unconscious logic; the narrator, instead of directly reacting to Melanctha's betrayal, displaces anger by multiplying scenes of violation without affect. A different reading might view the anger of the story as feminist anger, which is not so much repressed as camouflaged. The suppression of affect could be rhetorical rather than pathological, reflecting ideological rather than emotional conflict. The repetitive content may enable the narrator—or the author—to make some points about a woman's victimization without risking a straightforward polemic.

Marianne DeKoven has posited that the stories of *Three Lives* mask their own "powerful feminist morals."[41] This seems to me a plausible and very suggestive idea, particularly since Stein in an earlier phase of her life had openly entertained feminist ideas, which seem to have gone underground during or after her time in medical school.[42] I have been considering scenes of maternal failure and sexual violation at the margins of the love plot. Structurally, these scenes have the effect of undermining linear narrative. Their content—to consider it for a moment in isolation—is potentially feminist, in the sense of highlighting the situations of exploited or overlooked women. This content alone might account for the placement of this material at the margins.

In the context of James's psychology, Melanctha seems a defec-

[41]DeKoven, p. 32.

[42]During her first year in medical school, Stein gave a speech, "The Value of College Education for Women," modeled closely on ideas in Charlotte Perkins Gilman's *Women and Economics*. There is a copy of the speech in YCAL. But Elyse Blankley has shown that Stein did not ally herself wholeheartedly with women's causes. See "Beyond the 'Talent of Knowing': Gertrude Stein and the New Woman," in Michael J. Hoffman, ed., *Critical Essays on Gertrude Stein* (Boston: G. K. Hall, 1986), pp. 196–209. Catharine Stimpson discusses Stein's use of Gilman's ideas, in "The Mind, the Body, and Gertrude Stein," *Critical Inquiry* 3 (1977): 490.

tive member of the species, who never develops the practical interests that would save her. The story also gives a competing picture of her as the embodiment of a superior, disinterested wisdom. But a third possible view of her is neither as a failure nor as a wise woman but as a victim. The acts of violation that fill the background of the love plot are violations to which women, in the universe of "Melanctha," are peculiarly vulnerable.

Melanctha does not find an adequate mother; Rose, the hoped-for protector, repeats the rejecting behavior of Melanctha's own mother, who had "never cared much for this daughter" (110). Men, for their part—Jem Richards and Melanctha's father—treat her with a sexualized brutality. This pattern can be reconceived as follows: the women about Melanctha are too weak or uncaring to protect her from the damaging advances of men. If Rose had provided shelter and comfort, Melanctha would have avoided the ruinous affair with Jem. Again, if Melanctha's mother had been loving and attentive, she would have served as a buffer against the "unendurable" father who, about the time of the girl's puberty, begins to hover about her threateningly (90, 97). The father actually uses the mother's indifference to justify his own invasiveness: "A nice way she is going for a decent daughter. Why don't you see to that girl better you, ain't you her mother!" (94). His interest in his daughter, which flourishes just as she reaches puberty, seems incestuous; there is a disturbing vagueness in Rose's statement that Melanctha's father has done "some things so awful to her, she don't never want to tell nobody how bad he hurt her" (214). Her mother does nothing to protect Melanctha from his attacks.

One could see Melanctha's subsequent victimizations as issuing from her own pathology, for she chooses friends and lovers who reproduce her parents' damaging behavior. Rose Johnson is so patently self-centered that Melanctha is foolish to "cling to her" (233); Jem Richards is a bad choice too, for he makes no pretense of being anything but "fast" and mean (230). Melanctha seems masochistically to seek situations that recreate her early pain. At least once, in Jeff Campbell, she meets a kind man who is nothing like her father and who even has a warmly maternal side; he addresses her protectively as a "poor little girl," a "poor little, sweet, trembling baby" (141).[43] But she does not stay in this relationship, which might have ended the cycle of rejection and domination. Her next serious affair is with the destructive Jem.

Yet if Melanctha is masochistic, so, arguably, are the other heroines of *Three Lives*—which is to say that the sickness may be cultural.[44] The servant whose story is told in "The Good Anna" is so devoted to her subordinate role that she works herself to death. "She worked away her appetite, her health and strength, and always for the sake of those who begged her not to work so hard." Finally her "worn" body cannot withstand an operation, and she dies (32). Lena, of the final story, is passively good: she represses her own desires entirely, placing herself in the hands of people who put her in frightening and alienating positions. Ultimately she numbs herself fatally, forgetting her fear of childbirth. "Lena was not so much scared now when she had the babies. She did not seem to notice very much when they hurt her, and she never seemed to feel very much now about anything that happened to her" (278). She becomes pregnant with a fourth child and dies giving birth.

Either *Three Lives* portrays three masochistic pathologies, or— not an entirely inconsistent idea—the book gives a picture of a world that prompts self-punishing behavior in women. For the stories implicitly criticize a culture that does not always value women enough to teach them self-protection. All three stories contain instances of people (often women) who value boys more than girls. Anna, when she has two children in her charge, "naturally preferred the boy" (25); in general, she "loved to work for men" (37).[45] In "The Gentle Lena," the heroine's aunt "spoiled her boy" (243); later, Lena's husband "wanted badly that his baby should be a boy" (275). Lena herself is overlooked, for obscure but associated reasons, by her own parents, who willingly part with her since "Lena was not an important daughter in the family" (245).

[43]There is something unsettling, however, about the context of Jeff's pity for Melanctha: he has caused her pain.

[44]"What is clear in each plot [is] the defeat of a woman by dominant personality traits which are culturally defined as female." DeKoven, p. 32.

[45]The reason she gives in both instances is that males are a pleasure to feed (pp. 25, 37).

This motif, besides having something in common with Stein's own sense of having been insufficiently valued by her parents, sheds light on her heroine's self-destructive behavior. Melanctha's mother has always devalued Melanctha in favor of a brother who died young. "One day," Rose relates, "Melanctha was real little, and she heard her ma say to her pa, it was awful sad to her, Melanctha had not been the one the Lord had took from them stead of the little brother. . . . That hurt Melanctha awful" (213). I connect this rejection in favor of the brother with the remark that "Melanctha Herbert had not loved herself in childhood" (90).

In the context of William James, Melanctha seems the model of the "exuberant non-egoistic individual" who fails to take care of herself because she lacks a selective attention. But the marginal material about her family suggests a different source for her lack of egoism—that she was not valued enough as a child to feel worthy of care. Her response to this rejection is to devalue her own femininity. She not only ceases to love her mother—we hear that as a child "Melanctha had not liked her mother very well" (90)—but also traces her own insufficiency to her mother. She grows up wishing to be like her "virile" father, rather than to inherit her mother's passive, feminine traits: "Melanctha had a strong respect for any kind of successful power. It was this that always kept Melanctha nearer, in her feeling toward her virile and unendurable black father, than she ever was in her feeling for her pale yellow, sweet-appearing mother. The things she had in her of her mother, never made her feel respect" (96). This situation doubly explains the lack of a bond between Melanctha and her mother. The mother, simply, prefers a son, and the daughter reacts both by wishing to grow up to be manly and by feeling repelled by the mother's own feminine qualities. The lack of a maternal presence in Melanctha's childhood is due to familial values that favor males and make women repugnant to each other. This is the family scenario Freud naturalized as the female response to "castration."[46]

The two final crises repeat the pattern, this time outside the

[46]Sigmund Freud, "Some Psychical Consequences of the Anatomical Distinction between the Sexes," in *The Standard Edition of the Complete Psychological Works of Sigmund Freud*, trans. James Strachey (London: Hogarth Press, 1953–74), 19:253–54, hereafter cited as *SE*.

family. Rose fails to be an adequate friend partly because of the new primacy of a man in her thoughts: she considers Melanctha's presence a threat to her hold on her new husband, so she exiles her friend (231). Melanctha's response to this rejection is, again, to seek out a source of virile energy; Jem Richards, to whom she now turns, has the same "successful power" that Melanctha respected in her father (217).

But the irony is that by identifying with strong men, Melanctha, far from absorbing their power, only makes herself vulnerable to it. Her father is no kinder to her for her identification with him; perhaps her very admiration confirms his sense of his own superiority and thus his contempt for her. When she later turns to Jem, his toughness, according to the same paradox, is just what defeats her: "Jem . . . knew how to fight to win out, better. Melanctha really had already lost it" (223). For Jem's lasting ties are with men. He is "a man other men always trusted," "a straight man," who, in the exclusively male world of gambling and exchange, pays back what he owes (217). When he detaches himself from Melanctha, it is because he places his standing as a gambler above his relationship with any woman: "Jem Richards was not a kind of man to want a woman to be strong to him, when he was in trouble with his betting" (221).

Where male power commands exclusive respect, women's bonds among themselves, and their relationships with men, are troubled. The stories of *Three Lives* are feminist to the extent that the portraits of three overlooked and self-defeating women form a generalization about women's damaged self-image in a world of male privilege.

Yet the feminism is muffled, never articulated in such a generalization. In fact, some attention is required to notice issues of gender at all. The narrator of the stories either is innocent of critique or sees a pernicious social arrangement but resists taking an explicit stand on it, relying instead on the rhetorical effect of a bland accumulation of facts. The narrator—or perhaps Stein herself, as DeKoven suggests[47]—is passive to the status quo. Like the character Lena, the teller of these stories has an "unexpectant and

47DeKoven, p. 32.

unsuffering . . . patience" (239). One might call the stories near-feminist. But they fix the themes for Stein's later work, which is politically charged and precise. Between *Three Lives* in 1906 and the work of the teens Stein will develop a deeper understanding of the mechanism by which sexual arrangements are constructed, and will therefore be able to envision change.

The failure of maternal alliances is just what *Tender Buttons* and the other works of the teens will redeem. *Tender Buttons* not only portrays male privilege but also suggests how it perpetuates itself, and points to a means of subversion. The beginning of change, as envisioned in that text, is to reconstruct female bonds, the bonds that in *Three Lives* are shown in a damaged form. *Tender Buttons* explores the possibility of loving a "sister" who is "not a mister" (65) and of recovering, through her, a lost and degraded mother.

I have been talking about a number of features of "Melanctha" that stand outside the central love plot and complicate the relationship of Stein's thinking to the psychology of William James. But the tension between this last feature, Stein's latent feminism, and James's psychology needs some clarification. Nothing in that psychology *logically* stands in the way of a feminist politics, but the radical form Stein's feminism took, as the next chapters suggest, led her directly away from the things she had most valued in James.

Three Lives shows a Jamesian voice in dialogue for the first time with a feminist voice. The Jamesian romantic plot of "Melanctha" and the near-feminist material at the margins of the story point to antithetical views of mental and social life. Stein's story simultaneously encourages two ways of understanding the heroine and the world in which she struggles. The first notion is that success in life is a matter of individual will—that people thrive by "knowing what they want." According to this view, which is also James's view, a character like Jeff Campbell has a more active will or attention than Melanctha, and therefore is able to focus on things in a more productive way. Melanctha, seen from this perspective, is a sensualist who fashions her own doom by refusing to decide "what she wants," despite Jeff's attempts to persuade her to be more self-interested.

But the story is also susceptible to the view that the ability or inability to thrive is socially determined. Melanctha, viewed within her social context, seems to suffer not because of a feeble will but because of values within and beyond her family that minimize her as a woman and prompt a cycle of self-defeating behavior. The same ambiguity is apparent in the other two women's tales in *Three Lives*; and for the whole volume Stein chose an epigraph from Laforgue that perfectly suspends the question of blame: "Donc je suis un malheureux et ce n'est *ni* ma faute *ni* celle de la vie."[48] The two views of Melanctha—the Jamesian and the feminist views— are not absolutely contradictory. Quite plausibly, Melanctha, within a male-dominated culture, is orphaned emotionally and *hence* does not value herself enough to decide to thrive. But one's view of her own role in her failure changes as one moves from the debates with Jeff on the Jamesian theme of "knowing what one wants" to the account of her early brutalization by her family.

Stein's work of the next few years brings into sharper relief the tension between a Jamesian and a feminist ethics. The difference between the two is the difference between liberal or individualist values and radical critique. To speak more biographically, it is also the difference between a male and a female identification on Stein's part. To call James a "male" theorist would involve problems of definition, but in Stein's mind James was synonymous with an ideal of rugged masculinity. She referred to him as "a strong man willing to fight, to suffer and endure."[49] His is a psychology of the strong man; at the low end of the moral spectrum he sees the "weakling," and at the high end lies the ideal of the "*kräftige Seele*," which expresses itself in the "manly concrete deed."[50]

In "Melanctha," Stein reenvisioned herself according to that model—and as a man. Yet even as Stein made Jeff male, she dislodged him from the center of the story, and projected another part of herself onto a female character. Jeff was her self-idealization according to William James, but Melanctha absorbed features of

[48]"Therefore I am an unhappy person and it is *neither* my fault *nor* that of life" (emphases added).

[49]"Radcliffe Themes," p. 146.

[50]Letter quoted in Perry, *Thought and Character* 2:272. James is saying in this context that we are all "weakling[s]" except insofar as we "escape" from that state, moment by moment, through heroic acts that express (and earn us) a *kräftige Seele*. The reference to the "manly concrete deed" is from *P* 15.

her author's history as a self-alienated woman in a male culture. Stein bifurcated herself, that is, into a Jamesian male and a victimized woman. (At the same time, her story included but marginalized a further, crucial part of herself, her lesbianism: Melanctha has a homoerotic relationship with Jane Harden, but as an incidental episode on the way to her heterosexual self-discovery. Later, Stein will look past this heterosexist narrative.)

After "Melanctha," Stein's work never again places the manly and the female self-images in such precise counterpoint. "Melanctha" is the last and fullest expression of her bond with James and the first product of her incipient feminism. A male identification had pervaded her earlier writings: Stein had projected herself either into male protagonists or into women characters who disowned their gender, like Adele of *Q.E.D.* who was capable of the remark, "I always did thank God I wasn't born a woman" (58). After *Three Lives*, a female identification will move into view. Even in this later phase, Stein tends to think of herself as variously male and female; in her erotic relationship with Alice Toklas, for example, she pictures herself alternately as "sister" and "husband," and even as "king."[51] But once James fades as a presence, the texts never again have an ethics of manliness.

I have been describing the stories of *Three Lives* as near-feminist. Within seven years, Stein's writing will have an overt feminism, not in the sense of announcing its ideology—in fact the writing style suddenly becomes opaque—but in the sense of containing a coded account of what patriarchy is and how it works. In her poetry of the early teens, Stein brings out the strain of protest that is deflected and compromised in "Melanctha." More than that, she develops a view of female possibilities that is not only angry but also rhapsodic and freeing. She comes to envision women not simply as objects of pity but also as powerful agents of subversion. In order to begin to think in these terms, Stein must move beyond an unconscious equation of women with impotence and death, putting behind her the specter of the weak and victimized mother.

First, however, she makes a circuit, itself difficult and freeing,

[51]*TB* 29; Stein, "Lifting Belly," in *The Yale Gertrude Stein,* ed. Richard Kostelanetz (New Haven: Yale University Press, 1980), pp. 16, 49, 21.

through the father. *The Making of Americans* is a labor of brave self-analysis, in which Stein identifies some of her fears about her social and artistic roles and works past them toward new forms of self-trust.

2

The Making of Americans:
Modernism and Patricide

In *The Making of Americans*, Stein risked an emotional free-fall, one that entailed a fall into new language.[1] This novel releases the pressures contained and quieted in *Three Lives*. In *The Making of Americans*, Stein identifies and claims the rage that was distanced in *Three Lives*, and directs it particularly at her father. This emotional axis of the novel has not been seen before, but to know about it is also to know how to interpret *The Making of Americans* as an act of artistic innovation. For as Stein discharged anger at her own father, she also became intellectually a patricide, a "killer," as she would later say, of the nineteenth century that sired her. Her text produces its artistic newness over the corpse of the nineteenth century; in the course of discovering the creative implications of her patricidal anger, Stein invented the modern novel.

Stein could not have found her way to her private angers without this novel. The very fact that she was writing in a highly original way, channeling her feelings into what amounted to an artistic aggression, gave her the strength to explore the painful, unconscious, and familial meanings of her rage. This novel attests to the crucial role a woman's creative work can play in her difficult emancipation from a paternal specter. As the philosopher Mary Daly observes, a woman coming to consciousness "experiences a lessening of confusion, guilt, and despair, and an increasing sense

[1] I am borrowing the terms "free-fall" and "new language" from Adrienne Rich's "Transcendental Etude," *The Dream of a Common Language: Poems 1974–1977* (New York: Norton, 1978), p. 75.

of rage, of outrage. If she does not constantly convert the energy of this rage to creativity it pre-occupies her, pre-possesses her."[2]

Along with her anger, Stein experienced a rush of relief and self-acceptance. This was the novel in which she found her voice—not in the sense of perfecting a style ("Melanctha" is a more polished piece of work) but in the sense of identifying a shaping urge within her writing and claiming it as distinctively hers. Although her subtitle promises "A History of a Family's Progress," she gradually complicates the status of the story as narrative by revealing its sources in her own primitive desires. In the course of the novel she makes a journey into her unconscious, tapping—and then reflecting on—the various erotic processes that seem to her to motivate her act of composition. Her choice to affirm these erotic-artistic processes was an important step not only in her evolution as a modernist but also, privately, in her self-liberation from an internalized paternal censor.

A sentence from the chapter called "Martha Hersland" might serve as an epigraph to the novel: "This is now a little of what I love and how I write it."[3] *The Making of Americans* reflects Stein's growing faith in "what she loved," personally as well as artistically. For to allow herself to attend increasingly to her erotic and unconscious processes was to relinquish the controlled, "manly" persona of her previous writings. *The Making of Americans* represents a crucial phase in Stein's gradual exchange of a self-suppressing, male ideal for a positive view of herself as an embodied and sexual being. Soon this libidinous self-image will be folded into a female identification, in texts like *G.M.P.* and *Tender Buttons*.

Stein begins her novel with a manly voice, the voice of a respectful "son" of bourgeois culture. That voice is already crosscut by a rage at fathers, which intimates disturbances to come. This male, bourgeois persona gradually gives way to the image of a taboo self—sexual, impure, angry, also powerfully creative and loving. This transgressive self expresses what Stein calls her "earth feeling" (295), her growing sense of implication in material and

[2]Mary Daly, *Gyn/Ecology: The Metaethics of Radical Feminism* (Boston: Beacon Press, 1978), p. 348.

[3]Stein, *The Making of Americans: Being a History of a Family's Progress* (Paris: Contact Editions, 1925), p. 289, hereafter cited in the text.

nonrational activity. The formal consequence of earth feeling is a disruption of linear narrative, which anticipates the subsequent course of modernism: Stein's text is shaped by a friction between the demands of sequential, realist narrative and the speaker's own earthy or libidinal processes, which increasingly deform narrative in the direction of chant, circularity, and play. This tension resonates with a second, between the author's "clean" role of omniscient narrator—absent from the plot, guided by decorum—and her "dirty" role of self-indulgent speaker, seducing or tyrannizing her reader, or losing herself in an autoerotic discharge of words.

Another aspect of the turn to earth feeling is a transformed conception of human personality. While the view of identity developed in this novel still owes something to William James, it is crosscut by an alternative view, grounded in the desiring body—in fact, by a psychoanalytic view. There is a hidden debt to Freud in this novel, which has been missed in the past partly because of Stein's subsequent attempt to dissociate herself from psychoanalysis.

Earth feeling also had a special place in what for Stein were private issues of sexuality. At the time that she was working on *The Making of Americans*, she was becoming involved with Alice Toklas and beginning to accept herself as a sexual person—a feature of her emotional life henceforth inseparable from the forms of her literary daring, and entwined with her patricidal rage. Just as she was privately affirming her own sexual identity, and in the process freeing up her rage at her own prohibiting father, her novel unleashes erotic processes *in language* that deal a blow to the ideological universe of the nineteenth-century "fathers."

The Persona of the Angry Son

As *The Making of Americans* opens, one sense that Stein is approaching but reining in her explosive feelings. The first pages seem almost confused: in place of a single narrative voice are several unassimilated voices. The awkwardness registers an ambivalence, which Stein will ultimately transform from a liability into a suggestive theme. As she embarked on this project, she felt a mix of excitement and fear. She sensed that she was about to air transgressive and intimate feelings. The first few pages alternate between a wish to unleash her emotions and a self-protective impulse. She dangles provocative images before us, then withdraws into formality and tameness.

The first secret she half exposes in these pages is patricidal rage—a version of her own. This rage is the prelude, as it will later be the accompaniment, to the emergence of a passionate persona. The secret comes out in the brutal oedipal scenario that opens the novel and is set off from the text as a sort of epigraph: "Once an angry man dragged his father along the ground through his own orchard. 'Stop!' cried the groaning old man at last, 'Stop! I did not drag my father beyond this tree' " (3). How this joke about a son's anger bears on the rest of the text is not explained; a gloss that follows amounts to an evasion as much as a clarification:

> It is hard living down the tempers we are born with. We all begin well, for in our youth there is nothing we are more intolerant of than our own sins writ large in others and we fight them fiercely in ourselves; but we grow old and we see that these our sins are of all sins the really harmless ones to own, nay that they give a charm to any character, and so our struggle with them dies away. (3)

These two opening paragraphs sound like remnants of an early draft, neither well integrated into the text nor particularly coherent in themselves; the anecdote about filial violence does not square with the next thought about discovering the "charm" of one's "sins," since neither father nor son could plausibly perceive the anger they share as charming. But this material does make sense if regarded as a form of free association that exposes the conflicting pressures Stein felt as she began to put her novel together.

The narrator—who, as we will see, is so close to the author that it seems sensible to refer to her as Stein, with implied quotation marks—wavers between the thought of her anger and the idea that she is really harmless. She wishes both to proclaim and to disclaim her aggression, asking us first to identify with the figure of "an angry man," who is absorbed into a universal "we," then not to think of his or "our own" violent impulses as violations. For Stein was preparing in this novel to announce her own independence of paternal figures, notably her father, her brother Leo, and her mentor William James. And her angry self-assertion frightened her. She remarked in a notebook, as she was sketching plans to expose and kill off characters based on male relatives (Leo and her uncle Solomon Stein), "I am so nervous. . . . Jig is up" (*NB* 2.21). By opening the novel with an anecdote suggesting that vengeful feelings toward fathers are universal and not so harmful after all, perhaps even quaint, she signals her desire to stay within the fold.

This conflict will dissipate as Stein claims her violent feelings. I believe she used this text as an opportunity to scrutinize her inhibitions and her habits of self-censorship, to find ways to talk about these things, and ultimately to free herself by letting some repressed material to the surface—a lonely but exciting exploit. This first emotional note of rage at fathers had been present but heavily masked in *Three Lives*. What is odd is that now that Stein takes on her rage explicitly, it is not the feminist rage that *Three Lives* seemed to foreshadow. Stein identifies not with the figure of an angry daughter but with an oedipal son. At the moment her rebellious feelings emerge, her identity as a woman goes underground.

The oedipal son was a compromise persona, which suited her for this moment. I see in *Three Lives, The Making of Americans,* and the later texts of the teens a gradual radicalization, generating a series of increasingly subversive self-projections. The progression is from the persona of a good, manly daughter to that of a rebellious son, and finally, in the texts that follow *The Making of Americans,* to that of a rebellious daughter. In the earlier texts, *Three Lives* and *Q.E.D.,* Stein identifies with abused and passive women—Melanctha, Lena, Anna—and with the figure of the decent son or male-identified daughter, such as Jeff Campbell and Adele, upholders of bourgeois values who respect parents and the parent culture. These types have in common a reluctance to question the status quo in any focused way; they are susceptible to characterization as "gentle," "patient," and "good." The violent son we meet at the beginning of *The Making of Americans* is a middle term between that early figure of the obedient child and what in *Tender Buttons* will emerge as the voice of an angry daughter.

Woman-identified protest will be the last and riskiest stance, for it involves speaking from a position of cultural exile. *The Making of*

Americans initially adopts the safer persona of an oedipal son, for the son stands simultaneously outside and within the father's domain. He overthrows the father in order to become the father; the power that he challenges he inherits. That is the moral, after all, of the episode of the "angry man," a story, strangely, of bonding, as all oedipal stories are about the cementing of patriarchal relations. Stein's angry man opposes paternal constraints but not the system that confers his father's orchard on him.

The subject matter Stein chose for her novel brought into high relief these conflicts between rebellious rage and what amounts to a lurking conservatism. She begins her novel of self-definition as a book about ancestors. Her goal is to give a fictionalized chronicle of the immigrant families whose mores and professional successes shaped her identity as a middle-class American. She defines herself through and against these figures, who inspire two competing thoughts. She reveres them; yet she displaces them.

At first, she assumes the role of their devoted beneficiary:

> It has always seemed to me a rare privilege, this, of being an American, a real American, one whose tradition it has taken scarcely sixty years to create. We need only realise our parents, remember our grandparents and know ourselves and our history is complete.
>
> The old people in a new world, the new people made out of the old, that is the story that I mean to tell. (3)

Stein so overplays her debt to parents and grandparents, her sense of being "made out of" them, that the novel promises at this point to be little more than a conciliatory tribute. She is thoroughly defined by their "history."

Immediately, however, her role of narrator-descendant takes on an aggressive edge, for the same act of writing that enshrines her ancestors will overpower them. Stein diminishes her elders in fantasy in order to make room for herself: she announces a plan to portray her parents and grandparents either in their infancy or in their old age, reserving the strong role of "young grown men and women" for herself and her friends (6). Her reason is simply that it pleases her to do so, for she does not want an impotent role for herself. "To be ourself like an old man or an old woman to our feeling must be a horrid losing-self sense to be having"; she will impose that loss of self on her parents instead (5).

Quite like her "angry man," Stein as narrator is both her parents' indebted descendant and their rival. Her confession of these competitive feelings expands into a substantial aside that postpones the plot; the aside largely consists of restatements of her dread of "being to [herself] like children or like grown old men and women" and her need to confine her parents to that role (5). This sort of digression is risky, for it presumes that the reader will be as interested in the author's needs and fantasies as in the (still-deferred) plot. Stein will continue to take such risks; that is the nature of her experiment in *The Making of Americans*. The voice of a narrator telling a story is progressively invaded by the voice of an "author" who fractures the fictional illusion by exposing the private, often taboo wishes that motivate her aesthetic choices.

In the meantime a plot does get underway, one that itself foregrounds a theme of war with the father. The courtship of Alfred Hersland and Julia Dehning, the first episode in the family history, is set in a context of intergenerational struggle. The romance is triangulated by the strong presence of Julia's father Henry Dehning, an uncanny repetition of the initial figure of the revered but conquered parent. In this retelling, the story of a child's assault on the father has a peculiarly tame and happy quality.

Dehning objects to his daughter's engagement but then yields to the lovers' will. More than that, his initial resistance strengthens his daughter's powers of self-assertion, in which both he and she take pleasure. Their fights evolve into a kind of flirting. "She loved it in a way the struggle he made each day a new one for her. . . . They understood very well both of them how to please while they were combating with each other" (26). This image of a child locked pleasantly in battle with her father domesticates and sentimentalizes the original picture of warring generations in the tale of the angry man. Perhaps the mildness has something to do with the child's being a daughter in this case, although for all his children, male and female, Dehning is an oddly harmless patriarch. The role he takes is to stimulate their rebellion for the purpose of instructing and bonding with them: "This was a cheerful challenge to them for he liked it and they liked it too with him, to fight strongly against him" (9). Again, rebellion cements rather than dissolves the family.

Here, moreover, Stein envisions the possibility of being simultaneously opposed to a father and loyal to him. The episode offers a route past the conflicts of the other introductory sections, in which filial rage mixed unstably with feelings of devotion. What resolves the ambivalence is the image of a *loving* war between father and children. Now seemingly opposite feelings can merge in a way that seems psychologically coherent: "And so the young ones are firm to go on with their fighting. And always they stay with their father and listen to him" (10). Of course this resolution of the issue of filial anger is only temporary; a part of Stein continues to identify with the man who furiously dragged his father across the orchard. Her rebellious feelings resurface powerfully at a later moment when she feels bold enough to situate herself outside the orbit of fathers altogether.

These early explorations of the paternal theme show Stein approaching, directly and indirectly, issues of her own social and creative identity. The question she is asking, in different ways, is what it would mean to begin to define herself as an outsider. Is she, as the teller of her parents' story, a rebellious "son" or a loyal one? As a social being, is she sinful and strong, or harmless and acceptable, a member of the family?

These were important issues just now because Stein was reaching to claim her identity as an original—and eccentric—writer. Much of the rest of the novel has the quality of the monologue of an outsider, confronting for the first time (with mixed grandiosity and self-doubt) the "lonely feeling" that comes with "being a great author" (593). Stein now opts for her own voice at all costs, renouncing the figures of authority who might admire or be repelled by her work. In these early pages she pauses before taking on that kind of isolation. She toys, as she had in *Three Lives*, with images of people who remain their parents' loyal children. Her hesitations are compounded by the close association in her mind between the idiosyncratic literary voice she is developing and her lesbianism, the part of herself she thinks of as an affront to her (deceased) father and to the parent culture.

This last association, only half-conscious from the beginning of the novel to the end, appears in other early digressions. Stein rarely depicts lesbianism in the plot of The Making of Americans,[4] but she carries on a private conversation with herself about it, first in an odd polemic that interrupts her story of the Dehning-Hersland courtship. In this digression she assumes the status of a true outsider, rather than that of an inheritor. After describing the Dehning family, whose affectionate squabbling resolves or skirts the problem of children's anger at fathers, Stein places herself as narrator somewhere apart from that placid scene. She is an outcast from the world of the Dehnings, for she is a "Singular" (a cover term for her lesbianism). Having noted that her character Alfred Hersland has "a strain of singularity that yet keeps well within the limits of conventional respectability" (so that he intrigues his bride without threatening her middle-class values), Stein proceeds to a bitter digression on the failure of American culture to foster really "queer people," people stranger than Alfred Hersland—such as herself (21). She abruptly turns to address her fellow exiles: "Brother Singulars, we are misplaced in a generation that knows not Joseph. We flee before the disapproval of our cousins, the courageous condescension of our friends who gallantly sometimes agree to walk the streets with us, from all them who never any way can understand why such ways and not the others are so dear to us" (21).

"Singulars" are pariahs, as oedipal sons are not. Their personal battles lead to expulsion from, rather than initiation into, their culture. Stein's own expatriation exemplifies their fate. "We fly," she says, "to the kindly comfort of an older world accustomed to take all manner of strange forms into its bosom" (21). The "we" to which she now belongs is not the mass of fallen, ordinary humanity, as in the oedipal introduction, but a small band of lonely and displaced people. Like the biblical Joseph to whom she refers (who was sold into exile by his brothers), she has lost her sense of incorporation in a family. No longer the adoring daughter-granddaughter, she is an alien among her "cousins."

A reader unfamiliar with the author's life would not automatical-

---

[4]One of the episodes Stein wrote earliest, that of the Dounor-Charles-Redfern triangle, involves a homoerotic friendship between women that is disrupted by the seduction of one of the friends by a man.

ly connect the term *Singular* to the idea of lesbianism; the vague reference to "such ways," which "are so dear to us," does little to clarify what a Singular is and does. Stein is approaching, but obliquely, the subject of her sexual orientation—an important source of her feelings of alienation within bourgeois America, as her surrogate Adele had already intimated in *Q.E.D.* when she said, "I probably have the experience of all apostles, I am rejected by the class whose cause I preach."[5] Yet the Brother Singular is still a compromise identity, exposing the author's secrets but also disguising them. As a brother, Stein masks her gender once again, avoiding the double exclusion of speaking both as a "queer person" and as a woman. Her male persona is comforting because it still gives her membership in a small tribe.

One can easily imagine why a woman writing fiction in the first decade of the century, in avant-garde Paris or anywhere else, should hesitate to proclaim her identity as a lesbian; in spite of the existence of a lesbian community in Paris, "Paris's comforting lesbian 'islands,'" as Elyse Blankley has demonstrated, "were surrounded by treacherous waters indeed," whose dangers ranged from pernicious popular stereotypes to harassment.[6] But Stein's choice not to identify herself with the lesbian community had motivations that transcended the practical, as Shari Benstock has shown.[7] And in her novel, her self-camouflage was not only practically motivated.

She could, after all, have disguised her lesbianism by adopting the voice of a heterosexual woman, as easily as that of a "Singular" man. The fact is that Stein (as has been known for some time)[8] was inclined to think of herself as especially masculine. In *The Making of*

---

[5]*Q.E.D.*, in *Fernhurst*, p. 59.

[6]Elyse Blankley, "Return to Mytilène: Renée Vivien and the City of Women," in *Women Writers and the City: Essays in Feminist Literary Criticism*, ed. Susan Merrill Squier (Knoxville: University of Tennessee Press, 1984), p. 49.

[7]For an account of Stein's relationship to the Parisian lesbian community, see Shari Benstock, *Women of the Left Bank: Paris, 1900–1940* (Austin: University of Texas Press, 1986), pp. 173–77.

[8]See for example Catharine R. Stimpson, "Gertrude Stein and the Transposition of Gender," in *The Poetics of Gender*, ed. Nancy K. Miller (New York: Columbia University Press, 1986), pp. 5–6.

Americans, her self-transformation into a brother is not just a strategy to assure a readership but also the expression of a private wish.

Stein's notebooks from this period are filled with theorizing about the various "sexual types" (*NB* DB.61), from which develops part of the characterology of the novel. What is left out of the novel but prevalent in the notebooks is a disturbing misogyny. Stein likes to describe herself as a "masculine type" and therefore as exceptional. She speculates that Picasso, Matisse, and certain others "have a maleness that belongs to genius. Moi aussi, perhaps" (*NB* DB.26, C.21). Femininity, in the meantime, from which she dissociates herself, is linked not to things like genius but (often) to dirt, the body, slyness, stupidity, and half a dozen other stereotypical traits. Alice Toklas, for example, in the first phase of Stein's interest in her, is used, shockingly, to illustrate a "malicious unstable soulless feminine quality," which "wallows in filth" (*NB* C.15). Stein's elder sister, Bertha, is diagnosed as having too much "sloppy oozy female in her" (*NB* J.3).

This misogyny complicates the meaning of Stein's self-projection as male in the novel itself. A pattern in these early sections is a collision of incompatible self-images. Stein is at one moment an oedipal-aggressive son, at another a loyal and honorable one; similarly, her self-identification as one of the "Brother Singulars" approaches the intimate subject of her lesbianism, but at the same time alters her gender, erasing what she privately thought of as the baseness of femininity. These were the conflicts of a lesbian with a strong bourgeois (and male) identification, conflicts left over from *Q.E.D.* and "Melanctha" which have now moved to the surface and suffused the authorial persona. The clashing self-images are Stein's way of asking who she is, how "queer" she is, and whether she fits in anywhere.

These were artistic as well as personal questions. Having set out to write a novel of middle-class family life, Stein begins to wonder whether as a lesbian she is really of the group she is writing about. As an expatriate, she feels all the more out of place composing a paean to the American bourgeoisie she has left behind. Even more confusingly, her middle-class affiliation now makes her a stranger in the new milieu of avant-garde Paris. So she laments in another aside: "Middle-class, middle-class, I know no one of my friends who will admit it, one can find no one among you all to belong to it" (34). For "middle class is sordid material unillusioned unaspiring" (34). She is isolated, then, on all sides: the American bourgeois families she has deserted revile her as a "Singular," but her Parisian friends, she fears, will see her bourgeois identification itself as "sordid" and low.

Stein is directly identifying her feelings of intellectual loneliness. She wonders not only who her subject is but also who her audience is—a more anxious question, which will not go away after *The Making of Americans*. She is afraid that her sordid interests will alienate her readers; indeed, she wonders at times whether she has a reader at all. "Bear it in your mind my reader, but truly I never feel it that there ever can be for me any such a creature, no it is this scribbled and dirty and lined paper that is really to be to me always my receiver" (33). This sentence (which ends much later, after further interruptions) is shaped, or rather derailed, by Stein's need to confess her loneliness. Once again, she feels isolated and unclean, her only "receiver" a "dirty" piece of paper that mirrors her self-doubts.

This is the outcry of an emotional, self-concerned—and embodied—speaker, a particular writer "scribbling" on pieces of paper. Stein's feeling of attachment to the messy physical manuscript disturbs her—she has no authority, only soiled pieces of paper to show for herself—yet it also consoles her, for at least her scrawled-on pages are small but tangible presents for her reader. She speaks of her text as "this that I write down a little each day here on my scraps of paper for you" (33). As a person with a body and a writing hand, she can pass along traces of herself.

Stein slowly surmounts these anxieties about her audience; finally she decides, "I am writing for myself and strangers" (289). From that moment (as in all her later texts) there is no clear class identification, no "we" for whom she speaks; nor is there a clearly defined audience, either bourgeois or avant-garde. In the course of the novel, Stein writes her way past her need for a fixed group membership by revaluing her own idiosyncrasies, turning them from "dirt" into "gifts," and beginning to assume that in spite of her isolation there are readers somewhere who will encounter her with interest and recognition.

The Three Voices of *The Making of Americans*

Gradually, Stein's bourgeois persona in *The Making of Americans* is displaced. The voice of the good son, the chronicler of middle-class life, gives way to two other voices: that of a psychologist, who uses the characters to illustrate a theory of human nature with serious pretensions to truth, and the intimate voice of a hypnotized producer of sentences, someone with moods of her own and bodily rhythms that affect her way of putting words together.

I call these three axes "voices" and not just expressions of various goals Stein had for her novel because they have different inflections; more than that, they press in on one another, jarringly. No single overarching consciousness seems to monitor them. The subject speaking or writing the text amounts to the strain of these incongruous propulsions. It is tempting to imagine that Stein slowly acquires an embodied, emotional, and (therefore) authentic voice, which displaces the more "alienated" voices of the bourgeois chronicler and the psychological theorist. Yet this formulation seems wrong, not least because the intimate voice, once located, keeps slipping back into dialogue with the other two, which in fact are retained long after the third voice has joined them. Stein expresses "herself" as much through the conversation among the three as through her passages of seemingly unmediated self-revelation.

Her important works after *The Making of Americans* all have their own dialogisms; one after another, they invite and confound the question, who speaks this? Where there is self-disclosure, as there often is, it is cut across by some other texture or impulse. Even *The Autobiography of Alice B. Toklas*, Stein's leap into self-reporting and plain speech, is after all an elaborate act of ventriloquism.[9]

The three voices of *The Making of Americans* engulf and include

---

[9]On Stein's ventriloquism, see Lynn Z. Bloom, "Gertrude Is Alice Is Everybody: Innovation and Point of View in Gertrude Stein's Autobiographies," *Twentieth-Century Literature* 24 (1978): 81–93.

one another in turn. The plot, which is what the opening sections promise, is progressively overrun by the characterology; Stein the bourgeois narrator is (almost) consumed by Stein the psychological theorist. But simultaneously, both the plot and the characterology are dissolving into forms of pleasure; with increasing distinctness, we hear a speaker's "I want" guiding the movement of the text.

This is a crazily entertaining novel; its comedy has something to do with the destabilized narrator, someone who seems to want to be an integrated, orderly person but keeps succumbing to different internal tides. Stein's narrator is a descendant of Tristram Shandy, with the additional twentieth-century peculiarity of being in so uncertain a relation to the author that one is never sure how much of his or her mobile mental process is a transcription of Gertrude Stein's own thought. Often the novel is funny just because of the gap between two possible views of Stein, one as a somber psychologist-storyteller who is unaware that her text is getting absurdly out of control, and the other as someone carefully orchestrating the absurdity.

The plot traces the marriages, worldly fortunes, and interior lives of the members of the Hersland family and some of their acquaintances. A few episodes anchor the narrative: Alfred Hersland's courtship of Julia Dehning; the desertion of his sister Martha by an unfaithful husband; and the death from an unspecified ailment of a third sibling, David. From the start, however, this story exudes psychology—psychology of an unusual sort. Stein seems interested not so much in her characters' conscious interactions as in their ways of impinging on one another, rather as physical objects impinge on one another. People are not primarily centers of subjectivity but forces or motions, encountering other person-motions, which they either repel, besiege, or submit to. The courtship in the opening episode, for example, is presented as an instance of one person's "power" setting up residence inside someone else: Julia "never . . . did any very real thinking about Hersland as a man to be to her as a husband to control her. But, somehow, a little, he was *there in her as an unknown power* that might attack her" (32, emphasis added). Characters move into and out of one another, imbibe or expel one another. The elder David Hersland (the father of the David who dies) thrives only when "filled" with a combative woman: "In his latest living he needed a woman to fill him, later when he was shrunk away from the outside of him he needed a woman with sympathetic diplomatic domineering to, entering into him, to fill him" (155). This vision of people as quasi-physical masses in states of friction or fusion with one another evolves into an explicit psychological theory, which diverts attention from the plot and even from the fictional characters.

Stein is still imprinting her interest in psychology on her fiction, and far more openly than in "Melanctha." In fact, there are still traces of William James's psychology in her thinking. She gradually begins to speculate aloud that the world is divided into two types of people, "the attacking kind" and "the resisting kind." The two groups bear *some* connection to the Jamesian polarity that governed "Melanctha." There are resonances with James, for example, when Stein says that resisters are sluggish in their responses to stimuli. Their minds have a "slow resisting bottom" that muffles impressions so that "there is not in them a quick and poignant reaction" (343). Sometimes "a stimulation entering into the surface of the mass that is them to make an emotion does not get into it" (343): many stimuli are excluded from notice. Stein's resisting class has something like the Jamesian faculty of selective attention, the mental rigidity that filters out the swarm of sensation. The critical factor in selective attention is a mass of conventional names and ideas, which takes the place of immediate experience. Similarly, some of Stein's resisters are distanced from the world by a film of words and stock concepts. "There are in many of such ones aspirations and convictions due . . . to books they are reading, to the family tradition, to the lack of articulation of the meaning of the being in them" (463). Resisters are likely to be compulsive moralists and—especially—talkers, and some are so cerebral that they actually lack (or require from others) "enough stimulation to make them keep really alive inside them" (522).

Stein's resisters, then, are like her earlier character Jeff Campbell (in his first phase), in that "feeling about anything itself" is sometimes "not very much in" them (554). Attackers, on the other hand, often seem to repeat the features of Melanctha and of the promiscuous mental pole in James. They are characteristically "excited," as well as "poignant and quick [in] reaction"; "emotion in such of

them has the quickness and intensity of a sensation" (643, 343).
Like Melanctha, they also have "courage for living," or blind "daring" (654, 18).

Stein repeats as well the Jamesian idea that every mind achieves
its own balance between the two mental poles: "There is some
resisting and some attacking in every one" (253). She tries to define
each of her many characters' "bottom nature," the particular mix
(and quality) of resisting and attacking features in each. Finally, the
two types, as in "Melanctha," attract: "In all loving . . . mostly
there is one . . . [who] does attacking . . . and the other one then
is of them who have . . . resisting in them" (178). Once again Stein
dramatizes as affective play *between people* the play of faculties that
James attributed to the individual mind; many of the characters in
the novel, both major and minor, fall into pairs whose mutual
needs and complementarity Stein carefully describes. The corre-
spondence to James, however, is imperfect, partly because Stein's
imagery of persons-in-friction points to her characters' unconscious (erotic and aggressive) process, rather than to Jamesian issues of attention, and partly—as we will see—because as the novel
progresses her manner of describing personality types becomes
increasingly bizarre and subjective.

But to return from the Jamesian affinities to the larger question of
Stein's persona as psychologist, for a large portion of the novel she
expects her division of humanity into types (and into numerous
subclasses such as "engulfing murky resisting" [551]) to yield "a
history of every man and every woman and every kind of being
they ever have . . . in them" (175). Inflated as this goal for the
novel sounds, it seems to have been sincere. The notebooks show
Stein developing her classifications and devising charts fitting her
friends and acquaintances into various categories and subcatego-
ries. She had two very different aims for her novel, to tell a story
and to expound a quasi-scientific theory—the latter a strange thing
to attempt in a work of fiction. Rather than minimize the tension
between the two goals, she exaggerates it: her narrator splits into
two people, inhabiting and calling up different planes of reality.
The original narrator conveys fictional information in the past
tense about the Herslands, but the psychological theorist, who
keeps interrupting, speaks in the present tense about her sup-

posedly valid theories, illustrating them by reference to actual people whom she knows: "I was seeing one to-day who reminded me very much of another one. . . . they both [are] of the resisting kind" (607).

Stein wants us to hear this second narrator as a real person, an author, worthy of having her beliefs credited: "Sometime when I am all through all my writing, when . . . all my learning has been written, sometime then some will understand the being in all men and women" (348). She tries to propel herself past the fictional framework by insisting on the truth value of her claims: "This division [into resisters and attackers] has real meaning" (348) and "This is not just talking, this all has real meaning" (299).

But these protestations of meaning signal a narrative instability. The dual machinery Stein has set up for the novel is doomed to come unhinged. The further we read, the more copious the theorizing digressions become, and the more tenuous the plot—notwithstanding Stein's frequent halfhearted assurances to the effect that the thread of theory will somehow lead back to the story of the Herslands. "I will be wanting," she says, rather late in the novel, "to be going on writing the history of Alfred Hersland which will certainly be more interesting now that every one knows so very much more of resisting, of resisting engulfing being in men and women" (568). This is a particularly silly justification; Alfred Hersland's history in fact is not enriched, just endlessly delayed, by the repetitious and byzantine psychological speculations.

Stein either deliberately allows her psychological meanderings to crowd out her plot, as a kind of literary experiment, or simply loses control of her text. In fact the shapelessness is both unwilled and (then) made meaningful; Stein minds, then does not mind, that her novel is losing its original structure. She begins to see her text as something that "comes out of" her (323), with its own nonlinear but expressive shape. If she had doggedly adhered to the posture of a mental scientist, she would have produced a broken text—neither fiction nor compelling theory. But what saves the novel is a third voice that begins to make sense of the excesses and strains in the other voices. An introspective speaker emerges who rereads both her original plot-making and her will to theorize *as forms of her own desire.*

First Stein exposes a fantasy of omnipotence at the heart of her psychological theorizing: her typology is driven not in fact by a disinterested stake in the truth but by a primitive wish to "fill" the human race with life: "So then we go on . . . so that sometime there will be done a history of every one and every kind of one. . . . Every one then will be full then of the being a history of every one can give to them" (180). She wants not simply to classify people but to infuse "being" into them. Her ultimate (grandiose) goal is to give everyone who "ever was or is or will be living" the "last touch of being" that "a history of them can give to any one" (180).

As she fills people with life, she will also be filled by them: "More and more I know all there is of all being, . . . [and] some-time all history of all men and women will be inside some one"—the "someone" is herself (298). Stein has turned her vocabulary of body-masses on herself, unearthing her own urge to swallow the sum of human history. What seemed like a scientific project at first is actually an expression of her pleasure in the thought of filling and containing other people.

That her scheme is less a rational plan than the expression of a private need is evident also from the repetitive, almost drugged style in which she discusses it. Rather than execute her charac-terological scheme, she caresses it, suffusing herself with the pleas-ant feeling of being about to begin. She opens a paragraph, "Some time then there will be every kind of a history of every one"; the next paragraph seems to put these ideas into action with "This is *now* a history of a number of men and women"; but we move nowhere, for the next opens, "So then we go on to our beginning of giving a history of every one"; then, "And so to commence again with the"—still uncommenced—"history of many of them and all the kinds"; and finally, just to show that we have gone in a circle, "Sometime then there will be a history of every one of every man and every woman" (180, emphasis added).

Stein is exploring the feel of her overblown ambitions, rather than sublimating them and moving forward. The notebooks, as it happens, have none of this quality of self-hypnosis; outside the novel, Stein's thoughts are perfectly linear, and her attempt to classify people, while ambitious, is not grandiose. Paradoxically, she gets closer to her primitive fantasies in the public document, the novel; its strange style reflects not absentmindedness or self-indulgence but self-exploration.

At a crucial moment, a third of the way through the novel, the intimate "Stein" begins to talk more explicitly about herself. She opens the chapter called "Martha Hersland" by recasting her whole story as one of love. "There are many that I know and they know it. They are all of them repeating and I hear it. I love it and I tell it" (289). Her characterology is revealed to be the product, and the record, of her own love of the sound of other people's repeating. For it turns out that attacking and resisting, and their sub-classes, reflect in some unspecified way different "kinds and ways of repeating" (298); that is, each person's fundamental character reveals itself to Stein in his or her (perhaps not only spoken) repetitions. To the grandiose motives that Stein has unveiled behind her characterological scheme, she adds a motive of love, or pleasure; her interest in "looking and comparing and classifying" stems from her enchantment with people's ways of repeating (289).

In so exposing herself, Stein partially relinquishes the persona of hard scientist. As in "Melanctha," she is still a psychologist of sorts, schematically dividing the world into two types of people; now she has even announced that she is after a universal characterology. But a professional psychologist—William James, or Stein, had she followed the trajectory he had recommended to her—would not load a theoretical text with information about the private pleasures behind the science. The polarity in "Melanctha" of manly doctor and sensuous woman has broken down: the doctor is dissolving into the sensuous person, as if Jeff Campbell, having started to "wander" with Melanctha, never went back to his job.

Does this overlapping of the scientific and the pleasure-seeking person represent some sort of resolution of the conflicts in "Melanctha" between the things that Jeff and Melanctha embodied? It seems, instead, that the balance has shifted. Stein is beginning to explore and to claim more fully the forms of her own pleasure. One way in which she felt comfortable doing this was to remain in contact with the old, scientific voice of her Radcliffe days, although now in an exaggerated form bordering on self-parody. Instead of simply slipping away from her earlier scientific persona, an unmooring that might have seemed too threatening, she reinhabits that persona and uses the force of her own pleasure to break it open.

Her text is on the way to articulating its own erotics. The act of listening to repeating, she writes, gives her physical, almost sexual sensations. Repetition is a "pounding" in her; a person's repeating enters her, and "slowly it sounds louder and louder and louder inside me through my ears and eyes and feelings" (302, 300). It makes no sense to speak of this image in terms of erogenous zones; Stein's whole body is where the "pounding" happens. But sometimes the excitement is (as if) in the mouth: "Slowly [people's nature] comes out from them to the most delicate gradation, to the gentlest flavor of them. Always it comes out as repeating from them. . . . This is a joy to any one loving repeating" (293). Stein's pleasure becomes her text. Her love of repetition is the original stimulus for her characterology, and now her overt theme: "They are all of them repeating. . . . I love it *and now I will write it*" (289, emphasis added). But she also literally "writes it," writes repeating, takes her pleasure again, *in* the text. Her style, which to this point has been increasingly repetitive, now asks to be understood as a continuation of the "pounding" she loves to hear.

This first section of the Martha Hersland chapter raises the repetitive style to a new pitch. A very few thoughts are braided together, in changing sequences. These thoughts begin with, or are, the following sentences: "Sometime then there will be a complete history of every one" (294); "This is now a little description of having loving repeating as being" (295); "Every one always is repeating the whole of them" (293); "Always from the beginning there was to me all living as repeating" (300). Whenever one of these thoughts seems to have run its course, it lies in wait, to start over with minor additions or changes a few paragraphs later. There are smaller arcs of repeating as well: in the same pages Stein tries out a new prosody, rhythmic and condensed. The pair of sentences about the "many that I know" (which becomes a kind of refrain) "rhymes": "There are many that I know and they know it. They are all of them repeating and I hear it" (289). The sustained trochaic beat of the two sentences, their use of four identical words in identical places, and their virtual metrical identity make us hear them as a sound experiment based upon a simple form of repetition.

Thus, Stein emphasizes the texture of her medium, writing a prose close to poetry; her pleasure in repetition is her theme, but it flowers again as a stylistic imperative. We can think of the repetitive style as autoerotic. When Stein listens to people's repetitions, she feels a "pounding"—at times "irritating," at times pleasing, but always something she craves as someone who has "loving repeating being" (298). When she goes on to write repetition, she both creates and enjoys a new pounding. Her friend H. P. Roché, a man with literary aspirations, who had admired *Three Lives*, all but labeled some subsequent writing in the repetitive manner of *The Making of Americans* masturbatory: "More and more your style gets solitary. . . . Rhythm? oh yes. But that sort of rhythm is intoxicating for you—it is something like – – – – –."[10]

The novel courts, rather than hides from, the innuendo of Roché's five dashes. Stein's interminable repetitions void her sentences of their freight of information. What we hear most of all, after a certain point, is the author fondling her words: "I love it, I tell it. I love it, I live it and I tell it. Always I will tell it. They live it and I see it and I hear it and I feel it. They live it and I see it and I hear it and I feel it and I love it" (305).

Incantatory repetition is inherently erotic according to Roland Barthes, whose small book on textual pleasure is still one of the most sophisticated articulations we have of an erotics of the signifier. Repetition, he says, if extravagant, creates *jouissance*, the word (translated as "bliss") that refers to an author's pleasure-in-writing, which is then available to the reader.[11] There is *jouissance*

---

[10]Letter of February 6, 1912, Gallup, ed., *The Flowers of Friendship*, p. 56. Gallup speculates that the texts Stein had given Roché to read were portraits. I am indebted to Elena Yatzeck for suggesting, in a seminar paper, the implications of Roché's five dashes. On Roché, see Mellow, *Charmed Circle*, p. 112.

[11]"Repetition itself creates bliss." Roland Barthes, *The Pleasure of the Text*, trans. Richard Miller (New York: Farrar, Straus, and Giroux, 1975), p. 41, hereafter cited in the text. (These words are immediately preceded by a sentence I find obscure, but which may represent a qualification: "Yet one can make a claim for precisely the opposite (though I am not the one who would make such a claim)." In context, however, this statement seems to refer to the absence or "marginal[ity]" of erotically repetitive art "in our culture.") Barthes's book is about the varieties of a reader's pleasure, which he nonetheless says are impossible without the prior pleasure of the author: "If I read this sentence, this story, or this word with pleasure, it is because they were written in pleasure (such pleasure does not contradict the writer's complaints)" (p. 4). Hence his argument about the pleasure of reading contains

when the words themselves carry an erotic charge, in their irritating or delicious sounds, their rhythms, or their surprises of syntax and diction. Such words produce sexual feelings, whether or not they also refer to such feelings. The author's pleasure, and therefore the reader's, "leaps out of the frame" (57), affixing itself to the signifier rather than the signified.

One notion of how an author's pleasure in repetition or other stylistic play is sexual is as incest: if one thinks of a native language as a *"mother tongue,"* the writer, Barthes says, "is someone who plays with his mother's body . . . in order to glorify it, to embellish it, or in order to dismember it" (37). This formulation presupposes that all playful writers make an unconscious or conscious association of "language" and "mother." Whether or not such an association is universal, I find it in Stein—not in *The Making of Americans* but in *Tender Buttons,* where (as we will see) she conceives of her writing as an incestuous climb into the udder. Some of the violence, too, in Barthes's picture of what a writer does to or with language finds an analogue in the imagery of *Tender Buttons.*

But to remain with what *The Making of Americans* reveals about its own eroticism, we can think of the repetitive style as erotic without a sexual object, maternal or other—as autoerotic. Stein tells of her love of repeating and (re)lives it in the pulsations of her sentences; her style is a means of giving herself pleasure. On the other hand, the text does find an object of sorts in the reader. Stein pleases herself, but at the same time means to seduce a reader. "I want readers so strangers must do it"—so she declares, in the same section on love (289). Her repetition is an invitation to pleasure, not just an autoerotic act. "Now," she says, as she prepares for one of her repetitive paragraphs, "to begin again with it *as telling*" (299, emphasis added). Telling—unlike merely saying or stating—is an act of utterance in search of a listener. An effect of Stein's conveying the same information over and over is to draw attention to her sheer pleasure in "telling" us things; and if we like this redundant

---

an implicit argument about the pleasure of writing. For similar applications of Barthes's ideas to Stein's experimental writing, see DeKoven, *A Different Language,* especially p. 16; and Walker, *The Making of a Modernist,* p. 52 (the latter in the context of *The Making of Americans*).

style, it must be partly because there is also a pleasure in being told things, even when they keep echoing what we have heard a moment before.

Stein develops in this section a habit of reminding us that she knows we are there, absorbing her sentences; the chapter has a soothing metacommentary in which the speaker informs us of what she is about to do and asks us to share her momentum or her pleasure in pausing for a moment: "Now to slowly begin" (298) and "Now then" (306). Is her pleasure in telling, or ours in being told, erotic? At a very general level, the mouth and the ear can be thought of as erogenous zones, but the text itself has its own, different conception of the sexual dynamics of telling.

Loving Repeating: Anality and Style

The Making of Americans is a spectacularly anal text—knowingly so, although just subliminally enough to have escaped commentary. At one point Stein hints at the connection in her mind between telling and excreting: "I am not content, I have not had it come out without pressing the description of Mr. Arragon the musician. It should come out of me without pressing without any straining in me to be pressing. . . . Always each thing must come out completely from me leaving me inside me just then gently empty, so pleasantly and weakly gently empty" (586). This amusing passage on "straining" and "pressing" (from a much later part of the book than the Martha Hersland chapter) points to one sort of pleasure Stein's narrator takes in telling. To tell is to enjoy the feeling of filling up with material and then excreting it—onto the page or into the reader, or perhaps simply out of herself. That sort of anal pleasure is deeply coded in the Martha Hersland chapter too. When Stein says things like "Now to slowly begin," she is letting us know that she is about to fill up—and fill her paragraph—with information and sounds. Then she signals the release of that pressure with comments like "Now then"; at such moments she has exhausted a quantity of material and (to use the image from the later passage) is "pleasantly and weakly gently empty."

Stein experiences her telling as a form of rhythmic accumulation and release. She also offers her reader a version of that pleasure.

For from a reader's perspective, the only way to enjoy—or to endure—this novel is to succumb to it, yielding one's own pace to the
rhythm of Stein's paragraphs. As Roché wrote in his letter to her, "I
start reading your style only when I feel very strong & want in a
way to suffer."[12] *The Making of Americans* demands a relaxation of
many of the tendencies fiction normally activates: curiosity, the
need for a story, and the feeling of mastery that comes from being
able to peruse the text for information. We are always seduced back
into the rhythms of the medium.

Stein's vehicle, technically, for imposing rhythms of accumulation and release is the repetitive paragraph. Her paragraphs echo
one another, but always with something added or omitted, something tangled or changed. Yet by the end of each paragraph she has
expelled her tangle of thoughts, however unwieldy it has become.
She has finished; and there is a great pause before the next paragraph, an interval sometimes explicitly acknowledged by expressions of having finished—"So then" and "Now then." These
are the rhythms of an anal style—anal rather than sexual in some
other way because of Stein's consciousness of the mass of material
she is processing in each paragraph.

Karl Abraham, whose writings, along with Freud's, laid the
groundwork for the psychoanalytic concept of anality, theorized
that anal erotism involves two different sorts of pleasure: the excit-
ation associated with the "evacuation of the bowels" and an excita-
tion "based on a reverse process—the retention of the faeces."[13]
Stein's repetitive style involves both varieties of pleasure. The expressions of relief ("So then"), as well as the marked logical breaks
at the ends of paragraphs, bespeak the teller's pleasure in having
emptied herself; at the same time, her manner of reusing—and
adding—material from paragraph to paragraph strongly suggests
the pleasures of retention.

A brief example of Stein's repetitive technique (although any
illustration is both too little and too much, since this is the style of

12Gallup, p. 56.

13Karl Abraham, "A Short Study of the Development of the Libido, Viewed in the
Light of Mental Disorders," in *Selected Papers on Psycho-Analysis,* trans. Douglas
Bryan and Alix Strachey (London: Hogarth Press, 1948), p. 425. On Abraham's role
in helping to formulate the concept of anality, see Leonard Shengold, "Defensive
Anality and Anal Narcissism," *International Journal of Psycho-Analysis* 66 (1985): 49.

much of the novel) is a pair of like paragraphs, still from the section on love. The first reads, "Each one slowly comes to be a whole one to me. Each one slowly comes to be a whole one in me. This is now a description of learning one" (306). The second is, "Every one then sometimes comes to be a whole one to me. Each one sometimes comes to be a whole one in me. Always loving repeating is my way of being. This is now some description of my studying" (307). The second version adds a sentence and changes a few words, but manages to end in the same place as the first. The repeated final sentence, "This is now some description . . . ," signals that the thought, in its now slightly enlarged version, has again terminated. So the second paragraph "retains" material from the first and, indeed, retains the unit of thought for a longer time by virtue of the additions; yet the desire to retain is answered by the desire to expel or to finish. The moment at which the entire mass of material has again, as it were, passed through the speaker is the stylistic analogue to the "weakly gently empty" moment Stein describes herself as experiencing when a description has "come out" of her in the right way. (Thematically, these sentences incidentally seem to repeat the excretory metaphor, although they suggest even more strongly a picture of gestation. On the other hand, as Freud pointed out, at the level of the unconscious people make a close link between defecation and childbirth.)[14]

Stein's paragraphs, which fill with and then evacuate words as if they were faeces, also *play* with language in a manner reminiscent of the play of children during what classical psychoanalysis refers to as the anal phase. The anal, or "sadistic-anal," phase, as the psychoanalyst Lili E. Peller describes it (elaborating Freud), "is dominated by the drive for achieving mastery (*Bemächtigungstrieb*). Mouth, skeletal and ring muscles (anus, urethra) are highly charged with libido; they are the executive organs. The child strives primarily for mastery of his body."[15] The child in this phase is interested in learning to control his or her bodily functions. "Mastery and knowl-

---

[14]"The baby is regarded [by a child] as a 'lumf' (cf. the analysis of 'Little Hans'), as something which becomes detached from the body by passing through the bowel." "On Transformations of Instinct as Exemplified in Anal Erotism," *SE* 17:130.

[15]Lili E. Peller, "Comments on Libidinal Organizations and Child Development," *Journal of the American Psychoanalytic Association* 13 (1965): 737, hereafter cited in the text.

edge of his body functions—what he can do and how to do it—come to him through innumerable repetitions and their variations" (738). A form of repetitive play develops as a consequence, in which the child performs a "cycle of doing, stopping to look or listen, and then doing again" (740). This description reminds me of Stein's cyclical verbal play in *The Making of Americans,* in which a paragraph is followed by a pause—a "Now then"—and then by a new paragraph which does again what the first did, with small variations. Indeed, among the forms of play that evolve during the anal phase, Peller mentions a highly libidinized vocal experimentation: "The young child also plays with his voice, with sounds and intricate sound sequences." Once he has done something with his voice, "he *repeats* what he has just done" (738–39).

The suspense Stein creates about how and when she will finish off her thought-clusters accounts for much of the comedy of her style. When she seems stylistically funny, it is because her paragraphs provoke the question, will she manage to rid herself of everything she has built up? And will she continue playfully to "master" her material by keeping within the limits of grammar, in spite of the new material she adds from one paragraph to the next? For example, her refrain in this section—"There are many that I know and they know it. They are all of them repeating and I hear it"—goes through increasingly elaborate variations. Here is one version: "*There are many that I know* and I know it. They are many that I know *and they know it. They are all of them* themselves and they *repeat it and I hear it*" (303). Since we hear, with each variant, both the original (whose almost unchanged components I have italicized here) and the added material that draws it out, we are impatient to hear the familiar last words, whether because they seem inevitable or because we fear they may not be; when they do come, they produce a relief that is like (or is) a laugh.

It is striking enough to observe Stein puncturing the fictional illusion by grounding her novel in her own pleasure-in-writing—a sort of reflexiveness that we are used to finding in postmodern literature (and theory) but not in fiction of the early modern period. Yet it is hard to overstate the daring it took for Stein, furthermore, to associate that pleasure with anality. Defecation deserves to be called the last taboo; for an analogue to Stein's anal text we must look ahead a decade to *Ulysses* and then perhaps to Beckett's works. Joyce and Beckett, however (and even more their predecessors in a satiric vein, such as Aristophanes and Swift), put some distance between themselves and the scatological interests of their characters. Stein's novel bravely makes the narrator the person who does the "pressing" and "straining"—a narrator, moreover, whose distance from the author is just what the intrusive private voice keeps unsettling.

The erotically repetitive style dislodges the voice of the dutiful son, which governed the first sections of the novel. But why should it be anal eros in particular that breaks apart the linear narration of the good son? Why, that is, when Stein comes forward as an embodied, sensual "teller," is her pleasure so much (like) that of the bowel? As a preliminary answer, Stein is exposing an anality that is arguably a feature of literature generally. All literary genres depend on repetition of one sort or another; as Stein in *The Making of Americans* insistently attends to the sound of that repetition, and reproduces it in a raw form, she is playfully discovering something about the link between (all?) literary repetition and the primitive pleasure people take in filling up with and excreting matter. She is uncovering an archaic ground of narrative, and therefore she naturally slips beneath the civilized persona of the obedient son, someone who would not have been sensitive to the erotic dimension of his own writing.

But further than that, the anal voice is a revised version of that filial voice itself—or its underside. Stein's initial, pious persona contained and barely concealed feelings of rage at the father. That rage appears to have dissipated, as Stein has moved toward and into the chapter on love, but in fact the rage is *released* in her anal-erotic style. For the "teller" of this novel is no longer a cramped, indebted, and tentative daughter-son but an omnipotent digestive system, processing the universe through her own interior. Her excretory omnipotence gives her leverage against the father(s).

Thematically, her characterological scheme digests the world, so that "sometime all history of all men and women will be inside some one," herself (298). In other words, she is revenged on the parents and grandparents whose history seemed so thoroughly to define and control her in the opening pages, where she wrote, "We need only realise our parents, remember our grandparents and know ourselves and our history is complete" (3). Now, instead, all history is "inside" her; she has swallowed it. Similarly, whereas at first she was just one of "the new people made out of the old" (3), now she can virtually reverse the situation by showing how her characters (of all generations) are made out of her, like babies or like faeces: "Each one slowly comes to be a whole one in me" (306).

Stylistically, the anal-repetitive prose has a similar function, for it forces all things to pass through something like an authorial body. The teller refuses to use words as transparent signifiers conveying her thoughts; instead, she turns words into objects, which she churns and rechurns, audibly processing her sentences so they bear her peculiar stamp. She does not leave anything alone; any new datum she introduces (a word or a thought) must be rhyth-mically played with until it is assimilated to the sounds and the vocabulary of the previous paragraphs. The repetitive style be-comes what the psychoanalyst Janine Chasseguet-Smirgel, in an-other context, calls "an enormous grinding machine."[16]

Chasseguet-Smirgel's interesting essay, which explores the writ-ings of the Marquis de Sade, suggests how an author's fantasies of digestive and excretory omnipotence can amount to a revenge on the father. Her hypothesis—which is worth rehearsing for a mo-ment before I consider its relevance to Stein—is that Sade's writ-ings register a perverse wish to erode "the double difference be-tween the sexes and the generations" (294). The sexual scenarios Sade envisions involve acts and masquerades that fantastically turn men into women, women into men, and parents and children into members of the same generation. Furthermore, "a permuta-tion of the erotogenic zones and their functions also takes place and has the effect of making them interchangeable. *Mixture* could be considered the heading under which the whole of Sade's fan-tasy world is placed" (294).

Erosion of difference, in these various forms, challenges the dominance of the father. For a father's great victory over his child within the family triangle is that he, with his adult male organ, can

[16]Janine Chasseguet-Smirgel, "Perversion and the Universal Law," *International Review of Psycho-Analysis* 10 (1983): 295, hereafter cited in the text.

possess the mother sexually; the child who is coming to recognize sexual difference bemoans "his own [and we could as easily say 'her own'] smallness and inadequacy" by comparison (293). A "perverse" solution that the child, and later the adult, may adopt is to fantasize the abolition of all sexual and generational differences, so that the father is no longer the child's elder or sexual superior, and the penis in any case has no primacy over any other organ that might be used in a sexual act.

In particular, the child denies sexual difference by slipping back from the genital to the anal phase (concepts that Chasseguet-Smirgel adopts, of course, from Freud).[17] "The *perverse temptation* leads one to accept pregenital desire and satisfactions (attainable by the small boy) as being equal, or even superior, to genital desires and satisfactions (attainable only by the father)" (293–94). If the pleasures of the anus can be imagined to rival the pleasures of the (adult) penis, the child need not feel inferior to the father.

Let us recall in this context Stein's tremendous concern at the beginning of *The Making of Americans* with reversing the primacy of her elders. There she decides, as she tells us, to disempower her parents and grandparents by portraying them in their old age or their infancy, a bit of generational magic not unlike the reversals Chasseguet-Smirgel finds in Sade. I am also struck by another sort of leveling-out Stein achieves, for which again Chasseguet-Smirgel furnishes a vocabulary. Stein's characterological scheme, which slowly takes over the novel, is directed at uncovering the "bottom nature"—or, as she sometimes rephrases it, the "bottom"—in each person. The notable feature of each character is thus not membership in the class male or female (in fact some of her descriptions of "a one" or "this one" leave the gender indeterminate) but instead the sort of "bottom" the person has, as if Stein were unconsciously marginalizing genital sexual difference in favor of a weird and indistinct notion of anal identity. When Chasseguet-Smirgel observes this sort of orientation toward the anal zone in Sade, she thinks of it as representing a victory over the father's phallic pri-

---

[17]See especially the *Three Essays on the Theory of Sexuality* (*SE* 7:123–245), where Freud distinguishes oral, anal, and genital phases of early childhood; in each phase, a different organ (mouth, anus/intestines, then genitals) is particularly susceptible to sexual excitement.

macy. Perhaps for a daughter such a victory over sexual difference is a double one, for sexual difference disempowers a girl not only during her childhood, when she cannot compete with the father for the mother, but also for life.[18] So Stein's concern with the "bottom" in everyone, as well as her impulse to turn her parents into children (or old people), may be a way of contesting the supremacy of the father, who is such a dominating presence in the early pages of the novel.

Anality—to take up Chasseguet-Smirgel's argument again—not only provides a pleasure to rival the genital pleasures that only the father can receive and provide; it also itself abolishes difference. The "perverse" child or adult can believe his or her body capable of turning the universe to faeces and thus of eliminating the very distinction between the sexes. Chasseguet-Smirgel notes Sade's fascination with the image of nature as a "gigantic cauldron," absorbing bits of matter in one form and emitting them in another; the Sadian hero identifies with this "cruel and almighty mother," so that he himself "becomes the grinding machine, the cauldron in which the universe will be dissolved" (295). This fantasy exposes Sade's "one basic intention: *to reduce the universe to faeces,* or rather to annihilate the universe of differences (the genital universe) and put in its place the anal universe in which all parts are equal and interchangeable" (295).

This image of the self as a cauldron in which differences are dissolved suggests an interpretation not only of Stein's image of herself as absorbing and filling the universe, but also of the repetitive style of *The Making of Americans,* which homogenizes everything it touches, so that "all parts" (to reuse Chasseguet-Smirgel's phrase) become "equal and interchangeable." Stein makes of her language the sort of anal cauldron that Sade, according to Chasseguet-Smirgel, makes of his body. For example, when she transforms her sentence "There are many that I know and I know it" into "There are many that I know and they know it" (303), while we hear the contrast between the word *I* and the *they* that replaces it, we are

[18]For a discussion of girls' wish to compete with the father for sexual access to the mother, see Gayle Rubin, "The Traffic in Women: Notes on the 'Political Economy' of Sex," in *Toward an Anthropology of Women,* ed. Rayna R. Reiter (New York: Monthly Review Press, 1975), pp. 193–94.

also made aware of their syntactical and prosodic interchangeability. Their distinctness (to recur to Chasseguet-Smirgel's imagery) is partially stewed out of them by the repetitive style. The style of *The Making of Americans* has a rhythmic intensity, but it also has a lexical grayness, quite as if the author were in a position to "reduce the universe to faeces." The same sort of homogenization reappears in Stein's treatment of her characters, the vast majority of whom appear in the guise of a dehumanized, nonindividuated "some one," "a one," or "this one."

This all-powerful voice, then, which hums with the pleasures of producing matter and is not imposed upon by the reality or the dignity of other people, is the obverse of the timid and moralistic, but secretly enraged, good son of the first sections of the novel. Stein is exposing an aggressive and primitive fantasy beneath an initially civilized narration; in fact, she is uncovering an aggressivity that may be inherent in the act of narration itself, since all narrators (and authors) must derive some pleasure from their power to use characters and language as matter to be played with. If Stein's fantasy of anal omnipotence does amount to a challenge to the father's primacy, what she seems to me unconsciously to be protesting is not particularly the father's sexual access to the mother (an issue of which I see no traces in *The Making of Americans*) but simply the father's anteriority as her maker. The contested issue is, who is "made out of" whom? Her rage is a version of Satan's, a rage at having been authored by someone else. As an anal producer, she is able herself to become the maker (and remaker, and mixer-up) of the world.

I want to say something, in this context, about the other remarkable feature of the style of *The Making of Americans*, the famous "continuous present." This feature, which involves a heavy use of participles, gerunds, and progressive verb forms, represents another manner of "grinding" things into homogeneity. Rather than conjugate the information-bearing verb, Stein characteristically turns it into a gerund or a participle, which she attaches to a relatively common verb (to do, to have, to be) that she does inflect; thus, "she had to *do finishing*," or, "Repeating then *is* always *coming* out of every one" (198, emphases added). Sameness emerges not just from the proliferation of the verbs *do*, *be*, and *have* but also from the -*ing* that repeatedly terminates important verbs. Furthermore, the gerundial and participial forms remove the important verbs from time, effecting the grammatical equivalent of a collapse of generations; as Stein wrote of her earlier articulation of the "continuous present" in "Melanctha," "There was a marked direction in the direction of being in the present although naturally I had been accustomed to past present and future."[19] Her abolition of grammatical difference, or inflection, disturbs the linear time, the sequence of past-present-future, that symbolically supports the ever-anterior father.

Finally, the continuous present offers not only homogenization but also a potentially anti-paternal pleasure. Its emphasis is on process: characters do not simply "finish" something, for example, but "do finishing" (198). The father may own linear time, but the continuous present defies the closures of linear time by setting everything in motion. Is it possible that the continuous present replaces "linear-phallic time" (to borrow, perhaps too allusively, a phrase of Julia Kristeva's)[20] with some sort of bowel time, in keeping with the "perverse" wish described by Chasseguet-Smirgel? A remark Stein made about *The Making of Americans* prompts me to wonder whether the endless motion of her verbs had, for her, some of the meanings of the motion of the bowel. "It is something strictly American," she writes, "to conceive a space that is filled with moving, a space of time that is filled always filled with moving and my first real effort to express this thing which is an American thing began in writing The Making of Americans."[21] A "space of *time*" that is "filled always filled with moving" is the continuous present; but to think anatomically, a space of the body that is always filled with moving is the bowel. I would not want to make too much of this analogy; on the other hand, I do not want to overlook the instance of the continuous present in the title of Stein's novel—the gerund *making*, a word that children use to refer to defecation.

[19]Stein, "Composition as Explanation," in *Selected Writings of Gertrude Stein*, p. 517.

[20]See Julia Kristeva, "The Novel as Polylogue," in *Desire in Language: A Semiotic Approach to Literature and Art*, ed. Leon S. Roudiez, trans. Thomas Gora, Alice Jardine, and Leon S. Roudiez (New York: Columbia University Press, 1980), p. 201.

[21]Stein, "The Gradual Making of The Making of Americans," *Lectures*, p. 161.

(The possessive genitive also creates an ambiguity: this novel describes how Americans are made, but it can also represent how Americans, including the author, "make.")

My use of Chasseguet-Smirgel's concept of perversion is not meant to suggest that the experiment of *The Making of Americans* is grounded in pathology. As Chasseguet-Smirgel writes, "There is a 'perverse core' latent within each one of us that is capable of being activated under certain circumstances" (293); what Sade (or Stein) expresses, we all experience but ordinarily suppress in ourselves. More than that, if "the pervert," as Chasseguet-Smirgel writes, "is trying to free himself from the paternal universe and the law" (299), so is the artist, to the extent that art, whatever it overtly decides about "the paternal universe," protests limitation and death. If Stein's repetitive style and her grandiose fantasies were expressions of a mind gone awry, rather than of an unconscious tendency universally shared, her readers would not participate in the fantasy, succumb to the rhythmic style, or laugh along with the author's extravagant self-presentation.

Furthermore, if Stein's stylistic experimentation is anal-erotic and therefore (within Chasseguet-Smirgel's vocabulary) perverse, one could just as easily call it modernist instead. Much modernist experimentation involves passing linear prose through the cauldron of the unconscious. As Julia Kristeva has maintained, modern literature in one of its varieties exposes the "unceasing operation of the drives toward, in, and through language."[22] What Kristeva elsewhere, more generally, calls poetic language unsettles our experience of words as mere signs, turning them instead (or also) into sources of nonsymbolic *jouissance*: "The semiotic activity, which introduces wandering or fuzziness into language and, *a fortiori*, into poetic language is . . . a mark of the workings of drives (appropriation/rejection, orality/anality, love/hate, life/death)."[23] So the rhythmic, presymbolic (and anal) pleasure to which Stein's style "regresses" is of the essence of modernist experimentation. Perhaps regression is not even quite the word for it. Pinchas Noy's psychoanalytic work on the artistic process in-

---

[22]Julia Kristeva, *Revolution in Poetic Language*, trans. Margaret Waller (New York: Columbia University Press, 1984), p. 17.

[23]Kristeva, "From One Identity to an Other," in *Desire in Language*, p. 136.

terestingly contests the idea that an artist's use of formal features suggestive of archaic mental processes "is to be regarded as a *regression* to primitive-infantile levels of organization."[24]

The point that Kristeva powerfully makes is that language always partakes of archaic drives (for example, orality and anality), although these are normally repressed; but certain experimental writers interestingly excavate those drives within language. The experimental linguistic practice toward which Stein's anal orientation leads in *The Making of Americans*, incidentally, distinguishes her work from Sade's, where the anal fantasy occurs only at the level of the content and thus does not result in formal innovation.

The style of *The Making of Americans* is erotic or autoerotic. Is it "feminine" as well? The question seems relevant in the light of recent poststructuralist theory that associates textual erotics with femininity (theory that has influenced critical approaches to Stein).[25] Hélène Cixous, the best known theorist of the feminine body-text, writes, "Woman is body more than man is. Because he is invited to social success, to sublimation. More body hence more writing," in the Derridean sense of writing as textuality that opens up the free play of the signifier. Cixous believes that since male-dominated culture offers women slighter rewards than it offers men for repressing instinctual drives (they receive no oedipal inheritance and are subordinated by the social and linguistic codes repression makes possible), women have repressed incompletely and therefore have "furiously inhabited" their "sumptuous bodies"—in hysteria, for example, and soon, Cixous predicts, in a subversive writing that will bombard social and symbolic codes with "carnal, passionate body-words."[26]

Stein, ahead of her time, looks quite like the body-writer her-

---

[24]Pinchas Noy, "A Revision of the Psychoanalytic Theory of the Primary Process," *International Journal of Psycho-Analysis* 50 (1969): 157. Noy is writing not about anality but about features of art that seem to replicate "primary process." I believe, however, that his generalizations apply to other forms of seeming regression in artistic process as well.

[25]See particularly DeKoven, e.g., pp. xviii–xix, 21–23, 77.

[26]"Sorties," in Hélène Cixous and Catherine Clément, *The Newly Born Woman*, trans. Betsy Wing (Minneapolis: University of Minnesota Press, 1986), p. 95, hereafter cited in the text.

alded in 1975 by Cixous—as DeKoven notes too.[27] Cixous's descriptions fit the experimental style of Virginia Woolf perhaps, but even better the self-consciously erotic, anal-oral styles of *The Making of Americans* and (differently) *Tender Buttons*. "If woman," Cixous writes, "has always functioned 'within' man's discourse, . . . now it is time for her to displace this 'within,' explode it, overturn it, grab it, make it hers, take it in, take it into her women's [*sic*] mouth, bite its tongue with her women's teeth, make up her own tongue to get inside of it" (95–96). As Stein says in *Tender Buttons*, "It is a bite. Cut up alone the paved way which is harm" (48). A writer (to paraphrase *Tender Buttons* out of context once again) who enjoys her orality, or bites her words, cuts up the "paved way"— the symbolic system, an artificial thoroughfare to an absent signified—which is a source of "harm." In *The Making of Americans*, too, Stein self-consciously sexualizes her style, fondles and excretes her words or, in Cixous's phrase, invents "her own tongue" so that language becomes an erotic instrument.

A problem, of course, with calling this writing feminine is that men—Joyce for example, a favorite of Cixous's—can engage in it too; hence Cixous's own displeasure with the term *écriture féminine*, for which she substitutes the almost as troublesome idea of a "decipherable libidinal *femininity* which can be read in a writing produced by a male or a female."[28] Since there is no way to think in such terms without engaging in circular definitions or essentialism, I ultimately do not find it helpful to label the style of *The Making of Americans* exclusively feminine—any more than it was in 1912, when Stein's friend Roché, in the same letter complaining about her intoxication with rhythm, threw up his hands and asked, "Quantity! Quantity! Is thy name woman?"[29]

[27]See DeKoven, pp. xviii, 21. See also Harriet Scott Chessman, *The Public Is Invited to Dance: Representation, the Body, and Dialogue in Gertrude Stein* (Stanford: Stanford University Press, 1989), p. 5: "Stein's writing often resembles the post-modernist writings of *écriture féminine* to such an extent that her influence upon the French feminists has emerged as a subject inviting further exploration."

[28]"An Exchange with Hélène Cixous," in Verena Andermatt Conley, *Hélène Cixous: Writing the Feminine* (Lincoln: University of Nebraska Press, 1984), p. 129, emphasis added.

[29]Gallup, p. 56.

There is, however, much to say about how Stein genders *herself* and the activity of writing. *Tender Buttons*, for example, is a very different text, one that contemplates itself as a woman's writing. Since Stein embeds in both *The Making of Americans* and *Tender Buttons* her own complex associations about the sexualities of her voice, it makes sense to treat these associations as containing genuine, if mediated, information about the libidinal origins and processes of the texts. Significantly, *The Making of Americans* does furnish a term for its own erotic-repetitive style: not feminine but infantile.

Repeating is a passion of childhood. The section on love contains a story of sorts, not about the fictional characters but about the author-narrator herself. She recounts a piece of her personal history, revealing that her love of repetition was originally a feature of her childhood, lost as she matured but subsequently recovered. "Always from the beginning," she says, "there was to me all living as repeating" (300). Growing up, however, meant forgetting that early pleasure in repetition: "There was for many years a learning and talking and questioning in me and not listening to repeating in every one around me"—even though "loving repeating" was still "a bottom to me" (301), a basis of her character, *which had become unconscious.*

"Always at the bottom was loving repeating being, that was not then there to my conscious being" (302). I want to stress Stein's terminology—"not then there to my conscious being"—because of her explicit reliance on an idea of unconscious process. Her listening-to-repeating, she says, went underground; it continued, but without her awareness. "Many years I listened and did not know it. I heard it, I understood it some, I did not know I heard it" (303). More recently, she says, her love of repetition resurfaced, becoming once again "a *conscious* feeling in me" (301, emphasis added). At the present time, she actively listens to repeating. "Slowly I came to hear repeating. More and more then I came to listen, now always and always I listen" (302). Her novel issues from this listening.

Not only does Stein reveal here that the preoccupations of her novel as a whole owe everything to a recent resurgence of lost feelings from her childhood. More than that, her literary voice, with its own incantatory repetitions, can now be thought of as an attempt to bring to the surface this previously repressed, infantile dimension of her mental life. Stein's style replays in an intellectual, adult context what she as a child liked to hear and produce.

Perhaps her style at the same time addresses the child in her reader. For everyone, she says, once had and then buried the very love of repetition she has resurrected in herself (a hypothesis borne out by psychoanalytic work, such as Peller's, on children's use of repetitive play). "Loving repeating," Stein writes, "is *always* in children," but as in her own case, that repetition-pleasure is usually repressed in early adulthood: "Mostly when they are growing to be young men and women they have not it in them to have loving repeating being in them *as a conscious feeling*" (295, 296, emphases added). Her book, then, makes the unconscious conscious; the Martha Hersland chapter overtly reminds the reader of his or her long-repressed pleasure in repetition, and (a different thing) the incantatory style throughout, by reactivating the reader's infantile pleasure, undoes the repression. This is the lesson of the undervoice in *The Making of Americans*.

We are a long way from the two voices the novel originally set in play, the voice of bourgeois chronicler and that of psychological theorist. The Martha Hersland chapter clarifies the intimate voice that has been evolving in the interstices of the other two; Stein the author-narrator steps out of her fiction for a moment to tell us "what she loves," and what that has to do with the shape and sound of her text. She has separated herself from the male-identified posture of bourgeois inheritor, and from the image of the scientist as cool and authoritative; for the moment, her role seems to be to speak as herself.

Her text is driven by her various pleasures—her pleasure in listening to people's "pounding" repetitions, in producing pounding words of her own, in filling up with material and voiding it, in feeling as if she is suffusing or swallowing the human race. In a word, she has unveiled the unconscious of her text and made it conscious. She attributes the characterology of the previous sections to her own fascination with people's repetitions, a fascination that had been unconscious for most of her adult life. Her style too now becomes intelligible as an expression of a previously unconscious love of repeating; again, the earlier part of the text might now seem to have produced its repetitions unconsciously, without the speaker's having yet articulated to herself her love of repeating or connected it to a long-forgotten part of her childhood.

The two earlier voices, those of "narrator" and "theorist," will soon rejoin the conversation; from this point, however, they have a transparency, for they have become fixed in our minds as projections of a desiring teller who is filled with a new knowledge of herself.

James versus Freud

The new voice that emerges in the Martha Hersland chapter reflects a major transition in Stein's intellectual life. I am identifying a vocabulary of the unconscious in this material, one that suggests that Stein was approaching a psychoanalytic understanding of the mind. To speak in these terms is to run up against an idea of long standing about Stein, that she did not believe in the idea of an unconscious. This notion arose partly from her own comments in 1936 to the effect that her work was not produced through unconscious process, or "automatic writing"—comments prompted by an article by B. F. Skinner, who had found her Harvard psychology experiments, seen their discussion of automatic writing, and speculated that she had produced her own creative work by those means. "No," she wrote in response, "writing should be very exact."[30]

As Jayne Walker has intriguingly noted, however, there was a phase (just after *The Making of Americans*) when Stein repeatedly used the word *automatic* in her work in a way that suggests that she was indeed "thinking of her writing as a modified form of automatism."[31] Apart from this question of how she conceived of her own writing process, the idea that Stein rejected the concept of an unconscious sits oddly with her distinction of mental functions in *The Making of Americans* by the words *conscious* and *not-conscious*. Her later disclaimer was doubtless sincere, for she meant among other things to distinguish herself from the surrealists, whose completely free-associative manner of composition she had never

[30]Stein, *Everybody's Autobiography* (New York: Random House, 1937), p. 267.
[31]Walker, p. 121.

adopted.[32] She had also been affected over the years by the ridicule her seemingly irrational writings had sometimes provoked, and so took pains to dispel any association her earlier work had actually had with psychoanalytic thinking.

In fact, Freud is an unspoken presence in *The Making of Americans*. The distinction between conscious and not-conscious mental activity has a Freudian ring; although nineteenth-century theorists had had their own ideas of the unconscious, these had not included a notion of unconscious *process* such as we find in Stein's account of listening to repeating. The clearest link to Freud is Stein's identification of unconscious thinking with childhood; she believes that what each of us loves unconsciously as an adult we loved consciously as children, but have repressed. When she says that children experience repetition-love "as a conscious feeling *in so far as they can be said to have such a thing* in them," she seems to suggest, with Freud, that the very division into conscious and unconscious operations is the consequence of a repression that occurs during childhood (297, emphasis added).

Finally, the conflation, hinted at in her chapter, of the unconscious with the infantile and the *sexual* was part of Freud's unique contribution to modern psychology, and the very thing that made his early work controversial among his colleagues. The anal eroticism involved in repetition-love was Stein's own invention or discovery, rather than evidence that she had been reading Freud's *Three Essays on the Theory of Sexuality*; what sounds distinctly Freudian is not the anal orientation itself but Stein's idea that the pleasure of "loving repeating" is something that we indulge fully as children but later repress and experience only unconsciously.

Stein was encountering Freud's ideas through her brother Leo, who was at the time still her housemate and close intellectual friend. Leo had become a passionate devotee of Freud in 1909, just as his sister was about a third of the way through her intensive work on *The Making of Americans*.[33] Freud's idea of the unconscious

---

[32]Ibid.
[33]I assume from Stein's later remark that *The Making of Americans* had been the work of "almost three years" ("The Gradual Making," *Lectures*, p. 135) that the last three years, 1908–11, were the most important, but she had begun work on parts of the novel as early as 1903. See Leon Katz, "The First Making of *The Making of Americans*" (Ph.D. diss., Columbia University, 1963), pp. 35–37.

attracted Leo partly because it helped him to explain and justify his distaste for the profession of history, which he briefly considered for himself but ultimately condemned as "a mare's nest of illusory knowledge," unless a method could be devised "which could get behind the spoken word to the [historian's or historical figure's] real intention."[34] As his conversation began to fill up with Freud, his sister was quietly absorbing Freud's ideas and working them into her novel. In fact, her chapter on love, which suddenly introduces the vaguely Freudian terminology of the conscious and the not-conscious, was written in 1909, the very year of Leo's first enthusiasm for Freud.[35]

Besides the binary opposition of conscious and not-conscious, the word *repressed*, folded into the otherwise idiosyncratic characterology of *The Making of Americans*, attests to Stein's awareness of Freud's ideas. She writes of a type of "men and women whose nervous being is energy in them, from repression"; the word *repression* is then elaborated as "repressed active being or repressed loving being," what Freud might call repressed aggression and sexuality (363, 369).

Freud's name does not appear in Stein's notebooks, a fact that suggests that although she was selectively taking in his ideas, she was by no means a straightforward adherent who wished to align her unique psychological vision with Freud's theory or any other.[36] It looks very much as if Stein, like Faulkner some years later, opted to hear-and-not-hear Freud, finding resonances with some of her own intuitions but not wishing to compromise those intuitions by making a systematic excursion into psychoanalytic theory.[37] What

[34]Leo Stein, *Journey into the Self: Being the Letters, Papers and Journals of Leo Stein*, ed. Edmund Fuller (New York: Crown, 1950), quoted in Mellow, p. 51.

[35]According to Jayne Walker (*The Making of a Modernist*, p. 152), Leon Katz dates this part of *The Making of Americans* as having been written in the second half of 1909.

[36]Otto Weininger was an influence as well, but Leon Katz, who uncovered the influence, describes Stein's "way of absorbing" it as "aberrant and unusual." See Leon Katz, "Weininger and *The Making of Americans*," in Hoffman, ed., *Critical Essays on Gertrude Stein*, p. 141.

[37]Faulkner, like Stein, denied having been influenced by Freud, but see John Irwin's case for the probability that Faulkner did know about Freud but refused to read him because he "had learned enough about Freud's ideas to want to avoid the threat to his own creative energy and enterprise that might be posed by a sense of

emerges from the novel, in any case, is that she was now thinking in terms of conscious and not-conscious activity, as well as repression. In a word, she had departed, or was just now departing, from her earlier, Jamesian picture of how the mind works, in favor of a quasi-psychoanalytic view, which, though not dogmatically Freudian, could have emerged only in a milieu in which Freud was known.

The notebooks do register a shift away from James, whose work Stein was still following and discussing at the time, but with a new detachment. In the notebooks, the new term in her thinking, which clinches her resistance to James, is not psychoanalysis precisely but the same term she was using in the novel itself as a focus for her near-psychoanalytic ideas, namely, repetition. "When Leo," she writes, "said that all classification is teleological I knew I was not a pragmatist I do not believe that. . . . I believe in repetition" (*NB* D.11). This entry reveals, incidentally, how close Stein's account in the novel of an awakening to "loving repeating" was to the facts of her own recent life. She herself, that is, had just begun to define herself by the phrase, "I believe in repetition"—a position that somehow implied another, that she was not a "pragmatist" or a follower of James.

What exactly is the difference between "believing in repetition" and "being a pragmatist"? To answer this question is to define what distinguishes Stein's present intellectual commitments from those of a few years before, when her thinking had run (however ambivalently) in the direction of William James.

Pragmatism—James's philosophical system, as of 1907—begins with the idea that the meaning of a concept lies in its use or its practical consequences. Stein's notebook entry refers to this as the idea (Leo's, but not hers) "that all classification is teleological." In the last chapter we encountered a version of this teleological view of consciousness in James's previous work, the *Psychology*, and in Stein's "Melanctha," which mapped James's ideas onto the characterization of the practically oriented Jeff Campbell.

---

his own work having been anticipated by Freud's." *Doubling and Incest/Repetition and Revenge: A Speculative Reading of Faulkner* (Baltimore: Johns Hopkins University Press, 1975), p. 5.

As we also saw, however, "Melanctha" already contains a kind of syncopation, in the form of a cluster of anti-instrumental themes and formal strategies that make it something other than, and more than, a Jamesian allegory. By the time of *The Making of Americans*, Stein's subtle differences from James are moving to the surface. Stein is now dissenting from his ideas, in her notebooks overtly and in her novel implicitly. What distinguishes her present position from the Jamesian, or pragmatist, position is her belief "in repetition." For repetition, as she elaborates that idea in her novel, is a primitive love. Her chapter on loving repeating describes mental existence as shot through with pleasure, conscious or unconscious. All children, she suggests, know their own loving repeating; and adults, although they may repress that pleasure, still experience it. This is to say that anterior to instrumental concerns, a kind of erotic or pleasure-seeking activity, "pounding" and sensuous, is built into mental life. It may be repressed, but it always hums beneath the surface.[38]

James, however, conceives of the mind divested of practical concerns, or the infantile mind, not as a mechanism making its own pleasure but as a passive screen for sensory impressions. The teeming mass of sensations—James's picture of what makes up infantile experience—is "exciting," but he gives no picture of an active love or drive shaping the child's reception of that excitement. After early infancy, James suggests, we mediate between this passivity to impressions and associations and a more selective, active, and instrumental attention.

For James, the will to thrive drives the mind. No contending will to have pleasure gives its own different shape to mental events. Nothing in James's scheme would correspond to the sexualized inner pulsations Stein calls loving repeating. Another way of saying the same thing is to note that James's theory of the mind has no erotic axis. Freud, of course, was theorizing such an axis some

---

[38]There is some ambiguity in the text about this last point; the idea that most people in their young adulthood lose their love of repetition "as a conscious feeling" (296) could mean either that the feeling always becomes unconscious or, alternatively, that some people lose the feeling altogether. (In either case, Stein adds that the "consciousness of repeating" often returns in old age [p. 296].)

twenty years after James's *Psychology,* and we can think of Stein's novel as an attempt, contemporaneous with (though not identical to) Freud's, to uncover the "loving," or the erotic energy, motivating mental life.

This is the moment to note how modern Freud seems next to James; his emphasis on sexual and primitive thinking and on the shaping power of the unconscious makes him a contemporary of the modern novelists in a way James was not. Hence Freud was a fitting replacement for James in the background of Stein's development as a modernist. In *The Making of Americans* and the accompanying notebooks, we see Stein rejecting pragmatism, or an instrumental view of mental process, for what she calls repetition. To say, as shorthand, that she rejected James for Freud would almost fit the case if in any phase of her career she had taken psychological theory as dogma. But just as in her earlier work William James was a factor that contended with other factors, in her "psychoanalytic" period her connection to Freud is complicated. It ought not even to be called a debt; Stein did not so much embrace Freud as glance in his direction on the way to her own, often similar formulations.

A further measure of Stein's present distance from James—and her new resonance with Freud—is the idea of repression which now replaces what in her earlier work was a Jamesian discourse of *sup*pression, or selective attention. James in the *Psychology* describes (and Stein in *Three Lives* renders fictionally) the habits of attention that in adult life bring some data into relief at the expense of others. The data this sort of "selective attention" screens out (the "flies and beetles," for example, which James says no one, "save an entomologist," notices) are not relegated to another zone, an unconscious; they are not experienced at all; they are lost (*P* 39). But in *The Making of Americans* Stein envisions a different kind of forgetting, one that permits forbidden mental operations to continue somewhere out of sight. Her narrator tells of a time in her own life when an early love of repeating gave way to linear, logical functions such as "learning and talking and questioning" (301). Nonetheless, she says, she still unconsciously pursued the pleasures of childhood, by filling herself with the sound of repeating without knowingly processing what she heard. This image of a character whose apparent rationality masks unconscious pleasure is consonant with Freud's notion of repression—not with James's picture of selective attention.

Stein's earlier character Jeff Campbell, who like her present narrator is modeled on herself, has a similar phase of hyperrationality (before he meets Melanctha), but viewed in a Jamesian light; he is simply blinkered, so that he cannot take in new impressions. That image is an example of what selective attention looks like. The narrator of *The Making of Americans*, by contrast, describes herself as capable of having two conversations going on in her mind simultaneously, one attached to her conscious self-conception and one shaped by archaic impulses and hidden from her own awareness—in a word, repressed.

I have explained Stein's notebook entry in terms of a polarity: Stein herself and repetition (with links to Freud) on one side, and Jamesian pragmatism on the other. Another person, however, is mentioned in the entry, Leo. The voice of pragmatism in the notebook is Leo's voice: "When Leo said that all classification is teleological I knew I was not a pragmatist." Stein's rejection of pragmatism for repetition was part of her movement away from James and, at the same time, from Leo, who in spite of his new passion for Freud retained what had been an earlier attachment to James's ideas.[39] Leo occupied an ambiguous place in Stein's intellectual life at this moment. He was the source of much of her information about Freud, and thus (unbeknownst to himself) he enriched her present work; at the same time, he remained a proponent of the older, Jamesian views, which Stein's new psychoanalytic orientation was leading her to question.

Tellingly, Stein is outspoken in the notebook about her new intellectual opposition to Leo the pragmatist, yet silent about whatever debt she may have owed Leo the Freudian. This was just the period in which she was beginning to separate from her brother emotionally in a process that would soon dissolve their household.[40] She was irritated with him, personally and intellectually, and chan-

[39]See Katz, "The First Making," pp. 80–81, 291.

[40]For three descriptions of Stein's tensions with Leo, all of which view her *Two* as marking a breaking point, see Stimpson, "Gertrude Stein and the Transposition of Gender," p. 5; Benstock, pp. 154–58; Walker, pp. 117–19.

neled whatever engagement she had with his current psychoanalytic thinking not into an open conversation with him or even
into a one-sided conversation in the notebooks, where she might
have named him as a stimulus, but into a set of semitheoretical
reflections in the middle of the novel that she knew he, with his
contempt for her writing, would never read.

I do not wish, however, to overstate Stein's debt to Leo or, for
that matter, to Freud. For all the psychoanalytic resonances of her
evolving idea of repetition, the concept is not reducible to Freudian
theory. For one thing, it predates—and does not intersect in any
easy way with—Freud's own fully elaborated theory of repetition
in *Beyond the Pleasure Principle*. For another, Stein gives the term
repetition some resonances that simply transcend psychological theory. For her idea of loving repeating, although traversed by a near-
psychoanalytic vocabulary, was a formation not just of her changing psychological views but also of a cluster of private, almost
spiritual meanings.

These meanings are intimated in a clause I earlier elided from the
notebook entry on repetition: "I do not believe [what the pragmatist believes], *I believe in reality as Cezanne or Caliban believe in it.* I
believe in repetition" (*NB* D.11, emphasis added). Stein thinks of
repetition as a feature (or a version) of some essential "reality," and
as an object of "belief." Obscure as these terms are (even if we
bracket Cézanne and Caliban for the moment), they jog the word
repetition out of a psychoanalytic context, giving it a spiritual resonance—which Stein's next thought sustains, by associating her
own repetitive writing with worship. "Yes," she continues. "Always and always, Must write the *hymn* of repetition" (*NB* D.11,
emphasis added).

These are Stein's highly abbreviated notes to herself. One still
wonders what she means by "reality," and what that has to do with
repetition. She amplifies her terms in the novel, in the same chapter that has been my focus for some time. There she gives loving
repeating the alternative name of "earth feeling" (295). People who
powerfully hear repeating have what she calls an "earthy feeling of
being part of the solid dirt around them" (298). Here I interpolate
an idea that seems to make sense of this complex of thoughts: the
"earth," the "solid dirt"—the material universe—itself repeats.

This is how I understand a sentence that in various guises is part of the fabric of the chapter: "There is then always repeating in all living" (295). Matter—or living matter—is rhythmic, perhaps because whatever has links with "the solid dirt" is involved in cycles of reproduction, feeding, excretion, and death. As Neil Schmitz writes of the excremental metaphors in *Tender Buttons*, "For Gertrude Stein [dirt or excrement] is, humorously, the fundamental *rhythm of life*, one's consummate metaphor."[41]

In *The Making of Americans*, that rhythm is heard as repetition. The rhythms of matter reappear in the repeating that people do. Repeating is "in all living" *and* in people's minds. People, then, who love the repetitions produced by other people are able to overhear the repeating that pulses through all living things. Or, to translate all this back into the compressed vocabulary of the notebook, to hear and love repetition is to achieve contact with "reality."

My paraphrase of these three or four sentences is actually something of a collage, dependent on information from Stein's earlier and later works. "Melanctha," on one side of *The Making of Americans*, and *Tender Buttons*, on the other, envision the possibility of a near-mystical participation in a sort of life force whose sound is repetition. In "Melanctha," something called "real being" was associated with feelings bordering on "religion"; the character about whom those feelings circulated was the heroine, whose structural signpost in the story was repetition, and whose thematic signposts were an intimacy with the cycles of birth and death and a (similarly nonlinear, if not repetitive) wandering. The link, moreover, that Stein is now making between repetition and "dirt" or "earth" was intimated in "Melanctha," in the name of the repeating heroine— "black earth," etymologically—as well as in the imagery of "moist ground" which accompanied Jeff's initiation by Melanctha into wandering and "real being" (149).

To look ahead, on the other side, to the constellation earth/repetition in *Tender Buttons*—even if looking ahead to *Tender Buttons* means thinking about opaque word-clusters without a context— here is a bit of a poem called "Roastbeef": "In feeling there is

[41]Neil Schmitz, "Gertrude Stein as Post-Modernist: The Rhetoric of *Tender Buttons*," in Hoffman, ed., *Critical Essays on Gertrude Stein*, p. 123, emphasis added.

recurrence. . . . if there is singing then there is the resumption. The change the dirt" (33). These sentences mention "recurrence" and "resumption," forms of repetition, which are linked to "singing" because song is rhythmic—just as in the notebook for *The Making of Americans* Stein pictures herself writing a song, or "hymn," of repetition. These repetitions, in turn, are associated with "the change the dirt." Matter—what in *The Making of Americans* too is called "the solid dirt"—is where repeating happens. To feel "recurrence" is to know "the dirt."

It is also to know "the change." For material life, in its reproductive and alimentary cycles, repeats itself but is always in process. In *The Making of Americans,* Stein's reflections on the "repeating" of "living being" include an idea not just of recurrence but also of change: "In loving repeating being . . . there must always be a feeling for all changing, a feeling for living being" (301). As an artist of repetition, she herself "must admit all changing" (305). Thus her orientation toward excremental rhythms and themes—the very feature that is "infantile" and "erotic" from a psychoanalytic perspective—is, from a more spiritual perspective, an expression of Stein's reverential sense of participation in the mysterious workings of the natural world. She makes no sharp division herself between the excremental and the spiritual planes; the matter that she hymns is everywhere, including in the bowel.

Repetition, then, is a thread running through, but also before and after, the psychoanalytically oriented *Making of Americans*. It is a continuous part of Stein's conception of what she is about as an artist; all her work in one way or another "write[s] the hymn of repetition." In her chapter on repetition in *The Making of Americans,* we see her reflecting on her relation to repeating for the first time. That chapter gives us, among other things, a way of rethinking the form of "Melanctha"—and for all we know, Stein herself was thinking back to "Melanctha" when she wrote here of an earlier period in which she had only half-consciously loved (and written?) repetition. "Melanctha," as we know, puts an instrumental, Jamesian conception of consciousness—and of plot—in friction with patterns of repetition and unconscious process. Already in "Melanctha," that is, repetition is part of Stein's challenge to James. In the notebooks for *The Making of Americans,* Stein names these two contending principles of her earlier text—"teleological" thinking and "repetition." And now she makes it clear that the balance has tipped toward repetition. Her work after *The Making of Americans* will take up the same polarity and give it a new articulation. The major novelty will be a gendering of the two terms: the cluster "earth-repetition" will be assigned the new connotation "mother."

The tension between the two terms—instrumental thinking, on the one hand, and everything meant by "repetition," on the other—causes formal and stylistic polyphonies in every work I examine closely in this book. From *Three Lives* on, Stein claims her implication in earth feeling; yet she never ceases to write in a way that self-consciously crosses back and forth between the repetitive or unconscious "earth" processes and instrumental thinking. She uses a repetitive style in *The Making of Americans*, but one that, after all, would have no hold on our attention if it were not at the same time a vehicle for coherent themes. Her narrator at once loves to repeat and wants to communicate ideas to us. The meditation on repetition in the Martha Hersland chapter is itself hypnotically repetitive, but it is still a meditation *on* repetition; Stein has an intellectual agenda, even here. This is one of the most successful chapters of her book precisely because one feels so strongly the pull between quasi-theoretical content and stylistic seduction, between what Stein privately calls teleological classification and repetition.

Repetition is, so to speak, the trouble of Stein's text. It is what the part of Stein that does want to tell us things keeps dissolving into. This is to point to what Barthes and (differently) Kristeva have described as the pleasure of the avant-garde text; the truly "erotic" textual moment is the one in which repetition or another verbal pleasure cuts through rational speech.[42]

The Martha Hersland chapter, then, functions as a turning point in the novel as well as in Stein's oeuvre as a whole. She names here for the first time the drive behind her previous writing. The hidden motor for the earlier part of the book—and, I can now add, for her previous experimentation in *Three Lives*—was a repetition-love, at once autoerotic and seductive. Now we hear her talking aloud

[42]Barthes, p. 42.

about how she has been using and enjoying this source of pleasure all along. She exposes the sexuality of her text(s). Her plot to this point has been slowly collapsing into repetition; now she says why, and gives that counterlinear drag a meaning.

A near-psychoanalytic vocabulary appears at the same juncture; as Stein claims her writing as sexual, her thinking makes a swing away from the asexual psychology of William James and toward Freud. But I have suggested that the love of repetition she now locates has intimate meanings too, which transcend her psycho-analytic interests. Stein is claiming what she thinks of as a long-buried part of herself, her earth feeling, a set of internal pulsations that seems to echo the movements of matter. This sense of implication in the mysterious processes of earth will be one of the constants as her work later evolves in the direction of a spiritual feminism.

In the process of excavating her repetition-love, Stein became knowingly modern. Whereas deformation of linear narrative is a feature of experimental modern fiction generally, the texts that come to mind as similarly daring—*Ulysses, The Waves,* or *The Sound and the Fury*—postdate Stein's novel by at least a decade. Stein was breaking linear plot early, and in a uniquely self-analytic way. She worked in isolation; among her contemporaries it was not a fellow novelist or poet but Freud who helped her to think in terms of "writ[ing] the hymn of repetition."

She was not, however, so isolated artistically as she had been at the time of *Three Lives.* If not her literary contemporaries, her friends in the visual arts provided inspiration for her current experiments. Picasso, who had become a good friend in the years since *Three Lives,* and Matisse, with whom she had a less intimate friendship, gave her models for the sort of powerful work that could issue from what seemed to be a suspension of linear thinking in favor of internal drive.[43] In a notebook of 1908, she made what would be a recurring trio of herself and these two visual artists,

[43]According to the chronology in Bridgman (*Gertrude Stein in Pieces,* p. 361), Stein met Picasso three months or so before finishing *Three Lives.* For Stein's relationship with Matisse, see, for example, Alice Toklas's reminiscences: "Gertrude always spoke of Matisse as *le cher maître,* in derision of course." *What Is Remembered* (San Francisco: North Point Press, 1985), p. 38.

characterizing all three as deriving their genius from an irrational, unwilled "propulsion." "Leo does his [job]," she muses, "with his brains. . . . Matisse, Pablo, and I do not do ours with either brains or character we have all enough of both to do our job but our initiative comes from within a propulsion which we don't control, or create" (*NB* B.20). This propulsion that one doesn't control is like what her novel calls earth feeling; if psychoanalysis gave her theoretical confirmation of its reality, the example of her two friends helped to ground her sense of its value for artistic endeavors.

Matisse and Picasso also served Stein as wedges to drive between herself and Leo. Shari Benstock has described Picasso's role for Stein as that of "substitute brother";[44] and in her notebook, Stein uses Picasso against her brother, aligning herself with the party of propulsion, as against Leo, who works with "his brains" only. Her dismissal of Leo the arid intellectual is of a piece with her dismissal elsewhere of Leo the Jamesian or pragmatist, for she associated both Leo and William James with an antiseptic rationality, the opposite of "propulsion." "Leo and James," she observes in another notebook, "are clear by rationalising their material" (*NB* H.4). Her choice of a more instinctual, libidinous voice than she found in William James or in her brother would have been more difficult if she had not been able at the same time to identify herself with a group of creative people who seemed to her to embody alternative values and faculties. The opposition she is using refigures the polarity of brains and sensuality in "Melanctha," but the persona Stein now opposes to a figure like William James (or Jeff Campbell) is no longer that of a self-defeating and deserted priestess of the body but that of a strong artist.

Love and Patricide

In the background of the intellectual upheaval I have been charting, there is an emotional change. The Martha Hersland chapter of *The Making of Americans* exposes the hidden sexuality of the text. But Stein's account there of loving repeating screens other issues having to do with the form loving was literally taking in her life at

44Benstock, p. 153.

the time. The repetition theme does not quite take care of these other issues. Instead, it stirs them up, and they find their way into the next section of the novel, which is joyous, angry, and at the same time oblique.

The chapter on loving repeating, bold in its way, is followed by a shift in focus from questions of textuality (how Stein hears and writes her love of repeating) to more dangerous issues of sexual intimacy (how and whom she loves). She begins, that is, to write about her developing feelings for Alice Toklas, and about how those feelings interact with early, painful memories of an invasive father. At the same time she becomes indirect, expressing herself by suggestive juxtapositions and periphrasis. She does what she will continue to do in the next years, which is, if I may speak paradoxically, to come out of the closet—secretly.

The repetition chapter, with its celebration of earth feeling, resolves what was originally a conflict in the author between dirty and clean self-images. She has now claimed her connection to "the solid dirt," without the earlier need to compensate with a respectable self-projection such as the persona of the inheriting son. Her positive view of herself as earthy and dirty puts the initial quandary of the outsider behind her. Content now to distance herself from the disapproving bourgeois community, she resolves just to write for "myself and strangers."

The consequence is this: to be happily dirty is to be entitled to her sexual life. So, in the brooding digressions of the next chapter, Stein begins covertly to claim her identity as a lesbian in a way that is completely new for her. It is as if the act of revaluing her repetition-feeling—a buried, sensual part of herself, which no one else particularly loves—has heartened her for another affirmation, of her sexuality more broadly conceived. The artistic process itself, the activity of freeing up an incantatory, delicious prose, has released a new emotional awareness.

Toward the end of the Martha Hersland chapter, Stein moves in on the subject of her lesbianism by hinting that she has spent much of her recent life feeling lonely and misunderstood. "It is very hard for mostly every one to understand why another one has that way of loving, that way of being angry in them. . . . Some can never understand the queer ways in another one" (453). Someone—a version of the author—has been stigmatized because of her "way of loving" or her "queer ways." In the next chapter, whose nominal subjects are Alfred Hersland and Julia Dehning, she takes up her isolation as a major theme. She reflects on the courage it takes, in the face of such misunderstanding, to keep liking something other people do not like, "a low thing" in which one takes "pleasure" (488). The "thing" in question is for a while identified, safely, as a particular clock or handkerchief, low only in the sense of being distasteful to people of good breeding. But the list expands: "or you like eating something and liking it is a childish thing to every one or you like something that is a dirty thing and no one can really like that thing" (485).

With this statement about "eating," "childish" things, and "dirty" things, Stein seems to be working her way toward a theme of infantile oral eroticism. But other hints in the vicinity point to the possibility that the stigmatized "thing" is lesbian love (which, as we will see in *Tender Buttons*, is itself associated in Stein's mind with the oral pleasures of infancy). For example, Stein refers to the controversial handkerchief as "very gay"—perhaps a coded allusion to lesbianism, since the word *gay* already had its present connotation of homosexuality in her time.[45] She also expands the idea of the dirty thing to include "something that [certain people] have bought or made *or loved or are*," which they fear "no one will think . . . a nice thing" (485, emphasis added).

But someone comes into the picture who saves the isolated person by loving the same low things that she does. Loneliness, she says, is "one thing," but "another thing is the perfect joy of finding some one, any one really liking something you are liking, making, doing, being" (485). Stein herself had found such a "someone," in Alice Toklas. This part of *The Making of Americans* is heavily autobiographical; in her notebook from the same period, Stein was

[45]According to John Boswell, the Provençal word *gai* was used for homosexuals as early as the fourteenth century. By the early twentieth century, *gay* had acquired this connotation in English as well. *Christianity, Social Tolerance, and Homosexuality: Gay People in Western Europe from the Beginning of the Christian Era to the Fourteenth Century* (Chicago: University of Chicago Press, 1980), p. 43.

expressing identical sensations of relief and "joy," and connecting them to Toklas's presence in her life:

> The joy of when you are ashamed, after it is known then it is no longer a complete discovery to yourself of yourself.
>   . . . [G]o into . . . the joy of being recognised when you are ashamed and if any one has acknowledged it you can never again have that complete shame. . . .
> Also the way one builds up other people's convictions, other people's loving and virtue and religion, *saying good-night to Alice*. (NB 112, single page; emphasis added)

This entry is from 1910 or 1911, by which time Toklas had joined the Stein household at the rue de Fleurus.[46] "Saying good-night to Alice" is a mundane detail of Stein's present life, which she associates with "the joy of being recognised." She feels recognized now not just in the sense of being valued and appreciated but also in the sense of being known; one hears, in the notebook and in the novel as well, Stein's relief simply in having come out to someone. Although, as she says in this entry, she has felt "ashamed" of what she vaguely calls "it," now that she has shared her secret and "it is known," she "can never again have that complete shame." In retrospect one recognizes how lonely Stein must have been as a lesbian without a partner in a largely heterosexual circle, during her first four years in Paris.

The relief and self-acceptance Stein experienced at this moment were very different from the feelings that had gone along with her earlier relationship with May Bookstaver. In some ways, Alice seemed to her a reincarnation of May. "Her sexual base," Stein decided in a notebook, "is May, the elusive, finer purer flame of the prostitute" (*NB* B.5). But whereas May, in that first affair, had drawn Stein into a humiliating romantic triangle (charted in *Q.E.D.*), Alice had made a commitment and moved in with Stein. In the first relationship, moreover, May had adopted the pose of the sexual expert, putting Stein in the role of a novice embarrassing herself

---

[46]I am relying on Bridgman's chronology, p. 361, and on Leon Katz's dating of the various sections of the novel, as recorded in Walker, p. 152.

with sentences like, "I could undertake to be an efficient pupil if it were possible to find an efficient teacher" (a plea to which May responded by laughing).[47] While it is hard to know whether Stein reenacted that demeaning role in the early stages of her relationship with Alice Toklas—and her need to keep calling Toklas a prostitute in her notebooks suggests at least some insecurity on her part—the picture one gets from the entry on the "joy of being recognised" is not of two people filing away at each other's dignity but of people supporting and discovering each other, "build[ing] up" their "convictions" together.

Alice Toklas was recognizing Stein in another way as well, by applauding her literary endeavors. Another look at the passage in the novel about liking or doing something dirty shows that Stein lists her own book-in-progress in her inventory of dirty things: "or you like something that is a dirty thing and no one can really like that thing or you write a book and while you write it you are ashamed for every one must think you are a silly or a crazy one and yet you write it and you are ashamed, you know you will be laughed at or pitied by every one" (485). Her feeling of sexual shame blends in with her shame about her seemingly "crazy" book, just as in the beginning of the novel she was both a "Singular" sexually and a literary pariah without an audience. But "then," she goes on, "some one says yes to it, to something you are liking, or doing or making and then never again can you have completely such a feeling of being afraid and ashamed" (485). Toklas had "said yes," not just to Stein's sexual identity but also to the strange book she was writing. So in spite of Stein's declaration, "I am writing for *myself* and *strangers*," in reality there was an important third term in the equation, a companion who made Stein less afraid of the risks she was taking in her book.

Since the summer of 1908, Toklas had been typing *The Making of Americans* as Stein wrote it. The daily passing of the manuscript from hand to hand was a part of the couple's closeness; Toklas later recalled, "Doing the typing of *The Making of Americans* was a very

---

[47]The sentence is from *Q.E.D.*, in *Fernhurst*, p. 60. Katz, in his informative introduction to the volume, takes this to be a sentence Stein actually said to May Bookstaver, and adds that May's response to it (unlike that of her counterpart in the novelette) was to "burst out laughing" (*Fernhurst*, p. xiii).

happy time for me. [Each afternoon] Gertrude talked over her work of the day, which I typed the following morning. Frequently these were the characters or incidents of the previous day. It was like living history. I hoped it would go on forever."[48]

Courtship and creativity went together for Stein just now; one cannot dissociate the couple's romantic from their literary symbiosis, just as in the book itself Stein was conflating her sexual with her artistic self-acceptance. At the same time, Toklas's service as an amanuensis turned the novel into a shared secret. She was not only its first audience but also the only person in a position to unlock its references to the "characters or incidents" of each day. Thus when she joined the project, the book became two-tiered—unusually vague and abstract for the general reader, with its scores of characters called simply "one" or "someone," but for Alice Toklas a mine of gossipy conversation. The lonely teller of the first chapter suddenly had a completely sympathetic but hidden listener.

For the next few years, Stein would explore the meanings of this doubleness. The doubleness was part of her decision to write (but privately) as a lesbian; the indirect passages, for example, about liking something dirty and finding someone else who likes it contain an affectionate message for Toklas which few other readers would have been able to decipher. These passages are the first instances of the double speech, the veiled self-display, that develops in *Tender Buttons* into an elaborately coded writing.

A prohibiting father, in various guises, hung over the very first parts of *The Making of Americans*, as Stein tried on but did not fully claim a transgressive persona. He subsequently went underground. Now, as Stein embraces her identity as simultaneously strong and "queer," she brings this father back—in order to do away with him. She replays those early scenarios, but vengefully. Whether or not Stein was entirely conscious of what she was about, she yoked the self-affirmation of this moment in her novel and her life with patricide.

In what amounts to an explosive free association, she moves immediately from the passages of self-claiming to a murderous fantasy. The logical connective tissue is slight; after an unassimi-

[48]Toklas, *What Is Remembered*, p. 54.

lated paragraph on the difference between leaders and followers, and a vague hinge-thought running, "It happens very often that a man does something," a vignette begins as follows. "There was a man who was always writing to his daughter that she should not do things that were wrong that would disgrace him. . . . [I]n every letter he wrote to her that she should not do anything that was a disgraceful thing for her to be doing" (488–89). The scenario of the prohibiting father—familiar from the beginning of the novel—has now become sexualized: this patriarch demands of his daughter not just loyalty but chastity, or perhaps heterosexuality.

But Stein, having herself just broken through the taboos that made her think of her own sexuality as low or "disgraceful," has her surrogate of the moment turn on the disapproving father and reduce him to an impotent ghost:

> And then once she wrote back to him that he had not any right to write moral things in letters to her, that he had taught her that he had shown her that he had commenced in her the doing the things things that would disgrace her and he had said then when he had begun with her he had said he did it so that when she was older she could take care of herself with those who wished to make her do things that were wicked things and he would teach her and she would be stronger than such girls who had not any way of knowing better, and she wrote this letter and her father got the letter and he was a paralytic always after, it was a shock to him getting such a letter. (489)

The daughter's angry self-assertion magically paralyzes her father with a stroke. More than that, he imagines (or intuits) "that his daughter was trying to kill him and now she had done it"; he tells his wife, "she is killing me" (489).

This is the patricidal moment that the very early scenes of muted filial anger deferred. It corresponds to the moment in the notebooks when Stein wrote, "Jig is up." The episode does several kinds of work at once. First, the paralyzed father emblematizes Stein's having silenced in herself the oppressive voice that labeled her sexuality "disgraceful"—a voice that had been an internalized version of her own father's voice. The notebooks indicate that Stein at the time was remembering and reflecting on her father's disapproving and punitive behavior during her adolescence. She made these notes to herself: "Martha [Hersland, a character modeled on herself]. Also my high school experience and some of these friends"; and then, "Martha's friends come home late high-school experiences father angry hit her" (*NB* MA.20, 23). These recollected "experiences" have the same ambiguity as the scenes of a father's possessive fury in "Melanctha"; it is unclear just what made Daniel Stein angry, but one suspects it had something to do with his daughter's going out with friends at all.

Perhaps he intuited something about her sexual orientation as well, and bullied her especially for her close friendships with other girls. Her notebooks plot a suggestive scenario (never realized in the novel) involving David and Martha Hersland, portraits of herself and her father: "and then his constant downward turn always at outs with Martha . . . Martha's friends Tillie Brown and the bad one + May Bruchminster father angry the way pa was with me" (*NB* 11.4). The relationships that "father" forbids here are with two women (and an ungendered "bad one"); and of these, May Bookstaver (whom we see behind the gauzy pseudonym May Bruchminster) had actually been Stein's lover. This whole configuration—"+ May Bruchminster father angry the way pa was with me"—is startling, since Stein's father had in fact been dead for almost a decade when she met and fell in love with May Bookstaver.[49] What Stein is doing is to fantasize that her father had been alive to berate her when she had become sexually active.

He had in a sense been present to her, in the form of an internalized, self-punishing voice, the voice we heard in the inhibited and moralistic Stein character in *Q.E.D.* So in this projected episode, Stein's father becomes what he did not live to be in fact, his daughter's sexual censor, the type of the letter-writing father who found his way into the novel. Just as Stein paralyzed that fictional father, she vented her rage at her real father in this last notebook section by quietly plotting, "Death. father's slow death" (*NB* 11.4).

But the fictional daughter of the episode in *The Making of Americans*—to return to her—"kills" her father with a sexual accusation. What makes the whole episode shocking is its theme of incest; the

[49]Benstock dates the affair with May Bookstaver as having begun in 1900 (p. 147). Stein's father died in 1891.

father is the person who "commenced in [the daughter] the doing the things things that would disgrace her," on the weak pretext of preparing her for other men who might try "wicked things" with her. The image of the prohibiting father has changed drastically since the opening vignettes of the novel; no longer the benign patriarch perhaps opposing a daughter's marriage for a few weeks, he is a predator who owns his daughter sexually and then forbids her any other attachments.

Stein must just now have been seeing something in her own father that she had previously veiled from herself—a sexual possessiveness, for example, behind his irate scrutiny of her adolescent social life. From the material we have, there is no way of knowing whether Daniel Stein, like the father in the vignette, abused his daughter sexually; but Stein, by writing the episode, was at least discharging anger at her father for having subjected her to a sexualized possessiveness and violence. The notebooks also allude to an actual memory that may stand in for some (real or fantasized) act of paternal incest: Stein had once been approached in a vaguely sexual way by her father's brother, Sol. She plans the following fictional scenario: "[Bertha] stays with Herman [neither of these characters then appears in the novel] after death of [Herman's] wife and has scene like the kind I had with Sol" (NB 12.14). This (from another notebook, and in a fictionalized form) is what that "scene" had been like: "Herman sort of needs [Bertha] to take place of his wife [the word *father* is crossed out] in kinds of ways scare Bertha never went beyond pressure and coming in to her one night to come and keep him warm, she more dislike than terror" (NB 11.8).[50] One wonders whether Stein's father, too, may have somehow expected his daughters to "take place of his wife" when she died in Gertrude's fifteenth year.

Whatever we make of the scene with Sol, the episode of the paralyzed father in The Making of Americans represents a furious revaluation of the paternal figure who dominated the first parts of the novel. Stein's feelings of admiration and indebtedness are

---

[50]Katz draws attention to this passage, in "The First Making," p. 187. Along with the word *father*, a second reference to *wife* is crossed out. The character Bertha, incidentally, unlike Stein in the original incident, has a husband, to whom she reports the incident.

gone; the father who in the opening scenes embodied fine bourgeois values is now exposed as a sexual villain, and his crime
infects and discredits the whole paternal system of authority,
which had scapegoated the author-narrator as a "Singular." By way
of this brief but highly charged episode, Stein puts to rest the self-
punishing thoughts that had gone along with her equation of "father" with respectability and conscience. The fictional daughter's
vindictive letter turns Stein's initial thought—that she is a bad
daughter by her father's standards, either an ingrate or a sinner—
into an almost opposite thought: her father violated her. Self-
hatred has turned to rage; by writing the novel, Stein has freed
herself from the crippling emotional habits of the good daughter.

In a linked fantasy, she continues to expose and discredit the
patriarch. The incest vignette fades to a story about a young boy
who wishes to make an insect collection. His father gently dis-
suades him, pointing out the cruelty of "killing things to make
collections of them." Like the letter-writing father, this father mor-
alistically enforces self-restraint, telling the son that he "was a
noble boy to give up pleasure when it was a cruel one." But again
the father himself paradoxically indulges in the very pleasure he
taboos:

> The boy went to bed then and then the father when he got up in the
> early morning saw a wonderfully beautiful moth in the room and he
> caught him and he killed him and he pinned him and he woke up his
> son then and showed it to him and he said to him "see what a good
> father I am to have caught and killed this one," the boy was all mixed
> up inside him and then he said he would go on with his collecting.
> (489–90)

The wrong is a lesser one this time, but this father is just as confusing as the incestuous letter-writer. His son is "all mixed up" by the
conflicting signals the father sends. The father in the other vignette
tabooed and yet "taught" his child sex; this father taboos but teaches
violence. If one were to conflate these two paternal transgressions,
one would come up with an image of sexual violence—the very
thing that made Melanctha's father a hurtful parent, and something, again, that Stein was perhaps piecing together in her picture

of her own father's motivations. Significantly, the composite father she imagines here codes his lessons according to the gender of the child; the daughter is instructed in sexual pleasure and *submission*, while the son in the linked episode is instructed in the pleasures of appropriation and *killing*. There is a (still latent) feminist knowledge in these scenes.

Stein is discharging anger at a parent who was bewilderingly seductive and repressive at the same time. The cost of accusing a seductive parent is that one must admit to having been effectively seduced—as Stein in fact does, in these episodes. The son in her second episode is led by his father's example to keep doing the forbidden, pleasurable thing: "he said he would go on with his collecting." On a more explicitly sexual note, the daughter in the incest vignette traces her present erotic life to her father's earlier stimulation: he *"commenced in her* the doing the things things that would disgrace her" (489). Stein could have flattened out that episode in a consoling way by having the brutalized daughter renounce sex and then accuse her father from a position of unassailable respectability. But what she is after in this part of the novel is an acquaintance with her sexual identity, and she cannot pursue that without somehow exploring the continuity between the desires her father once "commenced in" her and the present desires she wishes to claim.

What are the personal meanings of the charge that the father "commenced" sexual behavior in his daughter? We could read this as Stein's version of the seduction fantasy that Freud says is universal: any child (in a nuclear family) believes he or she was sexually initiated by the parents, because the parents were the child's first sexual objects. (According to Freud a child will, for example, interpret the stimulation it receives while being bathed as seduction by the mother).[51] But it would be wrong to collapse this material into a seduction fantasy, just as it is wrong for Freud's own theory automatically to neutralize as "fantasy" incidents of actual seduction in families. Stein's observations about her father in the notebooks ("and then Martha's friends Tillie Brown and the bad one + May Bruchminster father angry the way pa was with me") suggest

[51]Freud, "Female Sexuality," *SE* 21:232.

the possibility that she was identifying a genuine sexual possessiveness on his part. Daniel Stein may well have been a confusing parent, in the way that the seductive fathers in these two
vignettes are confusing. He may have given his daughter some sort
of sexualized attention, then in her adolescence have been enraged
to find her developing as a sexual person.

If so, Stein now finds a way out of that tangle. By accusing her
father, and naming his possessiveness for what it was, she "paralyzes" his inhibiting influence. My basis for reading the daughter
and son in these linked episodes as emotional stand-ins for Stein is
that this material repeats the constellations of feelings in her private reflections on her "pa" in the notebooks. The incest episode,
moreover, is so odd and disturbing, and so unwarranted in terms
of the immediate demands of the plot or the characterology, that it
seems to call for interpretation in terms of its symbolic resonances
with the intensely autobiographical moment just before, when
Stein, speaking for herself, gave herself permission to like "dirty
things."

Stein's self-presentation becomes safely indirect just here. She
has suddenly shifted from the second person, which she wore as a
thin mask in the section on liking something dirty ("or *you* like
eating something and liking it is a childish thing"), to the further
remove of the third person, which, in a rare lapse into straight
narrative, transposes the burden of feeling onto fictional characters
("and then once *she* wrote back to him") (485, 489). This change
makes sense, since Stein is moving from a positive moment of self-
affirmation to connected but more troubling feelings of rage at her
father, mixed with a sense of sexual complicity with him. Third-
person narrative serves as a buffer, enabling her to finish discharging the anger that the act of claiming herself, just before, aroused.
And because of that displacement, she need not explain to the
reader the meaning of the incest story for herself, although the
reader will pick up some part of her feeling simply by coming upon
this startling episode just after the moment of self-affirmation.

The incest story has a positive as well as a disturbing meaning. It
contains its own moment of self-affirmation. The daughter, by accusing, frightening, and paralyzing her father, gets him to stop
invading her sexual privacy. It is as if the previous section on

"liking something dirty" left out a sentence that this episode then says aloud: it is a father (real or internalized) who was calling the narrator's sexual choices dirty, and now it is time to write him off. Stein, through the fictional daughter's paralyzing letter, is sending a message in fantasy to her own father. Although she in some sense "commenced" her sexual existence with him, she can now invest herself erotically wherever she likes, even if that means violating his rules by doing a "low" thing, falling in love with a woman.

Stein is disentangling her love of Alice Toklas from her bond with her father. Something is enabling her to say at this juncture in her life that she is allowed to take her love elsewhere. Her earlier romance with May Bookstaver had deferred this moment of angry independence; its triangulation had (conveniently?) prevented Stein from exploring the consequences of forming a true couple, and the role she assumed with May, that of an ingenue with an "almost puritanic horror" of "physical passion," had placed the burden of all the bad-sexual feelings on May, leaving Stein with the illusion of loving passively, by a kind of "inertia."[52] Now, in *The Making of Americans,* she has declared that the sexual feelings are hers as well, an idea that entails coming to terms with the specter of the censoring father and reversing his judgment that her sexuality is dirty.

A New Arrangement with the Father

I have discussed the innovations of *The Making of Americans* in terms of Stein's excavation of primitive, anal-erotic material, but then shifted away from those questions of "regression" toward seemingly opposite issues of Stein's self-realization and growth. It is worth spending a moment thinking about how to adjust these two images of Stein to each other—how to reconcile the image of the author as an archaeologist of the primitive, who slips back to a grandiose anality, with the image of the artist who uses her novel to move forward to a new self-awareness and strength.

[52]The quotations are from the fictionalized account of the relationship, in *Q.E.D.. Fernhurst,* pp. 59, 66.

The psychological arc of the novel, once again, is this: the early sections show Stein just beginning to measure herself against a powerful patriarch, whom she respects but half resents; then she slowly brings to the surface the erotic dimensions of her prose and the infantile ("anal" and grandiose) aspects of her fantasy life; finally, she makes her break with the patriarch, fully experiencing her rage at him and at the same time allowing herself her independent love of Alice Toklas. Somehow the circuit that she makes through loving repeating, with all the archaic material that journey involves, prepares for her moment of self-recognition and (quite adult) self-definition. I have been making sense of this sequence by conceiving of the section on loving repeating as initiating a new self-acceptance on Stein's part; she revalues a formerly suppressed, sensuous part of herself and therefore becomes able in the next section to claim her sexuality more broadly, putting to rest the censoring patriarch. The evolving self quite naturally looks backward and forward at the same time. As is inevitable during an important moment of emotional reorientation, various aspects of the psyche, the most ancient as well as the just-developing, are stirred up simultaneously.

But a different idea that I would like to propose as a tentative supplement is that the excursion through loving repeating, or the return to anality, is also Stein's way of *coping* with the otherwise overwhelming feelings of rage and erotic love that she knows she is about to release. She is about to make a dangerous leap forward, and a part of her slides backward as a way of holding herself together. The turn to a primitive anality defends her against the intensities of the growth-producing aspects of this moment.

Leonard Shengold, a psychoanalyst whose recent work on anality builds on Freud's and Abraham's theories, finds that psychic "danger situations" can provoke "a mobilization of anal erogeneity, mechanisms and symptoms."[53] For example, an analysand, when approaching disturbing feelings of rage connected to oedipal issues or to a threatened loss, may try to control this overwhelming affect by moving back to preoedipal, anal mechanisms, reducing the world and his or her own feelings to a kind of un-

---

[53]Shengold, "Defensive Anality," p. 52, hereafter cited in the text.

differentiated excrement that the patient can monitor and master. For such a person (at such a moment), "Emotions and body feelings involved with other people can be reduced to faeces that can be controlled by the psychic counterpart to the anal sphincter" (47). One patient, angry about a vacation the analyst is about to take—a desertion that revives a childhood loss—begins the hour "relatively 'open' about his anger," but then replaces the anger with "a mass of undifferentiated 'stuff.'" "His tone of voice became a drone. He was producing a list [of complaints and of people], obscured in a kind of hypnotic, petty, obsessive financial miasma," so that he can remark at the end of the hour, "I managed to turn this whole session to shit, didn't I?" (48, 47). Rage and vulnerability have given way to an affective grayness: "The exciting, chaotic, mysterious universe had, transiently but characteristically, become simplified, controlled and certain. Life, and specifically this bit of it ardently related to the analyst, consisted not of making love or making war but of making stool and making lists" (48).

Shengold's hypothesis of a "defensive anality" (52) is similar to Chasseguet-Smirgel's concept of anal "perversion" (which Shengold cites), but with the important difference that Chasseguet-Smirgel's "pervert" regresses to anality out of envy of the father's genitals, whereas the person Shengold describes uses anal mechanisms to master his or her own overwhelming affect at a particular instant of psychic stress. That Stein in The Making of Americans first exposes conflicting feelings of rage and devotion toward the father, then leaves these feelings behind as she moves to a list-making characterology and to a hypnotic, repetitive style suggests that her "anal" orientation may represent a means of mastering the initial conflict itself. As she embarked on The Making of Americans, she was preparing for the first interior crisis of her adult life, the break with her father, which enabled her to claim at once her sexuality and her "crazy" but (as she also knew) highly original literary voice. Perhaps in order to control the intense affect involved in this rupture with the father, she developed a mode of writing that is the stylistic analogue to what Shengold calls "making stool and making lists." Then, having made this descent into the anal-erotic world of loving repeating, she could resurface and challenge the father consciously, and this time successfully, in the section on finding a loving friend and in the episode of a daughter's revenge on an incestuous father. She went on, that is, to do just what Shengold's patient (in the session described) resists doing, "making love [and] making war."

It may seem strange to make this sort of link between a particular experimental style and the emotional needs of the author at the moment she evolved it. Modernism, after all, is characterized by widespread experimentation, whose motivations are primarily aesthetic; it is hardly the case that every time a modernist author brings anal or oral *jouissance* into his or her language, this excursion into the unconscious serves the author's needs at an instant of psychosexual crisis. Nor would I say that even for Stein the repetitive style always served this function; she invented it during a time of crisis, but thereafter it was independently interesting to her, and she continued to use it. On the other hand, an author delving into the unconscious has only his or her own unconscious to work with; any highly individual style must have private meanings for its author. It would be a mistake to overlook these private meanings on the grounds that the style (also) represents an important development within literary history.

Something happened in Stein as she worked on *The Making of Americans*, and I am asking how she was able to transform herself from the timid, overburdened daughter-son to the sensuous lover of "someone." Loving repeating, not just as a manner of listening but also as an artistic practice, was an important source of strength as she moved toward a new self-awareness. In a sense, loving repeating was a part of the new knowledge itself, but the repetitive style just may have had the secondary role of helping Stein to master the intensities of the dangerous material she was approaching.

With the story of the incestuous father, the emotional effort of the novel is complete. The pressures that formed Stein's initial persona are in abeyance; she has moved past her identification with paternal law, and the voice of the dutiful daughter-son has been replaced by that of an independent adult who is happily transgressive and sensual. Yet the incest episode has another set of meanings, which reorient rather than obliterate Stein's paternal identification. Ultimately, she is able to retain some good things from her father, without incurring the old cost of being his sexual property.

The angry daughter writes to her father that he "commenced"

sexual behavior "in her" (489). Perhaps he got her started sexually; yet the words could also be taken to suggest that she got her sexuality from him. Behind Stein's ambivalence about fathers in *The Making of Americans* there is her belief that the potent, sensual parts of herself were actually "commenced," or produced, in her by her father, as a sort of genetic inheritance. While she is busy writing off, or paralyzing, one paternal imago—that of the bourgeois patriarch who stood in the way of her lesbian sexuality—she covertly preserves another, that of an ally who passed along his own subversive powers to her.

Stein's happy revaluation of her sexual identity is connected to her exploration in the previous chapter of what she called her earth feeling. The things that come under the heading of earth feeling— her repetition-love and her sense of implication in the workings of matter—are continuous with her newly positive view of her sexuality; with Alice Toklas's help, she is "saying yes" to both parts of herself. But strangely—since Stein's father was a suffocating presence—she thinks of her earth feeling as coming from *him*. He is a dual figure, repressive yet also empowering. Like his daughter, he is (as she reconstructs him) a strange mix of bourgeois or patriarchal law—which, unlike her, he never renounced—and some other raw or taboo life principle.

In a notebook entry at which I glanced in the last chapter, she identifies the part of herself she owes to her father—what she calls "the Rabelaisian, nigger abandonment, Vollard, daddy side." She likes this daddy side: "bitter taste fond of it" (*NB* DB.47). Her father gave her something Rabelaisian—something dirty and bodily, perhaps even excremental, since that is a point of intersection between Rabelais and *The Making of Americans*. The association, furthermore, with "nigger abandonment" repeats the racist stereotype of "Melanctha" and reveals its place in Stein's own self-image: she has her own dangerous, sensual dimension, which she projects as blackness both in "Melanctha" and in her notebook. She thinks of that dimension of herself as her inheritance from her "daddy"—exactly, in fact, as her character Melanctha had. "Melanctha Herbert almost always hated her black father, but she loved very well the power in herself that came through him. And so her feeling was really closer to her black coarse father, than her feeling had ever been toward her pale yellow, sweet-appearing mother" (90).

The cluster power-black-coarse-father in "Melanctha" is just like what we find in the notebooks. In what amounts to a pernicious racial stereotype, thinly glossed over by idealization, Stein suggests that Melanctha's very "black" father has more power in him than the lighter-colored, "pale yellow" mother. Melanctha's ambivalence about her father, too, is a version of Stein's: Melanctha loves the traces of her father she inherits, but hates the abusive father himself. Just so, Stein had mixed feelings about owing so much that she valued in herself to someone she so resented. She mumbled to herself in a notebook, "Damn it all I go and find I am just like my father now & you know he just fixes it alright" (*NB* 2.5).[54]

In *The Making of Americans*, Stein saves for herself the empowering aspects of her bond with her father, at the same time that she paralyzes him as an authority figure. As a sort of fume rising from her angry confrontation with Daniel Stein the patriarch, we find a positive idealization of Daniel Stein the earthy man. She included a direct portrait of her father in the novel, in the character of the elder David Hersland: "It was all so simply to him as the world as all him, and it was this that gave him a big freedom and this big important feeling and the big way of beginning and so made a queer man of him, an eccentric from the others around him, and all that stopped it from making a god of him was his way of being impatient inside him" (51). The things that make Daniel-David an imposing figure—almost "a god"—are very like the things that Stein later in the novel identifies as the sources of her own transgressive energies. He is "queer," an "eccentric"—a feature that all his children inherit: "Later in their life they were queer too like him" (51). That queerness foreshadows Stein's more openly autobiographical exploration, midway through the novel, of the meanings of her own "queer ways" (453).

[54]The rest of this sentence, which is a bit opaque, is: "he takes [or "tells"] it so nice you think it bad to be right and I make a fuss and there I am just like my father." Stein's meaning here may be that she is like her father in creating a "fuss" or a fight with another person ("he"), even though—or just because—the other person takes her abuse "nice[ly]."

Good things accompany the father's queerness. David has an "abundant world embracing feeling," an unusual quality of fusion with the rest of the universe: "[One had] a kind of feeling that he was as big as all the world about him, one included the other in them, the world and him, the earth the sky the people around him the fruit the shops, it was all one and the same, all of it and him, . . . there were no separations of him or from him, and the whole world he lived in always lived inside him" (51). It is not a great leap from the (fictional) father's "world embracing feeling" to the earth feeling that later in the novel Stein the daughter-author identifies in herself. David's continuity with the material phenomena about him—"the earth the sky the people"—is rather like the repetition-lovers' (and the narrator's) "earthy feeling of being part of the solid dirt around them," their "feeling for living being" (298, 301).

But I am glancing back at a very early part of the novel, and there, for all Stein's idealization of her father, he is an extremely problematic figure. David Hersland is a model for his children, but an overpowering model who leaves no room for them, partly because he is such a large presence and partly because the ways of the "queer" person paradoxically mix in him with the domineering ways of the patriarch:

> The father David Hersland was in some ways a very splendid kind of person but he had some very uncertain things inside him. He too was very proud of his children but it was not easy for them to be free of him. Sometimes he was very angry with them. Sometimes it came to his doing very hard pounding on the table . . . , and ending with the angry word that he was the father, they were his children, they must obey him, he was master. (45)

Stein says perceptively that this bullying is hard on "the three big resentful children who knew very well what they needed to have given to them so that they could be free inside them" (45).

Her father never did "give" her the thing she needed in order to be free, but in the course of writing the novel she took it from him anyway. In subsequent chapters, as we have seen, she decides—as the Hersland children in this opening scenario are not strong enough to decide—that she can embrace her own queerness, brush aside the father who both gives it to her and forbids it, and yet still draw on him for sustenance. She can be indebted to him without being owned by him. We remember by contrast how isolated the character Melanctha was from both her parents; her father dominated her without simultaneously communicating strengths that she could use productively. Melanctha was cut adrift from her source. But in *The Making of Americans* Stein recovers a connection with her father which still allows her her angry independence, so that (to add emphases to a sentence I have already quoted) she can declare, "This is a little of what *I* love and how *I* write it" (289).

Stein will soon recover the mother too as a source, in *G.M.P.* and *Tender Buttons* (though she is not ready to do so in *The Making of Americans,* where Fanny Hersland, the character modeled directly on her mother, simply duplicates the wan, beaten, insubstantial mother of "Melanctha"). As would have happened in the course of a psychoanalysis, Stein gradually teaches herself to move closer to her remembered parents—both of them dangerous in their ways—without any longer fearing that they will co-opt, violate, or dissolve her.

A question the novel asks and then answers is how one can be an "earthy boy" (as Stein privately called herself) without being engulfed by the earthy man, or progenitor.[55] A pleasant outcome of Stein's new silent pact with her father was that it gave her further ammunition to use against Leo, for Leo was "not," within Stein's characterological scheme, "earthy" (*NB* B.19), not energetic and creative, but drily intellectual. Stein was creating herself as her father's spiritual heir in a way that she thought Leo could not be.

Stein's book and her relationship with Alice Toklas are things she has apart from her father. She has moved past the ambiguous position of the "angry man" in the very first story; she has gathered the strength to throw her father out of her orchard. She had not allowed herself to envision such an autonomy in her earlier works. The tyrannical father of "Melanctha" is an object of his daughter's hatred but not of her constructive anger; the daughter never renounces him as a figure of authority; and the whole story sub-

[55]"Me, not passionate adolescent   earthy boy." *NB* DB.22.

liminally conveys the message that to "wander" past the father's surveillance is to die. In *The Making of Americans,* Stein envisions an alternative cosmos for herself. This is not to say that she shakes off the paternal taboo entirely. In fact, she unconsciously brings it back in just these chapters, in the form of intermittent self-punishing thoughts. As if to atone for having expressed her self-love and independence, she sometimes broods aloud about the possibility that her whole characterological undertaking in the novel is a failure: "Sometimes I am almost despairing. Yes it is very hard, almost impossible I am feeling now in my despairing feeling to have completely a realising of the being in any one" (458).[56] This compensatory self-punishment is natural, but it does not prevent Stein from going ahead and producing the book and the life she wants for herself.

These tensions are not in themselves what makes *The Making of Americans* a good novel. But to understand them is to see where much of the passion and the artistic daring in the book come from. I have been thinking for the moment about how Stein made herself capable of writing this novel; the unspoken arrangement she was reaching with her father was freeing up her creativity *for* the book. In order to write a radically new text, she had to radicalize herself in intimate and difficult ways.

Killing the Nineteenth Century

What is the effect of reading *The Making of Americans?* Stein, the lesbian daughter, paralyzes her literal father, and as a modernist, she kills all the Victorian fathers, opening the way for a typically modern form of consciousness. The same rage that goes into Stein's refusal of her father's law becomes a part of her aggressive creativity as she shapes her place within modernism. Either way, and certainly in combination, *The Making of Americans* radicalizes the perceptive reader.

[56]It is hard to tell exactly when these sentences were written, since this particular part of the novel (the Dounor-Charles-Redfern episode) uses material written years earlier, in 1904 (Katz, Introduction to *Fernhurst,* p. xxxii). But since these "despairing" thoughts bleed into the next chapter ("[I am] a gently almost melancholy sulky one" [482]), I assume that they are a late addition, continuous with the material I have been discussing.

The remainder of *The Making of Americans*—and indeed the novel as a whole—amounts to a slow murder of the Victorian novel. Stein wrote in 1943 that "the nineteenth century is dead dead dead," and that for herself, "between babyhood and fourteen, I was there to begin to kill what was not dead, the nineteenth century which was so sure of evolution and prayers, and esperanto and their ideas."[57] *The Making of Americans* represents the crucial moment in Stein's career at which she recognizes herself as the murderer of the nineteenth century. Her literary experiment has the effect of unsettling key categories of Victorian thinking: objective history; science as "truth"; and character, or the integrated subject. But just as her familial rage is creative as well as destructive, so her novel puts something vibrant in the place of these inherited categories.

History, science, and character are the very things the author-narrator in the opening sections of the novel upheld. Stein started her novel in the exaggerated voice of a son of the nineteenth century; then, as her sensibility changed, she showed that figure exploding under the force of linguistic play. This linguistic play is modernism, or—in social terms—an instance of the textual *jouissance* that (according to Kristeva) attests in the modern period "to a 'crisis' of social structures and their ideological, coercive, and necrophilic manifestations."[58]

The subtitle of the novel, which Stein amusingly retains even after her novel has fractured its every meaning, conveys this crisis in thought and expression: "Being a History of a Family's Progress." The words *history* and *progress* do make perfect sense in the context of the opening section. There the narrator-descendant begins to record the history of his immigrant family, a history that easily folds itself into national or bourgeois history: "It has always seemed to me a rare privilege, this, of being an American, a real American, one whose tradition it has taken scarcely sixty years to create" (3). Tellingly, the "progress" of the family is defined in strictly bourgeois terms: "It was a substantial progress the family had made in wealth, in opportunity, in education" (42). But as Jayne Walker has compellingly shown, in an extensive interpreta-

[57]Stein, *Wars I Have Seen*, p. 21.
[58]Kristeva, *Revolution in Poetic Language*, p. 15.

tion that I will try to avoid duplicating at too great length, the linear family chronicle, as well as the sense of progressive history, gives way to a vision of history as repetition.[59]

Stein turns her assault on linear history into a joke. In the Martha Hersland chapter, as she replaces the bourgeois narrator with the voice of a transgressive lover of repetition, this is how she revises the meaning of the word *history*: "They repeat it and I hear it and I love it. This is now a history of the way they do it. This is now a history of the way I love it" (291). She has subordinated the "history" axis of her novel to the axis of "what I love." Her narrator is speaking no longer as a "real American" citizen but as a lone consciousness pulsating with various pleasures. Just as that new, intimate persona threatens to collapse the plot entirely into auto-erotic repetition, it also deforms and engulfs the category of objective history. The new stress on feeling, lyrical in intent, has destroyed the sense of narrative on which history must always rest.

In the remark of 1943, Stein speaks of herself as killing "the nineteenth century *which was so sure of evolution*." *The Making of Americans* dismantles Victorian ideas of evolution along with the bourgeois plot. Stein's earlier story, "Melanctha," had still enshrined evolution in the narrative of Jeff Campbell—a narrative whose contours literally reflected the nineteenth-century evolutionary thinking of William James. But even there, Jeff's story—at once a Darwinian and a bourgeois progress plot—had been countered by a narrative of repetition, failure, and death, in Melanctha's own story. In *The Making of Americans* that earlier counterpoint turns into a roar: stylistically and sometimes thematically, repetition besieges the progress story.

Stein does retain the vestigial plot of the family's "progress"; it is the object her repetition hammers at. Part of her brilliance is the realization that she cannot keep interestingly "killing the nineteenth century" if the victim stops moving. Structurally, what undoes the progress plot is drive, in the various forms of textual pleasure I have been noting. Kristeva has described modern literary experimentation as involving an explosion of rhythmic drive into language, disrupting existing ideologies and along with them

[59]See Walker, chap. 3.

the (ideologically inflected) notion of linear or familial time. "Since the family has its familial time—the time of reproduction, genera-tion, life and death, the linear-phallic time within which and in relation to which the familial son-daughter-subject thinks itself—shattering the family through rhythmic polylogue puts an end to that time."[60] This sentence could stand as a synopsis of Stein's unmaking of the family plot in *The Making of Americans*, where she slips from the role of "familial son-daughter-subject" to that of a subject traversed by "rhythmic" pleasure. Stein foreshadows Kristeva; she not only performs the modernist irruption of drive in language (as other modernists do) but also reflects on it, in quasi-theoretical moments like the section on loving repeating. One could say that *The Making of Americans* "knows" about modernism as a hunch what Kristeva explicates as theory.

The Making of Americans amounts to a genealogy of modern writ-ing. As inner drive progressively decenters what starts as an almost conventional nineteenth-century (and bourgeois) narrative, Stein places herself at the origin of modernism, dramatizing how modern-ism makes itself on the ruins of Victorian plot. This making-of-modernism amounts to a murder, in the sense that the infusion of drive into language represents a "shattering of discourse."[61] *The Making of Americans* makes its own unconscious or perhaps even coincidental pun on this killing. The progress plot moves from deterioration (under the pressure of repetition) to self-extermina-tion. As Walker notes, what begins as a "History of a Family's Progress" actually ends with the Hersland family's failures and partial extinction.[62] In a final, mocking turn on the word *history*, Stein comes to speak of "the history *of the ending* of the existing of the Hersland family" (457, emphasis added). The last chapter of her novel is about the death of the younger David Hersland. Stein has "killed" her plot.

She derived a mischievous excitement from ending her story in this way. According to her friend Janet Flanner, "One day when she was writing *The Making of Americans*, she suddenly killed off the

[60]Kristeva, "The Novel as Polylogue," in *Desire in Language*, p. 201.
[61]Kristeva, *Revolution in Poetic Language*, p. 15.
[62]Walker, p. 45.

hero. She went to tell a friend and said, 'I've killed him.' "[63] This is a variant of Stein's patricidal recognition in the notebook that the "jig is up." Hero-killing reflects her anger at her father and also, as Richard Bridgman has persuasively argued, at Leo, with whom the dying "hero" David shares features.[64] But the jig is up for the bourgeois plot as well. The death of the hero is a last blow to the family's linear success story. It dramatically unleashes what was eroding the plot all along, the play of drive in language, now in the form of an orgy of minimalist sentence-making.

"Everywhere something is done. Everywhere where that thing is done it is done by some one. Everywhere where the thing that is done by some one comes to be done it is done and done by some one" (920). These sentences, whose repetitions and incremental additions typify the anal style, have an egregious lack of informational content: "something is done" is just the prototypical subject-verb formation, emptied of specificity as to either agent or deed. These sentences do in exaggerated form what many of the paragraphs in this final chapter do: they function not primarily as carriers of meaning (although meaning never ceases entirely) but as acts or games motivated by the speaker's sheer pleasure in producing grammar. Still, beyond that pleasure is a larger claim of completion; Stein, as she winds up her novel, has a profound sense of what she herself has "done," "done," "done."

Stein, as a lesbian, is left out of bourgeois history and "family" reality, as she began at one point to tell us aloud in her small diatribe on being a "Singular." Yet aside from that early, brief, and not very effective polemic, her novel takes out its ideological rage furtively, in erotically pulsating sentences that dismantle bourgeois thinking and familial time without her ever openly staking out

[63]Janet Flanner, Foreword to Gertrude Stein, *Two: Gertrude Stein and Her Brother and Other Early Portraits (1908–12)* (New Haven: Yale University Press, 1951), p. xiii. The rest of the anecdote, which deflates some of the drama, is as follows: "'My God, why?' [asked the friend.] 'I know all about him,' she answered, 'and about them and about everybody in that story.' " Bridgman was the first to see the importance of the moment when Stein decided to kill her hero; see his remarks, p. 86. For a penetrating discussion of this decision and of the general collapse of history and family narrative in *The Making of Americans*, see Walker, pp. 43–54.

[64]Bridgman, p. 86.

(even to herself) an antibourgeois ideology.[65] Even on the last page of her novel, she uses the conservative phrase "family living" twenty-four times—as a tatter of the world of the bourgeois fathers to which she no longer belongs. Rather than argue with the phrase and all it implies ideologically, she grinds it down through orgiastic repetition: "Family living can be existing and every one can come to be a dead one and not any one then is remembering any such thing. Family living can be existing and every one can come to be a dead one and some are remembering some such thing. Family living can be existing and any one can come to be a dead one and every one is then a dead one and there are then not any more being living" (925). Although Stein need not have been entirely conscious of the politics of her text at this point, her paragraph takes a bourgeois idea, "family living," and makes it a counter in a grammatical game, disinfecting it of the sentimental associations and the aura of reality that normally give it its ideological grip on us.

A final assessment of the quality of *The Making of Americans* must cope with the power this novel has to rearrange our thinking. Although our experience of *The Making of Americans* is not always pleasurable, the novel, wherever we begin reading it—particularly if we are reading aloud—seems to have a unique capacity to convey us into a world at once lopsided and clarified. Even today *The Making of Americans* is likely to sound newer to readers than such landmarks of modernism as *The Waste Land* and *Mrs. Dalloway.* Laughter inevitably greets any public reading of Stein's novel, and this humor bespeaks at once a disorientation and a reorientation. The reinflections given to common language through repetition force a series of reconsiderations and turns upon established meanings. Stein's style, with its subversive drollery, releases our own aggression against the ideologically inflected "reality" that ordinarily binds us. If Stein had stated her lessons more baldly, we might refuse to follow her. We would not get the joke.

Along with neutral or disinterested history, Stein's novel up-

---

[65]DeKoven has described a parallel process in *Three Lives:* "Stein's rebellion [against a homophobic and male-dominated society] was channelled from content to linguistic structure itself" (p. 36).

holds, but then dissolves, the fiction of objective science. The characterology in *The Making of Americans* initially has pretensions to scientific truth, but these all but collapse into the narrator's grandiose fantasies and repetition-love. This collapse represents part of Stein's rebellion against the nineteenth century, in the person of William James. The characterology in *The Making of Americans* begins in the guise of a descriptive psychology, rather like James's (and, as Leon Katz has shown, like that of Otto Weininger),[66] but it ends in its own kind of outrageous play.

In the course of the novel, Stein's descriptions of the two types, resisters and attackers, become so imagistic and whimsical as to lose all authority as scientific truth: "This is a resisting earthy slow kind of them. . . . [T]he slow resisting bottom . . . in some can be solid, in some frozen, in some dried and cracked, in some muddy and engulfing, in some thicker, in some thinner, slimier, drier, very dry and not so dry. . . . [In some] the mud is dry and almost wooden . . . or metallic" (343). The author begins to let us know that her descriptions are coming from her immediate fantasies rather than from hard findings. *"I am thinking* of attacking being not as an earthy kind of substance but as a pulpy not dust not dirt but a more mixed up substance, it can be slimy, gelatinous, gluey, white opaquy kind of thing" (349, emphasis added). Her discoveries become mediated by the extravagant poetry of her own associations. Stein's vision of the attackers' essence as a "slimy, gelatinous, gluey, white opaquy kind of thing" is pretheoretical; she is letting her mind throw up preliminary associations around her subject.

Stein knowingly undermines her position as a detached theorist of character; she becomes tainted with (something like) her subjects' unconscious process. Increasingly, she allows herself to overidentify with her characters, imbibing or reproducing their emotions as her own. As she begins, for example, to write about certain people who are "going to be old ones," she stalls herself by letting their feelings seep into her: "I can feel myself in myself going to be being an old one" (671). She almost cannot write about characters without first feeling herself enveloping, incorporating, or "spread-

---

[66]Katz, "Weininger."

ing to" them: "I do not know yet very much about what any group of them are when they are young children. I am slowly spreading very slowly spreading to them, I have not yet spread to them, not at all reached to them yet in spreading out in knowing being in groups of men and women" (726). By so fusing with her subjects, Stein unsettles the authority of her science, in the same way that she demoted history from univocal truth to a part of her subjective experience of "what she loves."

A third object of Victorian belief that Stein unsettles is character. As an (extreme) instance of the nineteenth-century conception of "character," here again is a pronouncement of William James's: "Literature has no character when full of slack and wandering and superfluity. Neither does life. *Character* everywhere demands the stern and sacrificial mood as one of its factors. *The price must be paid.*"[67] To achieve character, one must suppress "slack and wandering and superfluity" in oneself. James, in spite of his fascination with such phenomena as the multiple self,[68] holds to the ideal of the focused will, which enables a person to bracket ambivalence and doubt and become a unified subject—as happened to James himself at a crucial momei . when he shook off a paralyzing depression by declaring to himself, "My first act of free will shall be to believe in free will."[69] The "mood" of the person of character, he writes, is "stern and sacrificial": selfhood is possible, for those who amputate discordant elements or otherness in themselves.

Stein comes to see that unified self as an oppressive fiction. What she does in myriad ways in *The Making of Americans* is to bring back all the "slack and wandering and superfluity" that "character" sacrifices. Freud's theories did a similar thing, as did other modern novels besides Stein's; stream-of-consciousness fiction represents an attack on ideas of character such as James's. *The Making of Americans*, however, in its emphasis on the very process of the birth of modernism, is unique (at least until the final pages of the "Oxen of the Sun" chapter of *Ulysses*). Stein's characterology

---

[67]James, "Is Life Worth Living?" quoted in Perry, *Thought and Character* 2:271.
[68]As an instance of James's interest in the split self, in 1896 he gave a series of lectures, "Abnormal Mental States," which included a talk titled "Multiple Personality." Perry, *Thought and Character* 2:169.
[69]Perry, *Thought and Character* 1:323.

begins by assuming the unitary self; people are "whole ones," and the narrator, too, starts off the novel as an integrated person. Then both the characters and the narrator slowly go to pieces, as Stein reaches toward very different truths.

At first, Stein conceives of human personality as a unity. In a characteristic moment of assurance, a third of the way through the novel, the author-narrator explains the dialectic by which she forms impressions of people. "There is," she believes, "a bottom nature in every one"; as that bottom nature reveals itself, a complete image of the individual emerges. When that picture is inadequate, Stein is alerted to the fact by conflicting data. But the alien elements then come "to have meaning"; gradually the person takes shape again as "a whole one to me" (309–10). But she adds a troubled note to this generalization. Certain people, it appears, never quite crystallize as "a whole one"; whenever she thinks she has fixed them, they "go to pieces again inside me," leaving the suspicion that even omniscience would be helpless to discover a unity (311).

It is not long before Stein's misgiving widens into a larger loss of certainty. Perhaps everyone, not only the eccentric few, is "in pieces"; there is little reason to suppose that even the fittest psychological formulations really capture their objects.[70] "Every one was a whole one in me and now a little every one is in fragments inside me. . . . Perhaps not any one really is a whole one" (519). The author-narrator's surmise that all her science has missed its object inspires a number of panicky monologues. By the end of the novel Stein is altogether discouraged with formulas, and makes what proves to be a lasting break with science. What began in an ambitious vein of characterology ends on a tentative and strangely interior note.

The fate of the narrator herself gives us a more precise, because interior, view of the self falling into "fragments." The narrator becomes a version of what Kristeva calls the subject-in-process, unsettled by the mobility of her unconscious and poetic activity.[71] The narrator-son of the very first paragraphs of The Making of Amer-

---

[70]See also the discussion in Walker, p. 68.
[71]Kristeva, "From One Identity to an Other," in Desire in Language, p. 135.

icans is nothing if not a unitary subject—a "real American," a respectful heir, and a focused ethical being. He has what one would call (a) character, and believes so himself, since he speaks in a sanguine way about the possibility of summarizing and "knowing" himself: "We need only realise our parents, remember our grandparents and know ourselves and our history is complete" (3). But as he—or (as soon becomes appropriate) she—starts to "know herself" better, the goal of self-summary looks farther and farther away. Otherness invades her, more rapidly than her powers of self-concentration can keep pace with.

Her narrative itself gradually becomes her enemy. It starts as a controlled expression of her complete "self" but then develops a will of its own that unsettles her wholeness.[72] More precisely, she *perceives* her own drive-to-tell as an alien thing in her that works against her sense of an integrated self. Stein's characterological theorizing, which was originally intended as a supplement to her history of herself and her family, ironically turns parasitic. Here is a hilarious sentence, too long to quote in its entirety (although that is part of the point), in which she tries to list conclusively all the different ways people have of "feeling living in them":

> Very many like it that they are doing something, living, working, loving, dressing, dreaming, waking, cleaning something, being a kind of a one, looking like some one, going to be doing something, being a nice one, being a not nice one, helping something, helping some one, . . . being one not liking any fresh air on them, being one not able to be breathing without much fresh air on them, being a funny one, being one not liking funny ones, one not liking queer ones in living, being one liking swimming, being one tired of ocean bathing before they have really been in more than twice in a season. (624–25)

The categories proliferate in such trivial and outlandish directions that an exhaustive inventory of the ways of "feeling living" quickly appears impossible. The narrator then speaks as if the endless data she is thus producing are coming from outside her and attacking

[72]Cf. Benstock: "She did what no other writer has had quite the courage to do: to relinquish the right to make language submit to the writer's will" (p. 159).

her: "There are all these ways then of having living having meaning and there are innumerable other ones, *do not crowd so on me* all
the other ones, I know very well there are very many other ones"
(625, emphasis added). The speaker is literally in pieces, having
split into a "me" that tries to keep its integrity, and "the other
ones," or the multiplying data, which she very strangely addresses
directly: "do not crowd so on me." The data-voice that crowds her
seems to be not a part of her self but an alien thing she hears:
"Now," she says, "I am always hearing of ways some have of
feeling living and they come crowding and I am resisting so that I
can be slowly realising" (625).

She does manage to resist or quiet that other voice in herself, by
telling herself (tautologically) that even if she cannot list here every
kind of personality, "I could know sometime, if I could know completely all I could be knowing, all the kinds there are of men and
women." That soothing thought stops the data mania and gives
her back her feeling of integrity: "I am comforting now my feeling
by saying this thing in my complete feeling again and again" (625).
Yet the whole dialogic episode has dramatized how precarious and
illusory the unitary self is. It will come apart again and again, in
other episodes of internal dialogue: "Certainly it is a trouble *to me*
to be doing this thing [exploring 'ways of realising and not realising thinking and feeling being']. I certainly cannot in any way
know it is a trouble *to you* to do this thing when *you* asked *me*
whether *you* should or should not do this thing" (772, emphases
added).

The self becomes single by "resisting" or repressing otherness.
Stein, by showing all the activity at the fringes, reverses the repression. Her picture of the dialogic subject is recognizably modernist;
for a fictional moment similar to these, one could look ahead six-
teen years, to Woolf's description of the jumble in Lily Briscoe's
mind in an instant of intense perception:

> How did one judge people, think of them? How did one add up this
> and that and conclude that it was liking one felt, or disliking? And to
> those words, what meaning attached, after all? Standing now, appar-
> ently transfixed, by the pear tree, impressions poured in upon her of
> those two men [Mr. Ramsay and William Bankes], and to follow her

thought was like following a voice which speaks too quickly to be taken down by one's pencil, and the voice was her own voice saying without prompting undeniable, everlasting, contradictory things.[73]

Like Lily Briscoe, Stein's narrator both sees the multiplicity in the people she observes and yields momentarily to fragmentation in herself. Stein's novel seems different from Woolf's, however, because of the extremely impure narrator, who herself, rather like a Beckett narrator, comically enacts the various splittings and reassemblies of the self. Woolf, for all her attention to the multiplicity of human personality, would not break the representational illusion by taking us through her own skirmishes with the things she must repress in order to keep writing linearly.

Stein's hero-murder in *The Making of Americans* is overdetermined. Her execution of David Hersland does business for multiple aggressions: for her anger at her father and Leo, for her subversion of the patrilineal and bourgeois social order, and finally for the creative violence she directs at the nineteenth century, which exalted and naturalized the categories of history, science, and character. In Stein's mind, a single phrase—"dead dead"—attached itself in protean ways to these different aggressions. Years after writing *The Making of Americans*, she would remark that "the nineteenth century is dead dead dead" and that she was one of its killers;[74] when she kills her hero in *The Making of Americans*, she takes as a refrain for her last chapter the sentence, "Old ones come to be dead" (923); and, before that, she in fact starts playing on the phrase "dead is dead" in connection with the climactic episode in which a daughter's letter paralyzes her incestuous father. "Such a one [as the father] then can have a paralytic stroke from the shock of realisation, of dead is dead" (499).[75] That moment in which she releases her private rage is continuous with her other, intellectual and aesthetic "murders."

[73]Virginia Woolf, *To the Lighthouse* (New York: Harcourt, Brace, and World, 1927), p. 40.

[74]Stein, *Wars I Have Seen*, p. 21.

[75]The phrase "dead is dead" also appears in other characterizations in these pages; Stein's general theme is the conflict in some people's minds between religion, which persuades them that "dead is not dead," and the shocking (or simply concrete) facts that can intrude to tell them on the contrary that "dead is dead."

Over the next few years, Stein comes to reconceive her creative struggle as a woman's struggle. As she does, her metaphor for her artistic task shifts from patricide to the recovery of a forgotten mother. She starts to fit more closely the paradigms we have for female authorship. Sandra Gilbert and Susan Gubar have challenged Harold Bloom's male paradigm of literary influence by describing women authors' need to reconstruct a "lost literary matrilineage."[76] Jane Marcus writes similarly of the necessity for all women writers of "thinking back through our mothers."[77] Although it will be many years before Stein identifies a specific historical foremother, a "mother of us all," her sense of her strength as an artist will soon depend on an image of connection to a lost mother.

But *The Making of Americans*, just before this phase, fits no familiar paradigm of authorship, male or female. Before Stein could start to unearth a mother, she felt a need to wage war on the father who seemed to stand in the way of all her erotic and creative powers. Incredibly, she also had to win—not as the oedipal literary son familiar from Bloom wins, for she neither identifies a specific poetic precursor nor inherits a place in the male lineage, but instead in a marginal and lonely way, deriving all her support from a single reader-companion. Then, strengthened by having defined herself against the paternal taboo, she could start to explore her exhilarating but threatening archaic memories of the mother.

[76]Sandra M. Gilbert and Susan Gubar, *The Madwoman in the Attic: The Woman Writer and the Nineteenth-Century Literary Imagination* (New Haven: Yale University Press, 1979), p. 53.

[77]Jane Marcus, "Thinking Back through Our Mothers," in Marcus, ed., *New Feminist Essays on Virginia Woolf* (Lincoln: University of Nebraska Press, 1981), p. 7. Marcus takes her title from a phrase of Woolf's.

3

G.M.P. and Others:
South to the Mother

Stein once commented on how slowly *The Making of Americans* had taken shape, how gradually the "preparation" for the novel "was made inside of me."[1] We have seen what that slow inner preparation amounted to, in emotional and artistic terms. But the next change in her work came rapidly; this time there was no need to prepare herself. *The Making of Americans* had left her with a strong sense of her identity and power as an artist. Soon she was taking new risks.

Within a year after finishing *The Making of Americans*, Stein started writing in a radically new style—fragmented, opaque, and image-rich. She had no fixed idea where this style would take her, but it moved her in new psychic directions. As she used this style in *G.M.P., A Long Gay Book*, and shorter pieces in the "portrait" genre, something new rose up from her unconscious—an archaic longing for her mother. Just as the repetitive style Stein developed in *The Making of Americans* had armed her for a confrontation with her father, the fragmented style that followed gave her access to feelings for her mother, feelings that had been entirely obscured in the patricidal scuffle of *The Making of Americans*.

The new works do not in fact leave that patricidal drama behind. Instead, they give patricide an altered meaning. Stein continues to circle about the thought "fathers are dead."[2] But the term opposite

[1]Stein, "The Gradual Making," *Lectures*, p. 135.
[2]Stein, *G.M.P.*, in *Matisse Picasso and Gertrude Stein*, p. 274, hereafter cited in the text. *G.M.P.* is Stein's own abbreviated title for the work she also called *Matisse Picasso and Gertrude Stein*.

"father" (which, in *The Making of Americans*, had been "repeating") now has a face, that of "mother." So to move past the father's law means, at the same time, to reach toward the mother. This new polarity of father and mother brings issues of gender to the fore, inaugurating in some of these texts a new kind of cultural critique. By the time of *Tender Buttons*, the work that culminates this phase, Stein's target is no longer the figure of the bourgeois patriarch, as in *The Making of Americans*, but, more broadly, patriarchy itself, the system of male dominion that contains a mechanism for its own perpetuation.

G.M.P., A Long Gay Book, Tender Buttons, and the many shorter works Stein composed in this opaque mode have been treated by most critics as stylistically important but largely impenetrable thematically. In fact, however, I find in them important ideas, including Stein's brilliant ruminations on the nature of patriarchy. Without trying to suggest the presence of a "code," in which every sentence has a single meaning to be unlocked, I trace in these texts what amounts to a series of reflections on how patriarchal relations are made: how the mother becomes taboo to us, how her presence is symbolically erased, and how women are subordinated in the social sphere.

At the same time, Stein offers a vision of escape and revolt. Once one sees women's subordination as a system, rather than as a fact of nature, one knows enough to slip through a crack in the system and to begin to challenge patriarchal thinking—something Stein had not been able to envision in *Three Lives*, where the women characters (and the passive narrator) were simply trapped. The image that Stein now uses for the woman poet's rupture with patriarchy is that of a recovery of the forbidden body of the mother.

The Experimental Style of 1911

Stein is not ordinarily called a feminist, and in her public commitments she was not one. Yet one can see traces of a feminist consciousness throughout her career, from her early speech called "The Value of College Education for Women" to creative works with such titles as "Patriarchal Poetry" and *The Mother of Us All*. In rare instances, she comes close to an overtly feminist voice, as when in *The Mother of Us All* she has Susan B. Anthony answer the remark, "Dear lady remember humanity comes first," with, "You mean men come first."[3] Furthermore, Stein's manipulation of language, particularly in the opaque style, seems "anti-patriarchal," an idea that has been elaborated recently in a number of Stein studies, most meticulously by DeKoven in *A Different Language*. As Catharine Stimpson also notes, "Stein is no ideological feminist, but she does [in the hovering of her language] foreshadow the pulsating, lyrical polemic of much contemporary feminist theory," such as Cixous's. Shari Benstock similarly finds that Stein "joined sexuality and textuality to refute the conservative patriarchal assumptions underlying Modernism's experimental claims"; and Ulla Dydo calls Stein's writing "subversive, anti-authoritarian, uncivilized." Finally, Harriet Chessman sees a "feminist project" as implicit in Stein's "poetics of dialogue, where dialogue presents an alternative to the possibility of patriarchal authoritarianism implicit in monologue, reliant upon the privileging of one voice, one narrator, or one significance."[4]

I believe that Stein is knowingly anti-patriarchal—that her themes themselves become feminist in this phase. Stein never produced a *Three Guineas*; her feminist voice, when it appears, is complicated by hermetic or dialogic literary forms. But beneath the surface of much of her hermetic work, intensive thinking is taking place. What I identify in the texts of 1911–1912 is an exploratory feminism, which is on the way to articulating itself. It is based not on theoretical propositions but on a set of tentative ideas, ideas so explosive and yet so preliminary that Stein felt safe with them only under the protection of a hieroglyphic style.

At the end of her career, she gave what may be a hint as to why she had never voiced her anti-patriarchal intuitions "out loud."

[3]Stein, *The Mother of Us All*, in *Last Operas and Plays*, ed. Carl Van Vechten (New York: Rinehart, 1949), p. 77.

[4]Stimpson, "Gertrude Stein and the Transposition of Gender," p. 10; Benstock, *Women of the Left Bank*, p. 187; Ulla E. Dydo, "Must Horses Drink; or, 'Any Language Is Funny if You Don't Understand It,'" *Tulsa Studies in Women's Literature* 4 (1985): 273; Chessman, *Public Is Invited*, pp. 2, 3. Similarly, Neil Schmitz calls Stein's poetic practice a contest between "Father and Demoiselle." *Of Huck and Alice: Humorous Writing in American Literature* (Minneapolis: University of Minnesota Press, 1983), p. 175.

She has Susan B. Anthony (again) say that while men are basically kind—"if I fall down in a faint, they will rush to pick me up"— they nonetheless "fear women, they fear each other." Another woman character asks Susan B. Anthony why she does not "say these things out loud" to the men. Her answer is: "Why not, because if I did they would not listen they not alone would not listen they would revenge themselves." Their "kindness would turn to hate."[5] These sentences, which Stein may have suddenly felt free to write when she knew she was approaching death,[6] offer a retrospective insight into her own hermetic style of 1911. She may well have chosen such a style partly in order to elude the "revenge" of the cultural censors; her works would seem simply impenetrable to anyone likely to be wholly unsympathetic to their ideas, but would slowly yield their pleasures and their subversive secrets to readers moved to stay with them for some time.

They reveal their secrets in different ways to different readers. That is another advantage of the experimental style. Whereas an already feminist reader might be especially alert to Stein's commentary on gender relations, other readers absorb the same material subliminally. Stein's mobile, ambiguous style is calculated to defuse not just the revenge of people who would oppose Stein's feminist ideas but also the internal censorship of readers whose minds might not yet be made up. Consciously or not, when we read a line like "Little sales ladies little sales ladies little saddles of mutton" (TB 27), we take in some kind of message about women's objectified status. Our interest may be hooked by these provocative musings, without our quite knowing why. Thus, much of the feminist content I locate in these works has already reached readers, subliminally, as an essential part of the experience of reading the texts.

Another reason for Stein's opacity is that her radical thinking was unfamiliar even to her—a "guess" or a "question" (TB 47, 52), which she kept trying out in an indirect, half-formulated way. It was a threatening guess, even to its guesser, and her linguistic play

[5]Stein, The Mother of Us All, p. 81.
[6]"She completed the text in March 1946, several months after she had begun to experience abdominal pain. The Mother of Us All gives every indication of being a valedictory." Bridgman, Gertrude Stein in Pieces, p. 341.

served her as a buffer and a protest against the disturbing truths she was unearthing within patriarchal culture. *Tender Buttons*, for example, even as it exposes a scene of rape-murder at the heart of gender relations—"A jack in kill her"—does so in a context filled with puns, byzantine jokes, and uncertain affect (29). The content is grim, but Stein's joking is a way of fighting back: she sends out wordplay as a not-to-be-"killed" energy in herself. That energy, in turn, works on the reader, stimulating the reader's own interpretive and creative energies. Thus, the style is much more than camouflage. Stein's formal experimentation, now as in *The Making of Americans*, is an indispensable part of her process of intellectual and spiritual discovery.

For these various reasons, the hermetic style is a medium suited to Stein's subversive thinking. But this highly imagistic style must be understood not just as a medium for certain powerful thoughts and insights but also as a dream medium, opening up a new kind of associative verbal play that is itself subversive. As Stein herself suggests (in some self-reflective poems I will look at), the challenge that her experimental style issues to univocal meaning is at the same time a challenge to the cultural fathers. Even in the many texts from this phase that have no feminist thoughts as part of their content, the innovative style itself performs a subversion that has much in common with expressly feminist content elsewhere.

Finally, the experimental style enables Stein to situate herself somewhere between discursive language and dream. The material that I explore in these last chapters contains a strand of sophisticated feminist thinking, but alongside this thinking there are articulations of the myth of the lost and recovered mother that take a half-conscious, more purely poetic form. At certain moments, therefore, it will make sense to speak of Stein's freeing, woman-centered imaginative vision, rather than of her feminist "ideas." But it is hard to draw a strict line between the mythical and the intellectual axes—or between Stein's unconscious mother-seeking and her theoretical challenge to patriarchy. While one can say that her work in this phase becomes progressively more intellectual, or more consciously feminist (with *Tender Buttons* representing a culmination), the intellectual and the unconscious motives exist side by side in all these texts. For there is no great distance between a poetic dream about a woman's challenge to patriarchy and a knowing polemic about it. Patriarchy is itself a bad dream, imprinted on the unconscious; and a poet who interestingly dreams its reversal is already on her way to a feminist insight.

I want to spend a few moments bringing the new style into focus before beginning to trace the woman-centered thinking it released. Stein's "Portrait of Constance Fletcher," a specimen in the portrait genre that spun off from *The Making of Americans*,[7] begins in the repetitive style of that novel but then—like *G.M.P.* and *A Long Gay Book*—breaks into an utterly new prose, vivid, fragmented, and imagistic. The first two pages of this piece are indistinguishable in style and, incidentally, in theme from portions of *The Making of Americans:* "She could be completely feeling having, having had family living. She was thinking in being one who could be completely feeling having had, having family living. She was feeling in being one who could be completely feeling having had, who could be completely feeling having family living."[8] As in *The Making of Americans*, the interest is in the grammatical permutations of the sentences and in their incremental additions and tiny shifts in vocabulary. The lexical palette is once again extremely limited; the locus of experimentation is the tissue of the sentence, not the properties of the individual word.

Then, about a quarter of the way through the portrait, an incongruous statement leaps out at us: "If they move in the shoe there is everything to do. They do not move in the shoe" (*GP* 159). Who are "they"? The context and even the facts under discussion are murky in a new way, somewhere between surreal and nonsensical. One cannot in practical reality get a "they" (moving or not) into a single shoe. "*The* shoe" is obscure, too, since there has been no prior reference to a shoe.[9]

What is the effect of this break in the prose? Stein shifts our attention from the ostensible topics of the portrait—the original

[7]On the portraits as the "progeny" of *The Making of Americans*, see Bridgman, pp. 91–98.

[8]Stein, "Portrait of Constance Fletcher," in *Geography and Plays* (Boston: Four Seas, 1922), pp. 157–58, hereafter cited in the text as *GP*.

[9]For a similar discussion of this stylistic break in the "Portrait of Constance Fletcher," see DeKoven, *A Different Language*, pp. 64–66.

"she" and her experiences of "family living"—to a dense word-surface that poses much more severe barriers to comprehension than the hypnotic, repetitive style of the earlier section. Here, although we know the meanings of the individual words, we cannot assemble their referents into a coherent fictional universe.

Marjorie Perloff and Jayne Walker, among others, have discussed this style as Stein's answer in a verbal medium to the techniques of collage that Picasso was developing at the same time in analytic cubism:

> In [Picasso's] *Ma Jolie*, the printed letters appear to shift and fade in space and yet they rest flatly upon the opaque plane of the canvas as if they were printed letters on a page. The painting invites us to identify familiar forms and objects . . . at the same time as it prevents us from applying the test of consistency. It is impossible to "read" such a painting as a coherent image of reality. . . .
>
> It is this tension between reference and compositional game, between a pointing system and a self-ordering system that we find in [Stein's] *Susie Asado*.[10]

Stein's "shoe" paragraph, like her prose from this period generally (and like analytic cubism), does exhibit various principles of organization, in spite of its opacity. The passage is not just a random assortment of words, picked out of a dictionary; we recognize it right away as wordplay, and play has its own rules. First, Stein maintains the sentence intact as a grammatical unit, creating a tension in fact between the obscurity of her subject matter and the lucidity of her syntax: the "if . . . then . . ." construction creates a strong logical framework, into which the second sentence fits as the expected supplement, since it tells whether the condition is met—whether "they" do indeed "move in the shoe." Another

[10]Perloff, *The Poetics of Indeterminacy*, p. 72; and see Walker, *The Making of a Modernist*, pp. 129–31; Schmitz, *Of Huck*, pp. 167–71; Chessman, *Public Is Invited*, pp. 88–111; and Randa Dubnick, *The Structure of Obscurity: Gertrude Stein, Language, and Cubism* (Urbana: University of Illinois Press, 1984), pp. 30–36. But Steiner and DeKoven contest the notion of making a literal analogy between Stein's writing and cubism. Steiner, *Exact Resemblance to Exact Resemblance*, pp. 159–60; DeKoven, "Gertrude Stein and Modern Painting: Beyond Literary Criticism," in Hoffman, ed., *Critical Essays on Gertrude Stein*, pp. 171–83.

principle of organization, here and in the new style generally, is soundplay. The first of Stein's "shoe" sentences rhymes and yields easily to scansion: "If they move in the shoe there is everything to do." (Indeed, one hears behind these words the nursery rhyme about the old woman who "lived *in a shoe*," and "had so many children she didn't know what *to do*.")[11] The second sentence almost fits the metrical pattern of the first.

The remainder of the "Portrait of Constance Fletcher," after this stylistic surprise, is written in the same formally playful vein. Sometimes Stein lets her wordplay strain her grammar to the limit—as in, "Oh sadly has the oak-tree not that sadness" (*GP* 160)—and sometimes past the limit: "If the way to say the turn is the turn the way that is the way to turn that way then all of the thing is in that thing" (*GP* 164–65). Surreal images continue to proliferate, typically in unions of abstract and very concrete nouns or adjectives, such as "the softening of the published soap," or "the origin of the penguin" (*GP* 161–62). The effect of these surrealistic juxtapositions is to alert us to the thing-ness of words, something we ordinarily lose track of in the instrumental use of language that necessarily displaces our attention from the feel of words onto their referents.[12] As I will soon be showing, this linguistic practice has meanings for Stein that are closely connected to her feminist themes.

Words-as-things, moreover, become in Stein's hands tools of semantic aggression: the vivid nouns "penguin," "oak-tree," and "soap," jutting out incongruously from their sentences, are mischievous assaults on the coherence of ordinary speech. These words fail to go with anything in their contexts, whereas language normally is a matter of going-with. Poking at the semantic proprieties is something in which children delight, since it releases their aggression against the rule-bound verbal system they are trying to master, which also masters them; and children would be entertained by many of Stein's surrealistic, nearly nonsensical sentences, such as this one from *Tender Buttons*, where coherency is sacrificed to the electrically incongruous images and the music of

11Cf. DeKoven, *A Different Language*, p. 68.
12See DeKoven, *A Different Language*, pp. 66–67.

the syllables. "Elephant beaten with candy and little pops and chews all bolts and reckless reckless rats, this is this" (26).

Just as Stein felt no embarrassment in *The Making of Americans* about bringing repetition, one of her own childish pleasures, into her prose, in this next phase she makes childlike jabs at the rules of grammar and diction. She herself thought of this new style as a reach back to infantile experience. She writes in *Tender Buttons*, "only excreate a no since" (58): her no-sense, or nonsense, is a recovered innocence (a-no-since). The phrase is from a piece called "Orange In"—a pun on "origin." Stein returns to infantile origins by way of an ex-creation or violent uncreation of the semantic world we know.

Her semantic deviancy is also a way of "excreating" or (true to a child's aggressive impulse) excreting on the orderly world of adult thinking. "Excreate a no since": to write no-sense is to excrete/ create. In other words, the innocent world that Stein's linguistic practice recreates is that of—among other things—anality, not too surprisingly after what we have seen in *The Making of Americans*. The rhythmically rich style of that novel and the new, semantically rich style could hardly be more different—and yet both represent experiments in pre-phallic speech, to borrow a term from classical Freudian theory. In the new texts, Stein is inventing—or rather reinventing—"a no since," that is, anus sense.

Lili Peller, in "Comments on Libidinal Organizations and Child Development," which I had occasion to quote in the last chapter, notes that in the anal-sadistic phase, the child "discovers and is proud of his body products," most notably his (or her) faeces but also "his voice," the production and control of which confers the same pleasure as the production and mastery of faeces. The child in the anal phase "plays with his voice, with sounds and intricate sound sequences. He produces them, not to communicate with us—this he does by simple sounds, crying and gestures—but for the joy of being their cause" (738).[13]

It is only in the next phase, the "phallic-oedipal phase," that

---

[13]Peller adds that the child libidinizes in this way not only the voice but also "his other body parts, and their functions" and even "his human and physical surround-ings" (739).

"proficiency in the *understanding* of language comes" (740). Stein's experimental style of 1911 depends on our "understanding" of the meanings of words; yet her sentences at the same time subvert the symbolic function by veering off into the sort of soundplay Peller associates with the preoedipal, anal phase. Hence Stein "excreate[s] a no" in the sense of undoing the father's "no," or prohibition, which initiates the oedipal phase. ("Since when?" she asks sarcastically.) In the present poem itself, she no sooner makes her own suggestive association of wordplay and excretion—"excreate a no since"—than she launches into a wild demonstration of excre(a)tory speech that fits Peller's notion of the child's pre-phallic joy in playing with sound sequences: "A no, a no since, a no since when, a no since when since, a no since when since a no since when since, a no since, a no since when since, a no since, a no, a no since a no since, a no since, a no since" (58).

But besides ex-creating or uncreating linear speech, Stein's prose creates. Although childlike in some of its effects and motivations, it is extremely sophisticated in others. Even as Stein dismantles ordinary thinking, she carefully puts together another kind of thinking. Her style itself combines primitive, presymbolic features and highly advanced thought processes. Whereas certain features of the style, such as the soundplay and the verbal surprises, bespeak childish pleasures, other aspects of this dense word-surface come from (and demand from the reader) a taut, analytic wit, as must already have been apparent from the multiple puns contained in the single phrase "excreate a no since."

Large portions of these texts contain ideas, suggestive and important in themselves. This is an unusual claim to make for Stein's experimental writing, but as she herself writes in *Tender Buttons*, "A mind under is exact and so it is necessary to have a mouth and eye glasses" (45). A mind that goes underground—by virtue either of exploring irrational processes or of thinking subversive thoughts— still must be "exact," or precise, and so, "it is necessary" for the underground poet to employ both her "mouth," the erotic organ that produces infantile wordplay, and her "eye glasses" or, metaphorically, her intellectual spectacles, the part of her adult self that scrutinizes and analyzes the world she sees. Another thing she says in *Tender Buttons* is "I spy" (52): Stein's job is not just to reintroduce us to the lost pleasures of childhood but to make stealthy observations of a social universe she has come to see as enemy territory.

The rest of this chapter is about what Stein sees with her "eye glasses." At the same time as she experiments with new language, she experiments with a new way of interpreting the world. The texts of 1911–1912 contain what amounts to an elaborate vision of how patriarchal relations make themselves, and how the individual woman can "spy" her way past them.

As I explore this material, the question of Stein's style sometimes moves into the background. I often interpret her sentences without commenting at length on their stylistic texture. My intention is by no means to minimize the density and the strangeness of the prose I am interpreting, but the ideas Stein is developing here are themselves so elaborate that it is essential to get at them in a continuous way, however discontinuous (and pleasantly bewildering) our immediate experience of the texts themselves is. I am helped by the extensive criticism that already exists on the style of these texts; if it were not for the illuminating work that other critics (particularly Marianne DeKoven, Marjorie Perloff, and Harriet Chessman) have done on the aims and effects of Stein's opaque style, my task in this chapter would be doubled.[14]

Nonetheless, the style often reenters as my theme, for among other things, it has an ethics of its own, which is closely linked to the content I am tracing. It makes sense, that is, that a person who had Stein's anti-patriarchal hunches would develop such a style. The style is itself the perfection of her hunch. While her themes point to a subversion of patriarchal relations, her style performs that subversion within language, initiating the reader in a new way of experiencing a text. Specifically, Stein shatters the reader's mastery of the signifier—a mastery that we ordinarily need and enjoy in our daily use of language, but that also holds in place a symbolic system that devalues and subordinates women.

[14]In addition to DeKoven, Perloff, and Chessman, see Stimpson, "Stein and the Transposition of Gender," p. 10; Dydo, p. 273; Benstock, pp. 158–61; Schmitz, *Of Huck,* pp. 175; Walker, pp. 127–49; and Dubnick, pp. 30–36.

Matter-Writing, Woman-Writing

The Making of Americans contained the kindling for a feminist idea, but the flame came later. In *The Making of Americans*, Stein excavated the ground of her narrative, identifying the love of repetition and the primitive fantasies that drove her text forward. It would be a small step from this attention to the (normally) repressed ground of a cultural product such as a novel to a feminist attention to woman as the repressed ground of culture. Just as narrative depends on but traditionally suppresses its connection to the author's moment-to-moment libidinal processes, so male-dominated culture depends on but tries to disinfect itself of women's bodies and work. In the texts that Stein went on to write in the early teens, she questions both sorts of repression at once. Woman becomes part of the "ground" she excavates.

A new feature in these texts is a vivid imagery of the female body, part of the female identification toward which Stein seems to be moving. Suddenly, she seems to enjoy focusing on the details of the female anatomy; furthermore, she starts to conceive of her own stylistic experimentation as a kind of feminine body-writing, in a manner that anticipates the theoretical formulations of Irigaray and Kristeva. Later, I want to do a speculative reading of *G.M.P.*, a text in which Stein thinks at length about the meaning of her "feminine" writing and places that writing in the context of a larger drama of the making and unmaking of patriarchy.

First, the female imagery. When Stein switched to the opaque style, she started to experiment with colorful images suggestive of women's anatomy. *A Long Gay Book*, *G.M.P.*, *Tender Buttons*, and the shorter pieces Stein wrote in the same period share certain key image-clusters, among them images of dirt and variations of the color red.[15] These images very often have anatomical associations. Red and roses, for example, suggest menstrual blood and the vagina, sometimes with a negative association of dirt or shame. A poem called "A Petticoat" in *Tender Buttons* describes a "rosy" stain on an undergarment: "A light white, a disgrace, an ink spot, a rosy charm" (22). (But if the stain is "a disgrace" according to one sys-

---

[15]Bridgman draws attention to the repeated symbolism of dirt and the color red in *Tender Buttons* (p. 126).

tem of valuation, according to another it has a "charm.") Elsewhere Stein compares the female genitalia to a red rose: "A shallow hole rose on red, a shallow hole in and in this makes ale less [Alice]" (*TB* 26). Alternatively, she mixes the colors red and white in a way that suggests the traditional image of a woman's body as a white flower, which intercourse "stamp[s]" or marks red: "A Red Stamp. If lilies are lily white . . . , if they dusty will dirt a surface. . . . if they do this they need a catalogue" (*TB* 14). "The white flower has not been bled," she writes in "Portrait of Constance Fletcher" (*GP* 162). In addition to images suggestive of menstruation and defloration, Stein makes abundant allusions to stains, spots, bleeding, and things secreted.[16] She is focusing on a taboo subject, the waste products of the body and, in many instances, of the female body.

She often associates these spots and secretions with her own writing process. For the first time Stein becomes, in some limited sense of the phrase, woman-identified. The attention to women's "rosy" bodies in these texts does not in itself attest to a female identification; a poet could use motifs like these without necessarily thinking of her own body or identity in feminine terms. But Stein's self-image, at least as an artist, does now take on feminine and even woman-affirming features. This development is anticipated by *Two* (1910); as Walker notes, "*Two*'s opposition between the sterile rationality of the male [a character based on Leo Stein] and the fluid creativity of the female [based on Stein's sister-in-law Sally Stein] in itself suggests a major change in Stein's conception of her role as an artist."[17]

In the opaque texts, Stein uses menstrual and uterine images to describe her writing. In "A Petticoat"—"A white light, a disgrace, an ink spot, a rosy charm"—the third term standing between the menstrual images of "a disgrace" and "a rosy charm" is "an ink spot." Stein is associating the ink spots she is making on the page with the rosy spots on a petticoat. The "white light" that precedes

[16]See, for example, *TB* 27, 39; *A Long Gay Book*, in *Matisse Picasso and Gertrude Stein*, p. 112; and *G.M.P.*, p. 277. Hereafter *A Long Gay Book* will be cited in the text, as *LGB*.

[17]Walker, p. 119. Bridgman (p. 91) dates *Two* as having been written (or at least begun) in 1910.

all three terms then refers doubly to the blank page and to the petticoat just before either is marked.[18]

What does it mean to compare one's writing to menstruation? Menstruation is a symbol and symptom of humanity's implication in the workings of matter; women's bodily cycles, as well as pregnancies, remind the species of its subjection to the rhythms of nature (although men, for just that reason, can imagine that they are farther from nature than women). Luce Irigaray notes that menstrual fluid serves in the Western imagination as a key symbol for the "prime matter"—shapeless, waiting-to-be-formed, and in itself waste. Western ontology conceives of this prime matter as secondary to God or intellection (or, symbolically, semen), which is seen as shaping matter and giving it value and definition. But, Irigaray continues, we can reverse this patriarchal ontology: "By coming back to the [menstrual, gestational] cycle of the mother, at least in potentiality, one will have turned again to the first matter and her mysteries."[19] Stein gives a poetic version of what such a return to the "the first matter" would look like; by conceiving of her writing as a menstrual "spot," she grounds her artistic activity in the body, and questions the priority of mind over material process. At the same time, she dismantles the false dichotomy of cultural products, such as literary texts, and (natural, female) bodily products.

Stein also compares her creativity to the embodied and feminine act of childbirth. In *G.M.P.*, she associates "song" or aural art (possibly her own art) with the mystery of pregnancy: "sing the song with the pleasure of the incubator" (255). An image like this reworks in a feminine vein the "earth feeling" that was already important to Stein's self-conception in *The Making of Americans*. In the notebooks for that novel Stein describes her work as the product of an unwilled "propulsion," a force she pictures in the novel itself in anal terms, although there may be a childbirth fantasy as

[18]In "'The Blank Page' and the Issues of Female Creativity," Susan Gubar discusses certain women writers' fantasies of writing with menstrual and other blood. In Elizabeth Abel, ed., *Writing and Sexual Difference* (Chicago: University of Chicago Press, 1982), pp. 73–93.

[19]Luce Irigaray, "How to Conceive (of) a Girl," *Speculum of the Other Woman*, trans. Gillian C. Gill (Ithaca: Cornell University Press, 1985), p. 166.

well. In this new material, Stein still uses anal imagery to describe her work, as was evident with the word *excreate*. She now (at least at one point) adds a urethral image: "A yellow happy thing is a gentle little tinkle that goes in all the way it has everything to say" (*LGB* 82). This idea of a "tinkle" that has something "to say" may suggest some sort of urinary speech, one that "goes in" someone's ear. In any case, Stein has now added to such images of expression-as-excretion an extensive, specifically feminine imagery, so that her writing can be a menstrual ink spot or an act of incubation.

"Menstrual writing" is an image; but what kind of writing corresponds to this image? Are Stein's own texts, in their methods or their effects, somehow menstrual or pregnant in a way that other texts are not? The imagery of writing as secretion suggests that she sees her self-expression as involving a partial relaxation of controlled intellectual processes—an extension of what she earlier called propulsion. She lets thoughts and images enter her mind and move from mind to page in an unselfconscious, half-willed way that is rather like what a body does when it gestates and expels a baby, or takes in food and emits waste. *Filling* and *emptying* are two of Stein's favorite words for her artistic process; as she says in *G.M.P.*, "emptying filling is creating [creative?] action" (215).[20] This is hardly to suggest that in practice Stein composes simply by free association or by automatic writing. She thinks about what she is doing, but she does not rule out the images and sounds that seem to enter her mind spontaneously from moment to moment. She writes in *A Long Gay Book*, "What is secretion, secretion is that amusement which every little mark shows as merit" (110). All literature, of course, uses the unconscious, but Stein's associative method, in which "every little mark" she makes on the page shows some kind of "merit," makes extreme concessions to the forces that I would call primary process and soundplay, and that she describes in terms of bodily feelings of filling and excretion.

[20]Opening-and-closing is another of Stein's favorite metaphors for self-expression: "Standing and expressing, opening and holding, turning and meaning, closing and folding, holding and meaning, . . . opening and holding" (*LGB* 86). For an interesting discussion of such images, see Joel Porte, "Gertrude Stein and the Rhythms of Life," *New Boston Review* 1 (June 1975): 16–18.

Writing about secretions and writing by a quasi secretion are similar activities. Both undermine the polarities of pure/impure and mental/material, polarities that are patriarchal in the sense that they tend to devalue woman along with matter. Stein, by focusing in a new way on bodily blots, erodes the boundary marking off a taboo or conventionally disgraceful topic. Similarly, by writing *with* spots—with what comes out of her—she disturbs the division between her conscious, higher processes and (what feel to her like) the rhythms of her body. In this feminine and anatomical focus is an incipient feminism: Stein is undoing a Cartesian dualism that historically has devalued and marginalized women.

Stein's is a bodily or material style in a second sense as well. In its effects, the opaque style brings to the surface the material aspects, or the "body," of language. Although Stein is not a theorist, she speculates aloud in an extraordinarily sophisticated way about the meanings of her style. In her own view, her poetic language is a matter-language or a waste-language, or—what she thinks of as the same thing—a feminine and woman-affirming language. We can trace these thoughts by looking closely at the poem "Cups," in *Tender Buttons.* "Cups," like the other material I have been examining, uses vaginal and uterine imagery. But in this poem Stein makes a further connection—consciously, I think—between women's devalued bodies and the presymbolic axis of language.

CUPS.

A single example of excellence is in the meat. A bent stick is surging and might all might is mental. A grand clothes is searching out a candle not that wheatly not that by more than an owl and a path. A ham is proud of cocoanut.

A cup is neglected by being all in size. It is a handle and meadows and sugar any sugar.

A cup is neglected by being full of size. It shows no shade, in come little wood cuts and blessing and nearly not that not with a wild bought in, not at all so polite, not nearly so behind.

Cups crane in. They need a pet oyster, they need it so hoary and nearly choice. The best slam is utter. Nearly be freeze.

Why is a cup a stir and a behave. Why is it so seen.

A cup is readily shaded, it has in between no sense that is to say music, memory, musical memory.

Peanuts blame, a half sand is holey and nearly. (49)

The first two paragraphs allude to the customary valuation of the phallus over the womb. Patriarchal thinking brands women's genitals a mere absence, as defined against the present and "excellent" male genitals: "A single example of excellence is in the meat. A bent stick is surging." But as this meat or stick surges up, the "cup is neglected," for it is "all in size," or all insides. By virtue of not being visible outside the body, the cup—vagina or uterus—is overlooked and devalued. This point about the neglected cup anticipates various feminist attacks on Freud's image of the female genitals as a mere absence, a "castrated" version of the male.[21] Stein herself is not challenging Freud in particular; the idea of woman as castrated is of such long standing that Irigaray, for example, believes it underwrites all of Western ontotheology.[22] But the woman-affirming sensibility that now appears in Stein's work sets her apart from Freud intellectually.

Stein thinks of women's bodies not as lacking but as different. In the next paragraph of her poem, she rewrites the words "all in size" as "full of size": "A cup is neglected by being full of size." The female genitals, that is, are in reality anything but an absence, even if still wrongly neglected. An "oyster" is mentioned: oysters have rounded exteriors and soft interiors, and can envelop precious things, pearls—the opposite of waste or absence. The cup or womb is "a stir and a behave"—astir and a beehive, a globe of secret life. (A beehive also contains a fertile, matriarchal queen bee.) The cup is astir as a site of fertility and perhaps also as a site of sexual pleasure, stimulated by "a stir" from a lover/spoon.

Then the poem goes on to make a complex connection between this region of hidden fertility and pleasure in the female body, and the hidden richness of the presymbolic dimension within language. The statement "A cup is readily shaded, it has in between no sense" makes an association between the cup, which has just been a figure for the womb, and the "in between no sense," or the rich non-sense that exists "in between" the lines of symbolic language—everything that "Orange In," the excreation poem, referred to, similarly, as "no since."

---

[21]See, for example, Irigaray, "The Blind Spot of an Old Dream of Symmetry," *Speculum*, pp. 11–129.

[22]See especially Irigaray, "Plato's *Hystera*," *Speculum*, pp. 241–364.

Language makes "sense"—each signifier has a signified—but language also has features extraneous to sense (and therefore, "no-sense"), such as its rhythm and its play of vowels and consonants. This aural dimension, which we repress from consciousness when we use words instrumentally, is like a cup of neglected vitality within language. (Hence, perhaps, the image of the cup as "readily shaded," in the sense of obscured.) Stein makes a further clarification: "A cup is readily shaded, it has in between no sense *that is to say music, memory, musical memory.*" The aural, or musical, features of our adult language retain a "memory" of our infantile existence, for as infants we appreciated words first as sounds, not as signifiers pointing to absent signifieds.

This presymbolic axis is just what the poem using the word *excreate* associated with excremental play. Here, however, the presymbolic axis is not so much anal as feminine, by an analogy between the social code that "neglects" women's cuplike bodies as mere absence and the linguistic code that neglects soundplay as mere waste.[23] Stein's poem recuperates the waste, in both senses. It exposes the fact that wombs are not absences but sites of delightful fertility; and it tells of the recovery of the musical axis of language, which is not waste but precious surplus. (Elsewhere she writes, "Any *extra* way is the way of speaking.")[24] More than that, the presymbolic is feminine in the sense of being the maternal register of language—an idea that Julia Kristeva has articulated theoretically, but that Stein, as we will see in the context of *G.M.P.*, intuited years before.

The present poem describes the "cup," or pocket of presymbolic activity within language, as having nearly been frozen—"Nearly be freeze." For just as the "surging" phallus almost erases the womb, the symbolic code almost erases the material aspect of language. Speech itself can be frozen; when the symbolic function is

[23]Cf. Benstock's discussion of Stein's "Arthur A Grammar": "Stein discovered that the equation supporting Western logic (signifier + signified = sign) always produces a remainder. . . . She discovered that one of the terms supporting this system—the signifier, the female—was devalued and considered unreliable" (p. 185).

[24]Stein, "Scenes. Actions and Disposition of Relations and Positions," *GP* 121, emphasis added.

emphasized exclusively, language-making as pleasurable (or aggressive) process is repressed. This repression is the analogy, in language, of the patriarchal privileging of mind over matter and male over female. The sentence "A bent stick is surging and might all might is mental," while describing the triumph of the phallus, also suggests a disembodied form of thought, "mental" in its seeming separation from matter. Signification that suppresses process is imaged as phallic—an idea with which we are familiar now from the (various) theories of Cixous, Kristeva, and Irigaray, but which was stunningly original for 1912, even in the oblique and poetic form in which we find it in Stein.

In spite of the near freezing of language, a "musical memory" persists. Language is always material and hence can be unfrozen, or infused once again with the stir of rhythm and drive. The cup can be made to "stir"; phallus can give way to womb—as it does in Stein's own poetic practice. "Be freeze" can turn into its opposite, "be frees"; Stein's mobile, punning style opens up the moment of nonsense or music "in between" our encounter with the immediate word and our transition to its meaning, and hence undoes the artificial subordination of the material to the mental. The style of the poem—and of all these texts—is of a piece with the antipatriarchal content. Stein not only questions (thematically) the valuation of phallus over vagina but also, and just as profoundly, stylistically unsettles the customary valuation of sense over nonsense, or signification over word-music.

In fact, true to form, she explodes the very distinction, for we are often unsure just where the sense in her prose leaves off and the nonsense begins. To use my own explication of "Cups" as an example, I have interpreted many of its phrases in a way that assigns them discursive content. But there are many other phrases for which I have no particular interpretation. One of these is "A grand clothes is searching out a candle not that wheatly not that by more than an owl and a path"; for all the attention I devote to *Tender Buttons,* I see in the text as a whole no grid of meaning that opens up any hidden significance in this sentence. It seems best (to me) to let it be, as nonsense, which one could analyze stylistically but not try to paraphrase. Furthermore, in between those moments when I see some continuous meaning in Stein's words and those when I do not, there is, ubiquitously, a third kind of moment when I falter at the boundary between paraphrasable sense and opacity. At such a moment, the boundary itself dissolves.

An example is the last sentence of the poem: "Peanuts blame, a half sand is nearly and holey." When I come to this sentence, having identified the meanings I have in the rest of the poem, I have a choice to make. Is it meaningful or relatively nonsensical? Does the word "peanuts," by some pun (penis? nuts?), fit with the imagery of male genitalia in the first part of the poem? In that case, could "peanuts blame" mean something like, "the male genitalia discredit the female"? Or is this the moment at which any attempt at interpretation amounts to overstraining? Similarly, I can wonder whether "holey" is an important pun that points to the "holiness" of the recovered feminine cup or "hole." But in that case, what is the "half sand" that is referred to as "holey"? Maybe "half sand" does have some latent relevance to the context, which I am missing; or maybe it is, instead, a pair of words placed here for their assonance or for their own surrealistic play (how can you get half a sand?), which has nothing to do with the rest of the poem.

Each reader of Stein's hermetic sentences must stop making sense somewhere; and no two readers will stop at the same place. The borderline will always be mobile, even for a single reader looking at the same words twice. That is Stein's way of forcing on us a truth about language generally, namely, that the distinction between sense and nonsense is troubled, since all signification contains something extra, some "in between no sense," in the play of the signifier. When, in ordinary conversation, for example, we hear the syllables *base ball*, we think of a game; but in doing so, we suppress the polyvalence of the words. We might just as easily hear the words as meaning "ignoble cotillion" or the even more nonsensical "bottom cotillion." Because of the polyvalence of language, nonsense floods us all the time; we just choose to suppress it.

The more familiar one becomes with Stein's hermetic texts, the less impenetrable they may seem; yet any reader perpetually crosses back and forth between the experiences of noticing continuous meanings and of seeing a vivid word-surface. Chessman writes of Stein's "creation of a literary language that invites our imaginative sense-making efforts as readers even as it successfully resists our desire either to master this language's meaning or to proclaim the language unreadable." Or as DeKoven notes, "The writing literally moves in and out of focus."[25] This continual crossing is part of our initiation in a new seeing; Stein may be describing her reader's unsettled but therefore creative and participatory experience when she writes, "a guess a whole guess is hanging" (*TB* 47). These texts are hard; they make us guess, or hang between one mode of interpretation and another. Just as their content sometimes calls into question patriarchal hierarchies, their linguistic practice subverts the (in Stein's image) phallic mastery that goes along with believing that one is in control of the signifier.

My own "guesses," as I interpret these texts, are not intended to fix a limit past which sense stops or before which all is sense; each reader of these pages will see thematic significance in many of Stein's words where I see only wordplay, and nonsense (and, very often, alternative senses) where I identify meanings. But wherever one locates the always-porous margin, Stein's texts are a great deal more responsive to their readers' sense-making than has been supposed.

G.M.P. and Mother-Loss

"Cups" depicts, in the space of a few paragraphs, a freezing and an unfreezing: the phallus surges, and the womb (very differently) stirs. I turn now to a text in which the same two things happen, in the same sequence, but across forty pages or so and in the context of broader meanings. In *G.M.P.* Stein thinks about the making and unmaking of patriarchy.

Of all the texts that I treat in this book, *G.M.P.* is the most resistant to sustained interpretation. *Tender Buttons* is every bit as experimental and difficult as *G.M.P.*, and yet in the case of *Tender Buttons*, something in the punning style and the density of thematic continuities suggests (to me) that the author is inviting readers to try to find paths through her multiple meanings. I see *G.M.P.* as a text with considerably less intellectual definition; here, Stein is just beginning to work with the new style, and she lets the fascina-

[25]Chessman, p. 15; DeKoven, *A Different Language*, p. 79.

tion of the wordplay take precedence over any notion that she might pattern her text in particular ways. I do not intend, therefore, anything like a comprehensive interpretation of *G.M.P.*; no such interpretation would be possible.

I do, however, see a motif in this text, which I wish to trace. I will attend to this motif only; were I to include analysis of the many sentences that bear no obvious connection to the motif, my approach to them would necessarily be formal—and in that case I would simply repeat what I have already said about Stein's style, with the most minor (and I am afraid uninteresting) variations. So for all those other sentences, the reader must simply go to the text. With these qualifications in mind, let me proceed.

I see in *G.M.P.* a series of reflections on how patriarchal thinking "freezes" itself into our minds, and on how our minds might then subversively thaw themselves. Briefly, patriarchy passes itself on at the moment a child renounces the mother's body; correspondingly, the poet who moves past patriarchal thinking transgressively recovers the mother's body. In a word, *G.M.P.* reaches toward psychological issues one could call oedipal. But to the extent that Stein knows something about the Oedipus complex, she knows it poetically rather than theoretically. The author of *G.M.P.* is not speculating about the Oedipus complex but unconsciously remembering it, in the sense in which other poets (before and after Freud) have remembered it—and yet still with an unusual, antipatriarchal orientation that borders on, and at times becomes, a feminist awareness. In *The Making of Americans*, Stein directly told us her thoughts about repeating and repression, and we could think in terms of her conversation with Freud. In *G.M.P.*, by contrast, Stein the psychologist has gone underground; her text, while intelligible in psychoanalytic terms, is not a piece of psychoanalytic thinking.

In *G.M.P.* Stein develops an intricate myth of mother-loss and repression. The myth is articulated unsystematically, but one can make out a motif involving a child's separation from the mother and entry into a world dominated and defined by the father. *G.M.P.* begins in the style of *The Making of Americans* but ends in the new, opaque style. The stylistic shift occurs about halfway through the text, and that is also where the story of mother-loss begins to construct itself. One of Stein's intentions for this work—whose longer title is *Matisse Picasso and Gertrude Stein*—must have been to explore connections between her artistic practice and that of her two important contemporaries in the visual arts. But however that intention might play itself out in the text (and it is by no means obvious to me how it does, since there are no clear allusions to either artist), what seeps into the text from another quarter, once Stein makes the transition to the opaque style, is a series of dream images that crystallize material from her unconscious. The second half of *G.M.P.* traces a cycle (to be repeated in *Tender Buttons*) involving the loss and recovery of the mother's body.

The cycle begins in an enclosed space—both "pink," because fleshy, and "green," because fertile: "Tender and not so blue, pink and white, not any shadow darker and anything green greener, . . . all the tightness is identified . . . and the space is enthusiastic. This and not so much passage is the beginning of that entry" (252). The "space" in question could be either the uterus or the first stage of life, "the beginning of that entry," before the child is differentiated from the mother: "all the tightness is identified." I say "child," but no clear picture of a male or female infant emerges; we find an imagistic rendition of the experiences of the infantile subject, but no representation of the subject him- or herself.

In this first stage of life, the child neither perceives the mother as separate nor distinguishes objects from one another: the world is a "lump of love, thick potato soup," and that sense of fusion and confusion is identified with the mother's body: "and all milk has a cream color" (250). The child has not yet learned to apply mental categories or to censor impressions by selective attention. To describe this phase of undifferentiated perception, Stein uses images of fluidity, darkness, cooking (since the world is like a stew in which things mingle), and abundant colors and tastes. They combine in passages like the following, which describes the pleasures of "home" for the infant:

> All the pouring of the rain, all the darkening in the evening, all the trains leaving and all the little fish-bones cooking, all the principal away and all the comfort of a home, all the pleasure of a pulpit, all the joke of wearing slippers, all the best dog to bark and all follow and

the pleasure in a lily, all the open space enclosing, all the listening to what is hearing, all of this and stay to go, that is one way to expect a person. (248–49)

The sense of abundance conveyed by the repeated *all*s, as well as the emphasis on small details like "little fish-bones," gives this passage a certain likeness to William James's picture of infancy as a period of undifferentiated perception; what he calls selective attention is learned gradually as a child acquires practical interests and a stake in the interests of society. Yet Stein's account has a gendered and familial component, which resonates less with James than with Freud. What she describes is not just infancy but the reign of the mother.

"The principal"—the father, perhaps—is "away." He could be the absent person referred to in the last clause, the "person" we "expect." Or that person could be the child, soon to be individuated. In either case, the father soon intervenes to disturb this primal unity. The shift from mother to father is precipitated by what looks quite a bit like a primal scene and an oedipal crisis.

The child observes a confusing scene: "Toss and spin and stay away and roll in hay in the center of the afternoon. . . . So then the union of the palm tree and the upside down one makes a lying woman escape handling" (253–54). The image of a "union of the palm tree and the upside down one" suggests a union of the penis with someone on her back, who then perhaps becomes "the lying woman." (Why she escapes handling is mysterious, however.) This witnessed act of intercourse marks a break in the child's life: "That was the period of that particular punctuation" (254). He or she now knows that "all the gate is open to a push"—the mother can be entered—"and more can come to stay there" (255). The child's reaction is the inevitable one: "A season of envy is a storm in the morning" (254).

At about this moment in the text, the child-subject's thinking changes. Because the father is now a rival, the child broods about "obedience" and "autocracy" (254, 256). At the same time, a set of values emerges in the child's mind, which elevates the phallus over the womb: "There is a tail. There is a bewildering distruction [destruction/distrust?] of simple linings" (257).

"Linings" is a uterine image. In a short piece called "Scenes," Stein refers to "a splendid piece of special soft sour and silk lining," and in the next sentence makes a rare use of the word *mother*: "the swift selling mother of colored clothing" (*GP* 121). The uterus is like a splendidly colored, enveloping piece of clothing, the mother's "lining." (Soon enough we will see how that lining can be associated with "selling.") The child in *G.M.P.*, then, notices the male organ, the "tail," and devalues the womb-lining. He or she may even forget the womb, or the "deep down" womblike communion the mother initially created. "So thoughtless are the plain painstaking principles. . . . How they do not stay in the deep down. How they do not" (257).

That obedience to the father entails a forgetting of the mother's body is a version of the oedipal drama, as Freud described it in males. I think that Stein, rather than applying her knowledge of psychoanalysis, is coming upon "oedipal" truths through her own poetic process. According to Freud, a boy, imagining that his father will punish him by castration for his desire for the mother, ultimately relinquishes his claim to her.[26] Perhaps Stein is thinking in terms of a boy child, for there is a reference, just before the primal scene, to a "pecker which is red, which has a colored head, which has a rose chin, which has a covering then" (253). It could be the boy's preoccupation with castration at this juncture that makes him focus on this part of his anatomy. However that may be, the child, after the primal scene, fears the father enough to repress desire for the mother. The "distruction of simple linings" points to a renunciation of the mother's body.

Castration is connected in a second way to the repression of the bond with the mother. When a child, male or female, sees the difference between men's and women's bodies—between, in Stein's phrases, the "palm tree" and the "lying woman"—he or she may assume that the female body is a castrated version of the male and devalue the female, privileging the "tail" over "simple linings." According to Freud, a male child also understands at this moment the *threat* of castration to himself. "The loss of his own penis becomes imaginable, and the threat of castration takes its

[26]See Freud, "The Dissolution of the Oedipus-Complex," *SE* 19:173–79.

deferred effect" in turning the boy away from the mother as an object.[27] Later on, moreover, "one thing that is left over in men from the influence of the Oedipus complex is a certain amount of disparagement in their attitude towards women, whom they regard as being castrated"—just as the child in Stein's account "distruct[s]" (distrusts or destroys) the mother's "linings."[28]

On the other hand, the author herself was a woman, who had had a girlhood rather than a boyhood, and to whatever extent she was replaying her own archaic memories in this scene, they were necessarily different from a boy's. A girl's attachment to the mother (according to Freud again) succumbs to the castration complex as well, but by a very different route from the boy's. For a girl as well as for a boy, a primal scene exposing the "palm tree" and the "lying woman" would lead to a privileging of "tail" over "linings." Freud's explanation, briefly, is that the girl, having noticed how the male anatomy differs from her own, feels disappointed for herself and sees her own "castration" as mysteriously traceable to the mother. In anger, combined with disgust at the mother's supposedly inferior anatomy, she transfers her love to her father.[29] While the castration complex *ends* the boy's Oedipus complex by leading him to renounce the mother as an object, the castration complex *begins* the girl's Oedipus complex by leading her to transfer her attachment from mother to father.[30] Hence, one could call this primal scene in *G.M.P.* oedipal, but in different senses for a boy and a girl subject.

In "Cups," however, we saw Stein contesting the whole idea of the female anatomy as castrated, or less than male. Castration is not a fact, which a child (male or female) simply observes, but—as Gayle Rubin and other women before and after her have maintained—a meaning that a male-dominated society attaches to the female genitals.[31] It is the world's idea, not initially the child's, to

[27]Ibid., 19:176.

[28]Freud, "Female Sexuality," *SE* 21:229.

[29]See Freud, "The Dissolution of the Oedipus-Complex," *SE* 19:177–79, and "Some Psychical Consequences," *SE* 19:243–58.

[30]Freud, "Some Psychical Consequences," *SE* 19:256.

[31]Rubin, "The Traffic in Women," in Reiter, ed., *Toward an Anthropology of Women,* esp. pp. 185–98.

exalt the male anatomy as the *"single* example of excellence"—
Stein's phrase from "Cups." Whereas a primal scene can have
oedipal meanings (for a child of either sex), patriarchy is parasitic
on the Oedipus complex. Thus at just the moment that Stein's
child-protagonist in *G.M.P.* discovers sexual difference, he or she
also gets lessons in hierarchical thinking and learns, from somewhere, that male things are higher than female things.

The child's tutor in this kind of polarized thinking is a person
symbolized by the sun—a crucial term in Stein's iconography, here
and in other texts. "Name and place and more besides makes the
time so gloomy, all the shade *is in the sun* and lessons have the place
of noon" (256, emphasis added). The child is beginning to apprehend things selectively and to rank them in importance. When,
in the maternal orbit, the world seemed a "thick potato soup,"
there were no categories of high and low; indeed, there were no
mental categories at all. But now the child is schooled in the
"name" for everything, and its "place." Symbolically speaking, it is
noon: a sun presides over these lessons in hierarchical thinking.
The sun is the sign of the father.

In the phase of the father's ascendancy, "no climb is so hot as the
half day when there is no mention of a moon" (263). The effect of
the father-sun is to replace the dark, mingling world of the mother
(a mother-moon?) with a field of vision in which everything is
differentiated because cast in a bright light. The ascending father
makes shade as well: "all the shade is in the sun," hence perhaps
the reference to this time as "gloomy." While the new consciousness associated with the father lights up some objects, its hierarchies simultaneously create a shadow world composed of things
pushed out of view. Thus the world of confused and abundant
colors, the world the child knew with the mother, gives way to a
simplified field of black and white, good and bad, important and
negligible. Stein is giving a new—and gendered—rendition of the
idea of selective attention that appeared earlier in "Melanctha."
Perhaps in "Melanctha" she was already half-consciously adding
gender to William James's idea of selective attention, since in that
story a man, Jeff, had the perceptual habits Stein is now associating
with the father's dominion, and the female heroine had something

like the form of perception here pictured as anterior and identified with the mother.

There is no confusion in Stein's saying that "all the shade is in the sun." The father is both the sun that exalts certain objects to notice and the source of a shadow that obscures or suppresses other objects. Two remarks, then, characterize this phase of life: "coloring was disappearing" and, mournfully perhaps, "why is it all so changed and so simple, why is there such a long shadow" (260, 264).

In "Cups" Stein reflects on the kind of thinking that exalts a glorious male "stick" and devalues the female "cup." G.M.P. suggests how that polarity first gets fixed in our minds, as each of us makes the transition into a gendered world. The model for all hierarchical oppositions is the opposition "tail"/"linings," which the child absorbs as the meaning of the primal scene. The father who comes into the picture at that moment to interrupt the mother-child dyad introduces not only triangulation, which is inevitable, but also, perniciously, the socially agreed-upon valuation of the male over the female. Onto that hierarchy is mapped a world of other hierarchies, so that the child's perceptual universe is reduced to two realms, sun and shadow.

"Coloring was disappearing" for another reason. Along with hierarchical thinking, the child absorbs a symbolic system that takes away the texture of things by branding them with sameness. "Copy-right and see a burst of sun shining" (260). The father-sun's influence suppresses the differences between objects that are called by the same name. Thus in G.M.P. two events are conflated—the child's detachment from the mother and the emergence in his or her mind of conceptual categories, "name and place."

The two phenomena are of a piece.[32] The child, formerly fused with the mother and with the surrounding world, is developing a

---

[32]Kristeva describes naming as "*a first victory over the mother*, a still uncertain distancing of the mother." "Place Names," *Desire in Language*, p. 289. Stein's narrative, however, like my account of it here, compresses into a single phase events that Kristeva divides between the mirror stage and the moment of the "discovery" of castration. See, for example, Kristeva, *Revolution in Poetic Language*, pp. 46–48.

stable self-image that enables him or her to mark the point at which the environment ends and the self begins. The mother, and the rest of the world, come to seem external to the child, and the externality of objects is fixed by naming them. "Signing that birthday means that the origin of every class is to be seen by that feeling" (254). Whatever else this sentence may mean, it makes a causal link ("origin") between the child's feeling of having a "birthday"—of acquiring an identity—and his or her use of mental categories, "every class." The first three words, "Signing that birthday," compress the point: the self is born when it uses signs.

It would be wrong to suppose that Stein sees either the separation from the mother or the birth of the signifying subject as inherently bad. She writes in *Tender Buttons*, "Practice measurement, practice the sign that means that really means a *necessary* betrayal" (18, emphasis added). It is necessary to use signs; to do so is to outgrow, or "betray," the presymbolic experience of the first stage of life. The infant-subject of *G.M.P.* enjoyed the preoedipal union with the mother and the accompanying sense of the world as "thick potato soup," but he or she enjoys emerging from this phase into signification as well. At least there is an understanding of the necessity of growing up. "To be older is not different than travelling. Travelling is necessary" (259).

But along with separation from the mother goes devaluation of her; in and through the Oedipus complex, gender hierarchy imposes itself. Besides a division from the mother, this phase involves a turning against her, a "distruction of simple linings." There is an aggression in the child's thinking, as he or she tries to become independent of the mother but also to get rid of her. For as the "sun" ascends in the child's mind, the first world, the dark world of the mother, is demeaned. Not only is the child's own woman-dominated, preoedipal existence pushed under, but the new mental habits he or she learns devalue and obscure women's bodies generally. Women—as a class—are viewed no longer as welcoming womb-spaces but as bearers of fetishized clothing; the clothes both stereotype them and literally cover them up: "There is a size corset"; "If the authority is mingled with a decent costume then there is no question that a woman is asking something" (257, 259). If one thinks of the child as a boy, this moment marks the beginning of his objectification of women; if as a girl, this is the beginning of her self-objectification and self-alienation in a male-dominated universe. At the same time, Stein starts in these pages to make reference to cultural norms (which the child is absorbing?) that turn women from social agents into silent objects. For the "woman" who "is asking something" turns out to be "asking to be listening." "No back talk means more than conviction. . . . It means something. . . . It means marriage" (259).

The images of a "corset" and "a decent costume" signify the quasi erasure of women's actual bodies, just as in "Cups" Stein describes the female genitals as "neglected." At the same time, there seems to be an obsessional fantasy of getting rid of all sorts of pollution by scrubbing: "So to clean that stinking has that odor." The goal is a "state when there is no dirt" (258). The fantasy is like the corset image; women's bodies are now among the things thought of as dirty, malodorous, and fit to be corseted or controlled.

The mania for cleanliness extends itself to other objects besides women's bodies. The mother who presided over the earlier phase of the child's life seemed to the child a cook, who threw everything into an earthy "potato soup." By contrast, the father inaugurates a bland cuisine, whose purpose is to sterilize. He boils. "Cooking is establishing a regulation which when it is suggested means that anything that is boiling is not withstanding cooking" (267). The point is to eliminate or lay claim to everything raw, uncivilized, outside the law or "regulation."

The paternal order brands certain things evil or dirty. What these examples suggest is that the one dirty thing (of which women's bodies are a subset) is, simply, matter—matter not yet appropriated by culture. Women's bodies are called dirty unless clothed in a "decent costume." And food is not acceptable unless subjected to a recipe, "boiled." Upon initiation into a social order whose representative in the family is the father, the child learns to dislike whatever is not quite reduced to a cultural product or symbol, whatever still "stinks" of matter.

It is of course an oppressive fiction that the female body bears the odor of matter in a way that the male does not. Perhaps the reason the child is now receptive to this association of women with dirt, and thinks in terms of corseting or suppressing the mother's and all women's bodies, is that the mother's was the body that the child loved specially before becoming a sign-using person and learning the difference between raw and cooked, or naked and clothed. Upon learning these distinctions, and learning to favor what has been entered into a cultural register, the child dismisses the mother, and the presymbolic bond with her, as dirty.

While the order of the father-sun labels the female raw or natural, the mother herself was originally pictured as a cook, who, with her impromptu way of putting things together, *mediated* between nature and culture, between raw materials and the dinner table, just as actual mothers mediate between their infants' bodily needs and drives, and the social universe. For Stein the very dichotomy between nature and culture is part of a patriarchal, polarizing language. Women "are" not in fact dirt but soup makers, agents of culture.

Along with boiling and cleaning, there are numerous references to a "bargain" or a sale during this episode of the child's transition from mother to father (257). Even time, in some obscure way, "was sold" (263). Things are valued insofar as one can own or use them. And a similar instrumentalism debases language. The mother, in the early part of the episode, had introduced the child to language, but to language-as-play. During this preoedipal phase, "a speech is so transferred that alas is not mentioned. . . . The whole time of trial is in the recitation of the vowels and also in the recitation of the figures" (251–52). The child recites words and numbers or "figures" for the pleasure of it, as an experiment or "trial" (as with the preoedipal, anal-phase child described in Peller's essay, who "produces [sound sequences], not to communicate with us . . . but for the joy of being their cause").[33] This activity was fun: there was no "alas." Language was enjoyed as music—as intonation and rhythm—rather than as a vehicle for meaning. "The *music* of the present tense has the presentation of more *accent* than the best intention multiplies" (252, emphases added). But in the next phase, the free play is lost. Words are things not to be enjoyed but to be used to refer to other things. Their music is suppressed. "*Limping in*

---

[33]Peller, "Comments on Libidinal Organizations," p. 738.

song, measuring a mile, . . . all this is autocracy" (256, emphasis added).

In other words, language too loses its body. For we repress our physical pleasure in making and hearing sound when we begin to think of words as interchangeable signifiers pointing to absent signifieds. We attend to the meaning at the expense of the sound, which we take to be incidental. What Stein suggests in *G.M.P.* is that this transition from language-as-music to language-as-signification (a shift pictured in "Cups" as a freezing of the word) is linked to the transition from mother to father. To the catalogue of matter sacrificed along with the mother's body during the Oedipus complex, we must add the materiality of language.

Kristeva writes of "the murder of soma" which makes signification possible, and describes this murder or repression of the materiality of language as correlative to the prohibition of incest.[34] Before the "mirror stage" (a concept Kristeva adopts from Lacan), the child's

> body is dependent vis-à-vis the mother. At the same time instinctual and maternal, semiotic processes prepare the future speaker for entrance into meaning and signification (the symbolic). But the symbolic (i.e., language as nomination, sign, and syntax) constitutes itself only by breaking with this anteriority, which is retrieved as "signifier," "primary processes," displacement and condensation, metaphor and metonymy, rhetorical figures—but which always remains subordinate—subjacent to the principal function of naming-predicating. *Language as symbolic function constitutes itself at the cost of repressing instinctual drive and continuous relation to the mother.*[35]

The mirror stage inaugurates this break with the mother's body and with drive-in-language, but "castration puts the finishing touches" on the break.[36] Stein, writing in the age of Freud, lacks the Kristevan vocabulary (which bridges psychoanalysis and semiotics), but her perceptions are uncannily close to Kristeva's ideas. The castration scene in *G.M.P.* precipitates the child's repression of

[34]Kristeva, *Revolution in Poetic Language*, p. 75, and see generally pp. 72–78.
[35]Kristeva, "From One Identity," *Desire in Language*, p. 136, emphasis added.
[36]Kristeva, *Revolution in Poetic Language*, p. 47.

language-as-sound; mother-loss is registered linguistically as music-loss.

For this child, "there was a time when all the teeth that were were so expressed that some effect was bitten and yet morally, and morally is not a repetition, and yet morally the synonym is not so excessive" (260). This sentence is confusing (it is itself playful language), but it contains potentially the following thoughts. "There was a time when all the teeth . . . were . . . expressed": in the preoedipal phase, utterance was expressive not of concepts but of the mouth, of the oral pleasure involved in articulating sounds. Speech was felt by the body, rather than used to point to concepts; it was "bitten." We remember that the speech the child shared with the mother involved the vocalization of vowels, meaningless in themselves. "And yet" now there has been a change, to a moral form of consciousness, dependent on ideas. "And morally is not a repetition": as the child's feeling of biting words diminishes, so does the pleasure in repetition or rhythm, which the child earlier experienced in the recitation of vowels and numbers. The drive to repeat works against the linear arrangement of ideas, so it is repressed.

In *The Making of Americans*, Stein articulated a similar idea much more straightforwardly. There, she said that repetition is a pleasure of childhood, which we later repress. But now her idea of the nature of the repression is much more complex. In what has become an oedipal scenario, a *father* taboos the mother's body and, along with that, the materiality of speech. This new framework may explain retrospectively something Stein did unconsciously in *The Making of Americans*, when she identified certain instinctive, sensuous parts of herself with repetition and thought of those features as somehow arming her against her father. Now, in *G.M.P.*, that idea of repetition, which was anti-paternal in *The Making of Americans*, gets attached to the figure of the mother, as Stein fleshes out the family triangle and its oedipal consequences.

The order of the father, as depicted in this episode, depends on the sacrifice of matter and the body. In many senses, the sacrifice is assisted by a repression of oral drive. As the child begins to use language symbolically, he or she represses the joy of biting words. The ubiquitous imagery of boiling suggests a loss of orality in another sphere; the food (or the mental sustenance) sanctioned by the father yields no tastes. But as we will soon see, orality, although it goes under, is never extinguished. The mouth remembers the mother and is a subversive point of access to her.

The story of the transition from mother to father is not exclusive to *G.M.P.* It is in the background of a number of Stein's texts in this period, texts that are not normally thought of as having discernible subjects at all. In passages that are superficially unintelligible, Stein repeats the tale. Here is a much briefer version in *A Long Gay Book:*

> Once upon a time there was a reverence for bleeding, at this time there was no search for what came. That which was winsome was unwinding and a clutter a single clutter showed the black white. It was so cautious and the reason why was that it was clear there had been here. All this was mightily stirring and littleness any littleness was engaged in spilling. Was there enough there was. Who was the shadow.
>
> The rest was left and all the language of thirty was in the truth. This made it choose just that establishment. . . . A likeness and no vacation. A regularity and obedience. Congratulations. (*LGB* 112–13)

The epoch referred to as "once upon a time" is the preoedipal phase, before the female body was trivialized. "There was a reverence for bleeding." Children do not revere menstrual fluid, but the sentence retrospectively captures a child's awe of the seemingly all-powerful maternal body. "At this time," there was no selective attention, "no search for what came." Instead, the world was perceived whole, like a great clutter. It was "single clutter" because undifferentiated. Black and white were not yet defined. The clutter was so profound that it "showed the black white," confusing the contraries. In short, everything was fluid, "mightily stirring" and "spilling." As in the passages from *G.M.P.*, whoever is experiencing this state finds the perceptual abundance thoroughly satisfying: "Was there enough there was."

But this first paragraph ends ominously: "Who was the shadow." The shadow, as before, is the father. As he looms into view, everything changes. He ushers in new sensations of "regularity and obedience," and his medium is language. It is "a language of thirty"; if this phrase is meant to recall the betrayal of Christ for thirty pieces of silver,[37] Stein is giving her theme of sale or sacrifice a mythic coloring, as she will again in *Tender Buttons*. Nothing, in this stage, goes unclassified: there is "no vacation" from "likeness" or conformity. "The rest was left": whatever does not conform to the new order is left behind or repressed. The narrator's wry comment: "Congratulations."

Yet the word "vacation" hints at the possibility of a holiday from paternal law. In fact, the dominion of the father is always partial and reversible.

G.M.P.: The Daughter-Poet's Flight

G.M.P. ends not in fact with the oedipal drama I have just traced but with its reversal, in a long episode of escape which amounts to a holiday from the law of the father:

Fathers are dead. What are fathers, they are different. The casual silence and the joke, the sad supper and the boiling tree, why are bells mightily and stopped because food is not refused because not any food is refused, because when the moment and the rejoicing and the elevation and the relief do not make a surface sober, when all that is exchanged and any intermediary is a sacrificed surfeit, when elaboration has no towel and the season to sow consists in the dark and no titular remembrance, does being weather beaten mean more weather and does it not show a sudden result of not enduring, does it not bestow a resolution to abstain in silence and move South and almost certainly have a ticket. Perhaps it does nightly, certainly it does daily and raw much raw sampling is not succored by the sun.

A wonder in a break, a whole wonder and more rascality in a slight waste. (274–75)

"Fathers," as we know, make a "sad supper" by boiling everything into conformity. The "boiling *tree*" is a version of the phallus, like the stick that Stein refers to in "Cups" as the "single example of

[37]I am indebted to William Veeder and (independently) Robert Ferguson for this association.

excellence." The phallus is boiling in two senses: it boils or sim-
plifies, turning people's individual and different bodies into mere
male presence and female absence; and it is itself boiled, a material
penis reduced to a disembodied symbol of male dominance. Yet
suddenly, "fathers are dead."

For some unidentified person, perhaps the same subject who
previously entered the paternal order through the Oedipus complex—but let us just say a daughter—moves beyond the reach of
all fathers. She feels "weather beaten," or oppressed by the father-
sun. The "sudden result" is one "of not enduring": the daughter
disclaims the father, resolving "to abstain in silence." As Stein
writes shortly before this passage, "The best way to disappear is to
undertake to refuse to stay and at the same time to go away" (273).

Now, there is "no titular remembrance" or patrilineal loyalty.
Instead, the daughter makes "a break," one that amounts to "a
whole wonder": wonderfully, and with "rascality," she can break
away from the father. She does not overthrow him, in the sense of
taking him on directly and assuming his power (as would have
been the way with the oedipal-son persona of *The Making of Americans*); instead, she "under throw[s]" him, taking "exception" to
patriarchal power altogether: "Make the exception unanimous and
under thrown" (277).

In its psychic meanings, this moment is analogous to the moment in *The Making of Americans* when Stein turned on her own
father and, in fantasy, paralyzed him, making room for her own
creativity and erotic life. But this time, patricide, or a making-
"dead" of the father, involves a mediated recovery of the world of
the mother. Escape is simple: one need only go underground, or
"move South." For the father cannot claim everything; the sun
cannot shine everywhere. There is still the shadow world, the
suppressed maternal zone "not succored by the sun," which one
can explore at will. Down there, nothing is boiled or regulated;
there is only "raw much raw sampling." The pleasures of the
mouth revive.

Immediate or raw perception is repressed under the father but
never destroyed. Throughout adulthood, part of us continues to
perceive things as an infant does. While our survival and our as-
similation to a social order depend on conceptual grids that "boil"

the flavor out of everything, we can relax our categories from time to time and see that our minds are full of pristine data. At such an instant we take pleasure in the sheer abundance of impressions, useless from a practical standpoint but invigorating. We stop selecting. The burden of instrumental existence is lifted, and we feel "the moment and the rejoicing and the elevation and the relief." This shift in perception amounts to a recovery of the domain of the mother, a return to the mental state Stein earlier symbolized as an enveloping darkness and now as a dark seed-space. "The season to sow consists in the dark."

In "Melanctha," Stein rendered a version of William James's idea that a healthy mental existence depends on the periodic rupture of categories by fresh data. But within the context of the family triangle, rupture is synonymous with the violation of taboo. To recover raw thinking, one must slip past the rule of the father. And what returns is not simply a mass of sensory data but (also) the mother's outlawed body.

The corset that was earlier imposed on the maternal body is now done away with:

> All is good in cooking, all is good in shaking, all is good in sacrificing a nut and corsets.
> All is behind a closed dark scuttle, all is priced in sucking solemn sardines and outrageously, outrageously quickly soon. (278)

Stein connects the daughter's release from the paternal taboo with her release from sensual inhibition. The corset (along with a nut, whose significance is obscure, although it suggests a testicle) is sacrificed. At the same time, there is a reference to "sucking solemn sardines and outrageously." "Sucking" suggests regression, either to the mother's breast, now that the negating corset is gone, or more generally to the oral eroticism that was part of the first phase of life. This sucking is "outrageous," in all the senses of the word: it is extravagant; it transgresses standards of decency; it commits an outrage against the father's law; it is erotic but also aggressive, as infantile pleasures are. The daughter-subject is moving "behind a closed dark scuttle," into a small hidden space with a lid on it; she is descending, that is, into the unconscious, or into the womb, or (the same thing) into a refuge from the father-sun.

What does this regression to the mother mean? One can never in actual fact return to the mother's body, nor would anyone want to. Certain experiences, however, can render permeable the boundary between adult existence and the drives enjoyed openly in infancy. For Stein, two experiences in particular bring back repressed pre-oedipal pleasures and memories: lesbian love and experimental writing.

While "sacrificing corsets" suggests a recovered memory of closeness to the mother's body, the same words could describe women undressing together. Many of Stein's images suggest both reunion with the mother and erotic activity between two women. "All this shows in wounding and in loving all the mound. All this shows a widening and excessively excessive round"; "Cups, when are cups splendid. . . . They are always splendid entirely" (270, 277). These sentences could communicate the daughter's recovered sense of communion with the "round," "mound"-like body of the mother, and the uterine "cup" (or the breast-as-cup) that was the place of origin. On the other hand, "loving all the mound" sounds sexual; it suggests loving the mons or loving each other's curves. (In her later erotic poem, "Lifting Belly," Stein calls herself *Mount Fatty.*)[38] And "wounding" (paired with "loving") could be a reference to aggressive sexual touching. Similarly, the reference to "cups" as "splendid," while it could allude to the mother's splendid interior (which was earlier dismissed but is now revalued), could also be an expression of admiration for a lover's body.

There is no need to decide between these two interpretations, since the two realms of experience were closely allied in Stein's mind: her erotic feelings for Alice Toklas had an unabashed infantile component. Enjoying Alice sexually was like being Alice's ("hubbie" and "king," but also) baby, as well as having Alice for her own baby. In "Lifting Belly," she writes, "Baby is so good to baby." That poem is filled both with erotic details and with baby talk and childish pleasures. "Sweet little bun dear little bun good little bun for my bunny."[39]

The daughter-subject "moves South" in two senses, as a voyager

[38]Stein, "Lifting Belly," *Yale Gertrude Stein,* p. 36, emphasis added.
[39]"Lifting Belly," pp. 49, 21, 24, 41.

into an archaic, maternal zone and as a sexual escapee from the father. I observed earlier how important Alice Toklas was as a presence behind the aesthetic and personal risks Stein took in *The Making of Americans*. In this new material, the relationship with Toklas is again an essential part of Stein's vision of artistic and sexual freedom. Biographically, Toklas was the person with whom Stein discovered her sexuality; she was also the person through whom Stein began to remember the pleasure of being close to a mother's body. The episode of escape at the end of *G.M.P.* contains a veiled reference to Toklas: in the paragraph that seems to me to mark the beginning of this whole movement, Stein writes, "there was a friend and a closet" (265). The scuttle she has crept into is not just a hidden part of her own mind but also the autonomous sphere that she and Toklas share (if Stein is anticipating current usage by thinking of her friend as inhabiting the "closet" with her). They are free of "fathers" together.

The radicalism that was observable just emerging in *The Making of Americans* has now tilted in a woman-oriented direction. In *The Making of Americans*, the central emotional drama, Stein's struggle with the father, was not self-consciously a woman's struggle, however much the brief but crucial episode about the letter-writing daughter hinted at an emerging female identification. In this new material, by contrast, Stein makes gender central, challenging the father's order by imagining a zone of specifically female "outrage" or transgression. She is farther than ever before from kinship with an imagined group of "*Brother* Singulars."

While lesbian existence, for Stein, was one route of escape from fathers to everything connoted by mother, writing experimental prose was another. In the same paragraph that mentions "a friend and a closet," she describes a return of music, associating her lover either with a renewed memory of the presymbolic, "musical" era of the mother or with a sensuous and musical poetic practice—or both. "Suppose there was nothing done at any rate singing is not more than reciting and reciting is not more than dancing. In any case a swelling has plenty of the same endearment and the peace of an organ is that which is most handled" (265). Through a series of puns, these sentences conflate music and sex. The words "sing-ing-reciting-swelling-organ" convey an idea of swelling sound, produced by singers and an organist. But if we make a constellation of "endearment-swelling-handled," we picture a sexual act, and the "peace of an organ" turns into a piece of an anatomical organ, while "swelling" connotes arousal. The subject who has gone south gets her "organ" back, in both senses; the return of her sexual appetite is accompanied by a return of "singing," a recovery of her ability to enjoy and produce luscious sound. Her "friend" is an enabling presence in both developments.

Singing, recitals, and organ music involve not just sound but artistic sound, and Stein is describing, among other things, her own poetic activity. While the paternal order taboos the mother's flesh and with it the "flesh" or materiality of words, the daughter for whom "fathers are dead" is in a position to rediscover the mother *and* to write a prose that brings back the lost flesh of language. In "Cups," Stein pictures herself recovering, through poetic soundplay, a "musical memory"; *G.M.P.* shows the content of that "musical memory." The features of Stein's language that I discussed earlier under the heading of matter-writing have the meaning, within the familial drama, of incest; matter-writing is like a violation of the taboo on the mother's body.[40]

Stein writes, in the same phase of escape, "A discharge, every discharge is within matter" (271). The word *discharge* puns in several directions. The daughter-subject's "discharge" from confinement by the father is achieved through a "discharge," or explosion, "within matter": her sexuality and her poetry alike release material energies, which free her. (Both also release "discharges," in the sense of bodily—and linguistic—secretions.) At one point Stein ecstatically repeats the phrase, "all the animal": "all the animal which is the same as a tick, all the animal which is the same as a Hindoo, all the animal which is breakfast"; then she writes, "All the animal is silent in left over bundles, in the box of bundles, in the ride on returned bundles" (276–77). Within language, the "ani-

---

[40]"If it is true that the prohibition of incest constitutes, at the same time, language as communicative code and women as exchange objects in order for a society to be established, *poetic language would be* for its questionable subject-in-process the *equivalent of incest*: it is within the economy of signification itself that the questionable subject-in-process appropriates to itself this archaic, instinctual, and maternal territory." Kristeva, "From One Identity," p. 136.

mal"—that is, bodily drive, which expresses itself through sound-play—is usually "silent" or overlooked; it is merely waste, extra, or "left over." But the "left over bundles" of presymbolic pleasure can come back into prominence; the animal makes a "ride" back in (or we ride the animal) "on *returned* bundles," or on the now returning presymbolic surplus in language.

Strangely, the sun, the sign of the father, is still in the picture, as G.M.P. and this scenario of escape come to a close. "Plunging into the middle mingling, wedding the worrying, and teasing the trying, meddling with more and *fathering a single sunshine,* all this makes much hut and more much more" (278, emphasis added). "Plunging into the middle mingling" is a fine description of everything the underground daughter-poet is up to; but is she also "fathering a single sunshine"? She seemed to have escaped to a maternal zone "not succored by the sun." Yet now it appears that the father-sun has followed her there. And she may be somehow father*ing*, or assuming the paternal function herself.

For she is still a user of language, not in fact an infant; to that extent, she carries the phallus herself. As she comments nearby, "The pen within is more there than before" (278). This sentence could have a maternal meaning: the "pen within," in the sense of an interior enclosure (like the "scuttle" she slipped into), is more present to her "than before." But the pen is also her writing implement, civilized in function and phallic in shape—an association that may well have been present in Stein's mind.[41] In that case, the sentence suggests that she feels the "pen within," or the phallic power within herself (and also within some sort of womb?), even more "than before."

Her poetic process empowers her not by taking her back to infantile chatter (which would be no empowerment at all) but by letting her cross back and forth *between* the unconscious, material, infantile bases of language and the signifying functions. Stein is concerned to recover and honor the continuity between symbolic thinking and the body, or between an adult self that has consciousness and a social role, and an infant self that lives in the flesh. Her prose hovers between (what Kristeva would similarly

---

[41]For an image of pencil as phallus, see *Tender Buttons*, p. 29.

call) the paternal and maternal registers of language, or between sun and darkness. She immerses us in the material feel of words, yet does not write nonsense or pure word-music. She tempts us to make sense of her words.

Hence she sees herself, in this last movement of *G.M.P.*, as a cook, someone whose work makes her a conduit between raw matter and the social order. "What is a cook a cook is a cross between odor and perfume. What is an odor and what is perfume. An odor is a singular glance and milk and lightning, a perfume is an article and an expected space and even an authority" (275). "A cook is a cross," or perhaps someone who crosses, "between odor and perfume." An odor is a natural fact (whose "stinking" the father earlier tried to clean, or subordinate to the cultural order), and its association here with milk may suggest a connection between odor and the preoedipal mother. A perfume, on the other hand, in the sense of a bottled scent, "is an article" or a commodity. Perfume—as odor transformed into a cultural product—is identified with "an authority." Then "a cross *between* odor and perfume" means a crossing between the animal fact and the civilized article. Stein compares this "cross" to "a cook," for cooking is a liminal process, which makes a bridge between matter and symbol, or between natural and social objects (without, here, the negative associations that went along with the father's overcooking, or "boiling").

Although we know that Toklas, not Stein, was actually the cook in the couple, Stein as a writer imagines herself at the site of cooking in *G.M.P.*, as she will again in *Tender Buttons*.[42] She is a sign-cook, using words in the way a (good) cook uses meat; she makes an artistic product of them, but without boiling away their material richness, their "odors" so to speak. That image gives us another way of thinking about the crossing Stein makes us do as readers. She situates us somewhere between odor and perfume, between the material and the symbolic registers of language. She gives us texts whose sounds we must encounter—whose body we must

[42]Neil Schmitz too has noted the analogy. In *Tender Buttons*, he writes, "like the potato, words and phrases have several states, can be sliced and cooked, changed in character." "Gertrude Stein as Post-Modernist," in Hoffman, ed., *Critical Essays on Gertrude Stein*, p. 125.

acquaint ourselves with—before we can go on to master their meanings rationally. Nor can her texts ever become entirely "perfume" to us (controlled, sweet, and appropriate); they are polysemous in a way that ensures that any paraphrase we devise will omit something, leaving a taboo or inviolable textual remainder, something like an untransmutable "odor" or a "left over bundle."

In *The Making of Americans,* Stein paralyzed or silenced her own father, but she also allowed herself to take from him certain powers that she saw as essential for her art. We find the same pattern in this next phase, a year or two later: as the subversive daughter-poet, she moves to a place in which "fathers are dead"; yet the work that she does there still makes a circuit through the father, so that she herself can think of "fathering a single sunshine." Still, the meanings of *father* have changed dramatically since *The Making of Americans.* Here, the word *father,* while still associated with sexual and social repressiveness, has also become a term in an elaborate statement about the nature of language. Stein is still defining herself against her real father, Daniel Stein, and perhaps even imagining that she can "father a single s[o]nshine," author herself as son (a remnant of the male-oedipal identification of *The Making of Americans*). But at the same time she is thinking in a general way about what it means for poets to "under throw" the paternal-symbolic function of language.

Thus her compromise with the father has a new meaning. In *The Making of Americans,* she saw herself as inheriting her individual father's gusto; in *G.M.P.,* what she inherits is the ability to father a sunshine, which is to say that like all experimental writers, she questions, but still wields, the phallus. In *Tender Buttons,* it will be apparent that this implication in the symbolic or paternal function complicates the ethical meaning of her act of poetic subversion: ultimately, there is no utopian world of the daughters that is not colored by patriarchal "sacrifice."

From Leo to Alice

In *G.M.P.,* as in *The Making of Americans,* Stein remains interested in issues of repression, and asks what it means for a repression to be lifted or "under thrown." But her work has now developed a feminist component. Onto the idea of repression, she has mapped ideas of social oppression, and onto a drama of childhood, she has mapped a vision of a child's transit into a male-dominated world.

What was happening in the intellectual and personal life of Gertrude Stein, to account for these changes in her thinking? As with *Three Lives* and *The Making of Americans*, a major stimulus was the work of painters she admired, whose experiments she could echo in a verbal medium. The major inspiration for the opaque style, as I have already indicated, was Picasso's development of collage techniques within analytic cubism. Walker has observed how closely timed the two developments were: "Within months after Picasso created his first [cubist] collage, Stein invented the newly concrete, logically disjunctive style that culminated in *Tender Buttons*."[43] But what I have discerned at every stage is that Stein's formal experimentation, once underway, released new material in her that had little to do with what she was absorbing from the visual arts. Her emphasis, in the opaque texts, on questions of language may mirror the cubists' foregrounding of the properties of the medium; but the familial drama that attached itself to her linguistic themes was original to her, and resembles nothing so closely as the theories of Kristeva in our own time. Furthermore, the opaque style, which Stein developed as a literary analogue to analytical cubism, enabled her to begin to express ideas about gender that were hers alone. The new opaque style not only made these ideas safe (in ways I suggested at the beginning of this chapter); it also conveyed its own matter-loving and "feminine" meanings, which paralleled the issues Stein was exploring thematically.

Why was Stein ready for a feminist orientation just now? It is not as if the ideas that emerged at this moment had been fully developed in her mind, simply waiting for the right stylistic vehicle. Something had happened to prompt so radical a shift away from the male persona of her earliest work, and even from the persona that had broken through in *The Making of Americans*—the sensuous lover of repetition who momentarily slipped into the role of a daughter but whose gender was for the most part indeterminate. Many years before, during medical school, Stein had espoused

[43]Walker, p. 130.

feminist ideas, which had owed something to the thought of Charlotte Perkins Gilman. But her feminism had subsequently either cloaked itself or vanished altogether—during the decade or so, in fact, when she lived with Leo, separated from the community of ambitious and intellectual women she had known in Baltimore.[44] Leo himself espoused antifeminist ideas. According to Leon Katz, who interviewed the Steins' friend H. P. Roché, "Leo responded for a time [starting in 1908] to [Otto] Weininger's antifeminism, and at the peak of his interest in him, declared that if one could take women's minds off their wombs, they might be helped to some kind of development after all."[45] Stein herself had shared her brother's admiration for Weininger, during her last years of work on *The Making of Americans*.

But in 1911 she was ready to try out feminist thinking once again—just in the period in which she was breaking away from Leo's depressing influence and forming a couple with Alice Toklas. Toklas had joined the Stein household in 1909; Leo had slowly become the outsider in the trio, and he made his final departure from 27, rue de Fleurus in 1912 or 1913. As early as the spring of 1912, Toklas was Stein's primary companion, for the two spent a great deal of their time traveling together, apart from Leo.[46]

Thus, at the very moment that Stein found in Picasso a new formal model, she was undergoing a momentous reorientation in her affections. The two events meshed in a strikingly new literary practice. Catharine Stimpson has written about the importance of Stein's changing her allegiance "from male mentor to female companion, from one who was, at best, indifferent to her writing to one who was utterly supportive."[47] And as Shari Benstock notes, "Gertrude Stein's writing . . . became openly sexual and erotic as well as increasingly domestic after her brother moved out."[48] A

[44]For descriptions of Stein's circle of friends in Baltimore, see Mellow, *Charmed Circle*, pp. 58–63; and Katz, Introduction to *Fernhurst*, pp. xi–xiii. For a discussion of Stein's espousal of feminist ideas (particularly those of Charlotte Perkins Stetson, later Gilman) in the late 1890s, see Stimpson, "The Mind, the Body," pp. 490–91.

[45]Katz, "Weininger," in Hoffman, ed., *Critical Essays on Gertrude Stein*, p. 140.

[46]For a discussion of different scholars' views on when the break took place, see Bridgman, p. 107.

[47]Stimpson, "The Mind, the Body," p. 495.

[48]Benstock, pp. 156–57.

new woman-identification appears at just this juncture. Once Leo's inhibiting influence was gone (as it had not quite been for *The Making of Americans*), Stein allowed a new feminism to articulate itself in her work, and her "cubist" style developed as a knowingly anti-patriarchal mode.

Beyond the external facts of the household, a new range of feeling was opening up in Stein. Her works from this period bespeak a wandering toward the mother. I think that Alice Toklas's presence made this emotional swing possible. Stein, in order to envision a preoedipal phase of experience as she did in *G.M.P.*, had to excavate an archaic maternal memory in herself. Freud himself had not yet developed a clear picture of "this early, pre-Oedipus, phase in girls";[49] Stein's thinking in this phase anticipates him rather than draws on him, and its sources are in her own unconscious. Her reconstruction now of the child's preoedipal bond with the mother filled in what had been a tremendous blank in her previous work.

In *Three Lives* and *The Making of Americans*, mothers had been all but invisible. Melanctha's mother had quietly died without causing her daughter to mourn, and the relationship was described as having always been loveless on both sides. The heroine-mother of "The Gentle Lena" also died quietly, without causing a disruption in her family. In *The Making of Americans*, Fanny Hersland, Stein's portrait of her own mother, was a similarly negligible presence; her children "had no deep loving feeling in them for her"; she "had never been really important to any of them" (54, 114). When Fanny started to ail, as Stein's mother had with cancer in Stein's girlhood, "mostly they forgot about her, slowly she died away among them. . . . [N]ow she died away among them and they never thought about her" (114). Like Melanctha, and like Stein herself, the Hersland children identified with their strong father, rather than with this wan and uninteresting woman.

But in *G.M.P.*, Stein unearths a time when her mother had been a powerful and lovable presence. Every infant loves its mother intensely, whether or not the feeling is adequately returned; and in *G.M.P.*, Stein reversed a powerful censorship in her own mind when she recovered an awareness of that early love. She may have

[49]Freud, "Female Sexuality" (1931), *SE* 21:226.

been approaching this memory in a way that was still only half-conscious; she uses innumerable maternal images, but it is unclear to what extent the thought of her own mother consciously entered her mind. Nonetheless, the maternal memory was directing her imagination; something was making the memory approachable for the first time.

Alice Toklas made the difference, for she repaired certain emotional wounds that had previously made maternal themes unsafe for Stein. Stein relived with Toklas some of her feelings for her mother, but in a way that remedied an ancient hurt inflicted by her mother, so that Stein could think her way back now without feeling immobilized by pain. From Stein's notebooks for *The Making of Americans*, one can derive a faint picture of Amelia Stein and discern the features in Alice Toklas that reminded Stein of her mother. "There is a certain vanity connected with [Alice's] sexual bottom [that is, her deepest nature] . . . not an aggressive vanity like her denial vanity [whose meaning is obscure] but a passive one *like in our mother*" (*NB* B.9, emphasis added).

As a young child, Gertrude Stein had reacted to what she perceived as her mother's "vanity" by trying to woo her, as two notebook entries in particular intimate. In one of these, Stein sketches out her plans for Fanny Hersland, the portrait of her own mother:

Work it out carefully that Madeleine Weiman [Wyman, the family's governess in the novel] and Mrs. Hersland were the same kind and Madeleine owned her by letting her be important to her and so possessed her and her memory completely to the infuriation of her children. *the* [sic] *gentleness and timidity and beauty of her appealed to her to make her own her.* A complicated but interesting study. Finish up with that here and then *more about it in Martha* etc. (*NB* 81, single page; emphasis added)

The phrase "more about it in Martha" raises the possibility that Stein herself (the model for Martha) had experienced "it," or the emotion attributed to the governess—specifically, an attraction to her mother because of "the gentleness and timidity and beauty of her." The added phrase, about the the governess wanting to "own" the mother, sounds very like the feelings Stein had for Alice

Toklas in the period of courtship these notebooks chart. "My attack on Alice . . . always a forward pressure till the final achievement"; "Have to do miracle on another [person] to win her, the worldly side of her, the appeal to her admiration of success" (*NB* C.46, 41). This romantic "attack" on Alice may well have been a version of an attack that Gertrude Stein, as a girl, had wished to make on her mother, overcoming the mother's seeming self-involvement and claiming her sexually.

In a second notebook entry, Stein thinks about a group of (actual) women whose mothers discounted them in favor of sons—a situation that sounds so much like Melanctha's case that one wonders whether this pattern interested Stein because of some resonance with her own history.

> The Sally-Emma group idealise and idolise mother who usually have [*sic*] another for a favorite child. . . . [U]sually taken by lady quality of mother they being otherwise. In every case it is a son that is the favorite. . . . Daughters usually are like the fathers, mothers respect daughters and husbands but don't love them, make lovers of their sons then bad marriages [of the sons]. (*NB* DB.11–12)

These women are "like [their] fathers," as Stein perceived herself to be; and perhaps Stein too, at a very young age, had idolized her mother for a "lady quality" missing in herself, only to be rejected in favor of one of her brothers. Whether or not this was indeed the case, we know from *Everybody's Autobiography* that Stein had experienced an insult that was in some ways similar: as a child she had felt "funny" knowing that two previous children had "died in babyhood or else I would not have come nor my brother."[50] Her feeling of being second choice may possibly have been reinforced by her mother's preference for one of the sons.

From these entries, a picture dimly emerges: Amelia Stein had been a vain and absent mother, and as a girl Gertrude Stein, to spare herself further injury, had decided (like the character Melanctha) that her mother was a nonentity, and had chosen to identify almost exclusively with her father. Later, when Stein met Alice Toklas, Toklas had repeated the mother's traits of vanity and seem-

[50]Stein, *Everybody's Autobiography*, p. 134.

ing indifference; but those traits, far from repelling Stein, lured her to try to "win" Alice, as she had never been able to win her mother. Stein writes in a notebook, "Alice attention and not interest, . . . no interest excepting in what catches attention" (*NB* I.10). Even though this wavering attention contributed to Stein's idea of Toklas as an example of "the most sordid unillumined undramatic unimaginative prostitute type" (*NB* DB.56), the prospect of finally conquering the prostitute excited her.

As she and Toklas got to know each other, Stein enjoyed capturing Toklas's attention, and in fact dominating her. My guess is that in making Toklas submit to her, Stein was unconsciously taking revenge on her uninvolved mother. As she observes in a notebook, "I impressed [Alice] the first day I was made into an idol. Then she got on top out of relation as always, *then I impressed with an axe*, and she has never quite lost that, after that she . . . [closed up] by getting scared to death."[51] Or again, "Alice would not come over alone, very sassy until you give her hell and then caves right in" (*NB* DB.59). If Stein's need to dominate her friend was indeed linked to her early disappointment by her mother, what we see in these entries is not a resolution of those deep maternal issues but a solution that on a superficial level worked. Happily—although surely not always happily for Toklas—Stein could force from her lover the attention that Amelia Stein had denied her. Stein even found herself now in the much desired role of the adored son. She writes in her love poem "Lifting Belly," "Dear little bun I'm her sunny [sonny]."[52]

Helene Deutsch, in the 1932 article "On Female Homosexuality," suggests that certain love relationships can furnish just this sort of compensation for an early deprivation by the mother. Of one patient, who entered analysis for the treatment of depressive symptoms, she writes, "Her mother had been a stern and distant individual whom the patient had quite consciously hated all her life." But the patient was cured of her depressions, not so much by the analysis (which did play an enabling role) as by a lesbian rela-

[51]*NB* 46.2, emphasis added. In this entry, Stein is probably referring to her (later famous) explosion at Toklas for arriving half an hour late for their first arranged meeting.

[52]Stein, "Lifting Belly," p. 41.

tionship after the analysis was interrupted. Deutsch, despite her predictable bias in favor of heterosexuality as the "more favorable solution" in such a case, remarks on the positive effects of the affair, which turned the former patient into a "vivid, radiant person." The relationship enabled her to rescript her experience with her mother. "[The] homosexual relationship was quite consciously acted out" (as Stein and Toklas's was) "as if it were a mother-child situation, in which sometimes one, sometimes the other played the mother." Deutsch's former patient was relieved of her neurotic depressions by this "mother-substitute object," who "paid off the infantile grievances by granting her sexual satisfactions."[53]

Toklas's presence similarly "paid off" her lover's early rejection by the mother. Thus, as Stein and Toklas became increasingly secure together, Stein was able to admit to herself, if only in her writings and half-consciously, how important her mother had once been to her. Her early hunger for her mother, which texts like "Melanctha" and *The Making of Americans* had suppressed, was a less dangerous theme now that the sense of loss which had gone along with it was in some provisional sense behind her. The scenario that ends *G.M.P.*—in which an early mother-loss is repaired, partly through the presence of "a friend and a closet"—had private meanings involving the particular mother who had let Stein down long ago and whose deficiencies Alice Toklas now compensated for.

Stein minimized the figure of the mother in her earlier texts not only because her mother had hurt her but also because her mother represented a threatening model. There is every sign that Stein feared that identifying with her mother would mean dying as her mother had. Melanctha inherits her "wandering" from her mother; then, like her mother, she dies. *The Making of Americans* contains portraits of both of Stein's parents, but while Stein is busy confronting her father there and turning him into a source for herself, she is still discounting her mother, in the person of Fanny Hissen. Amelia Stein, the model for Fanny, had also been an inspiration for the character of Melanctha's mother, and in her portrait as Fanny

[53]Helene Deutsch, "On Female Homosexuality," *Psychoanalytic Quarterly* 1 (1932): 486, 490, 491.

we can see why she represented a dangerous example. "The father David Hersland was in some ways a very splendid kind of person but he had some very uncertain things inside him. . . . Sometimes he was very angry with [his children]. Sometimes it came to his doing very hard pounding on the table . . . , and ending with the angry word that he was the father, they were his children, they must obey him, he was master" (45). This picture of the father is familiar from *The Making of Americans*—but in the background, there is in fact a "little" mother. "Such scenes were very hard on the little gentle mother woman who was all lost in between the angry father and the three big resentful children" (45). In other words, Fanny-Amelia is cowed by her husband, and then even by her children as they become strong enough to resist the father. She is a "gentle scared little thing," who is "lost among them" (113). And she dies: "Then she died away and the gentle scared little woman was all that they ever after remembered of her" (114).

Daniel Stein was too dominating a presence for his wife to survive; that is the image Stein conveys in these portraits of her parents. She also links the mother's death to the father's simple indifference: "and she more and more died away and left him and then she was not in any way important to him, he needed more beginning in his loving feeling to fill him than anything that she could give him, he mostly then forgot about her and that was the end of her living" (156). It is understandable that in her early fiction Stein chose to identify with her father, who had won these grim battles, rather than with the mother who had seemed simply to succumb and die. The mother was not just a "scared" but a scary figure, whom the daughter had no wish to emulate.

Stein would always sustain her paternal identification. Yet in the opaque texts, she resurrects the mother, making her a far from trivial figure. In *G.M.P.* the mother does not drag the daughter to impotence and death with her but, instead, communicates her own sort of power. By remembering the mother, the daughter-poet grounds herself again in matter and in the linguistic substratum of the presymbolic. Now the mother too has become a source. At the same time, Stein begins to identify with the mother, turning to maternal and feminine images to describe her own artistic activity.

Stein could dream of herself as a mother in her art because she was becoming less and less afraid of turning into her mother in reality. She could explore a feminine identification now that she had replaced Leo and become the quasi male of the household. Stimpson has described the contradictions involved in Stein and Toklas's simultaneous liberation from, and repetition of, the patterns of heterosexual marriage:

> Paradoxically, as their naked erotic impulses broke boundaries, they clothed them in language that redrew those very lines. . . . We, who value freedom and options and flexibility, must accept the possibility that the very firmness of their roles helped them to surmount the difficulties of their deviancies. Most problematically, Stein was husband, Toklas wife. Not only did Stein write, and Toklas type and edit, but Stein ate, and Toklas cooked and served.[54]

By a similar paradox, Stein became strong enough to start to explore feminine themes only once she was secure in a "marriage" that in its own structure was far from feminist. And she could let herself drift back in fantasy to an infantile communion with the mother just when her control of Toklas was secure. This strange mental balancing act is reflected in "Lifting Belly" (of 1917), where Stein assumes multiple erotic roles, with "baby" at one end and "Caesar," or emperor, at the other.[55] It is "Caesar" that makes "baby" possible.

Similarly, although within the opaque texts Stein was letting her self-image develop in a feminine direction, publicly she did not define herself in feminine terms. To have done so would have undermined her prestige in a largely male-defined artistic community.[56] Indeed, the very title of the text in which I have uncovered the anti-patriarchal, mother-oriented story is *Matisse Picasso and Gertrude Stein* (which Stein shortened to *G.M.P.*): she was still deriving a sense of power from her association with male genius, as

[54]Stimpson, "Gertrice/Altrude: Stein, Toklas, and the Paradox of the Happy Marriage," in Ruth Perry and Martine Watson Brownley, eds., *Mothering the Mind: Twelve Studies of Writers and Their Silent Partners* (New York and London: Holmes and Meier, 1984), pp. 126–30.

[55]Stein, "Lifting Belly," pp. 24, 27.

[56]"She had to renounce her womanhood in order to acknowledge a genius that was grounded *in* her womanhood." Benstock, p. 188.

she had at the time of *The Making of Americans*. The title bears no obvious connection to what happens in the text, but it has its own function as a banner announcing Stein's membership in a brotherhood, which is just the identification she disclaims in the text. (Perhaps her putting her own initial first in the abbreviated title was at the same time a slight self-assertion against her two male colleagues.)[57] The more secure Stein felt in her male professional persona, the freer she felt, within her dense texts, to burrow into an infantile and maternal territory and to challenge habits of thinking connected with male dominance.

G.M.P. emerged from a special moment of equilibrium, in which Stein found the courage to explore archaic memories from which she had earlier been protecting herself. The equilibrium was precarious. It was shattered, in my view, by the First World War. The war that represented such a creative stimulus for many of Stein's male colleagues in the literary arts seems in her case to have temporarily dampened her inspiration; even after the war her writings, however fine in new ways, would never again have the same introspective daring. But before this moment of balance ended, it produced *Tender Buttons*, Stein's masterpiece in the opaque style.

[57] I am indebted to Marianne Eismann for this suggestion.

4

Tender Buttons:
Woman and Gnosis

G.M.P. was an exploratory text, in which Stein made the switch to an opaque style and pieced together a new, woman-affirming vision. Just afterward, in a rush of creativity in the spring and summer of 1912, she wrote *Tender Buttons,* her most original work.[1] Here she elaborated the anti-patriarchal vision developed in *G.M.P.* But she was able, as she had not been in *G.M.P.,* to write a book that, for all its difficulty, invites us in.

The witty, riddling structures of *Tender Buttons* amount to a lure as well as an obstacle. These short prose poems, which have simple declarative titles ("Milk," "A Purse") but punning, elusive texts, sit before us like nuts we are meant to crack. And since Richard Bridgman's important study in 1970, Stein's critics have been tempted to crack into *Tender Buttons,* although, like Bridgman, they have been alert to the dangers of looking for "an infallible pass-key."[2]

I intend to show that *Tender Buttons* can be unlocked, to a far greater extent than has been supposed. Various critics have made inroads into isolated sentences and poems in *Tender Buttons;* to pick a single example, the last poem of the "Objects" section, called "This Is This Dress, Aider," has been interpreted interestingly (and variously) by Bridgman, Catharine Stimpson, Marjorie Perloff, and

---

[1]Bridgman, *Gertrude Stein in Pieces,* p. 125.
[2]Ibid.

Neil Schmitz.[3] Furthermore, some readers have identified a lesbian "code," and one has interpreted *Tender Buttons* as a hieroglyphic account of Stein's disengagement from Leo and attachment to Alice.[4] But for the most part, *Tender Buttons* has been viewed as impenetrable, however dazzling stylistically.

I find what amounts to a set of powerful feminist reflections in this text. *Tender Buttons* represents Stein's fully developed vision of the making and unmaking of patriarchy. An idea that she develops here for the first time is that patriarchy constitutes itself by a sacrifice, real or mythic—a crucifixion, a choking, or a live burial. What *Tender Buttons* then suggests is that once one sees male dominance as dependent on sacrifice, one is in a position to undo sacrifice and to transcend patriarchal thinking. The way to reverse sacrifice is to revive what sacrifice kills, or to decide to remember, and see, what sacrifice makes invisible.

As Stein contemplated the meanings of sacrifice, her thinking moved in a startling new direction. In *Tender Buttons* a woman-centered, revisionary spirituality, which was just latent in Stein's earlier work, breaks through. This spirituality has been missed by her critics, although it is one of the most remarkable facets of *Tender Buttons* and helps to explain why this work grips us subliminally. I have found no definite source for Stein's woman-centered spiritual

[3]Ibid., pp. 129–30; Stimpson, "Gertrude Stein and the Transposition of Gender," pp. 15–16; Stimpson, "The Somagrams of Gertrude Stein," in Hoffman, ed., *Critical Essays on Gertrude Stein*, p. 190; Perloff, *Poetics of Indeterminacy*, p. 107; Schmitz, "Gertrude Stein as Post-Modernist," in Hoffman, ed., *Critical Essays*, pp. 123–24; Schmitz, *Of Huck*, pp. 166–67.

[4]Pamela Hadas, "Spreading the Difference: One Way to Read Gertrude Stein's *Tender Buttons*," *Twentieth-Century Literature* 24 (1978): 57–75. The most compelling account of a lesbian code in Stein's writings (of a slightly later date) is Elizabeth Fifer, "Is Flesh Advisable? The Interior Theater of Gertrude Stein," *Signs* 4 (1979): 472–83. On the lesbian code in *Tender Buttons*, see Doris T. Wright, "Woman as Eros-Rose in Gertrude Stein's *Tender Buttons* and Contemporaneous Portraits," *Transactions of the Wisconsin Academy of Sciences, Arts, and Letters* 74 (1986): 34–40; Schmitz, "Gertrude Stein as Post-Modernist," pp. 123–24; Stimpson, "Somagrams," p. 190; Benstock, *Women of the Left Bank*, pp. 162–63. For an entirely different reading, which views *Tender Buttons* in Jungian terms as a mandala or "magic circle," see Allegra Stewart, *Gertrude Stein and the Present* (Cambridge: Harvard University Press, 1967), pp. 69–139.

vision, although I will consider some likely inspirations. The other chapters of this book have identified contributors to Stein's intellectual and artistic development, ranging from William James to Freud to Picasso. With *Tender Buttons*, however, Stein was moving into territory so radically new that no one quite ushered her there. Her revisionary spirituality was the effect of her own brilliant "guess."

"Vegetable" and the Crucifixion of Matter

Tender Buttons contains a great deal of verbal experimentation, indulged in for its own sake and interesting in its own right. I hope to bring aspects of this experimentation into view, but it is not my primary focus. What interests me about *Tender Buttons* is that in addition to being an extremely original inquiry into the nature of language, this text provokes us to think new thoughts. Stein here not only experiments with the properties of her linguistic medium but also (more knowingly than in *G.M.P.*) tells us things—things about language, indeed, but other things as well. What I emphasize in *Tender Buttons* is a series of ideas (and I am aware that it is controversial to use the term *ideas* here) about the sacrificial origins of patriarchal culture. *Tender Buttons* as a whole has no one unifying *structure* and, indeed, interestingly contests notions of textual unity; yet it seems to me that at important moments the text follows particular ideas to such an extent as to begin to fall into what one could call movements. I locate two such movements in the text, two phases of crisis—a phase of sacrifice, followed by a phase of repair in which the sacrifice is undone. The first of these crises occurs at the end of the first section of the text, called "Objects," and the second, countersacrificial crisis falls at the end of the second section, "Food."

There is, of course, a third section, "Rooms" (comprising not a series of titled poems but a single long poem). Although I turn to material from "Rooms" from time to time, that part of the text does not have the same status in my argument as "Objects" and "Food." In spite of its placement at the end, "Rooms" was almost certainly composed before the other two sections,[5] and it represents, in my

[5]See DeKoven, *A Different Language:* "It is my belief, based on manuscript evidence, style, and on what she says in *The Autobiography of Alice B. Toklas,* that the

view, a preliminary sketch initiating certain thoughts that the two subsequently composed sections transform into something quite a bit more daring, not only stylistically but also intellectually. Although each reader of *Tender Buttons* will have an independent judgment of the relative merits of the three sections, my own (necessarily subjective) opinion is that "Rooms" is not quite as fine or interesting a piece of work as "Objects" and "Food"—just as the earlier *G.M.P.*, which "Rooms" quite resembles stylistically, does not rival *Tender Buttons* as a whole. Rather, therefore, than devote the same close attention to "Rooms" that I do to the other two sections, I intermittently take up portions of "Rooms" that indicate tendencies in Stein's thought as she was reaching toward the greater illuminations of "Objects" and "Food."

In *Tender Buttons*, as at other moments, we see Stein's intellectual leaps following from, rather than generating, her formal innovations. She began composing "Rooms" with no particular subject in mind. If "Rooms" has a recurring theme, it is, in fact, the unanchored quality of its own linguistic play; its first sentence announces a polylogic practice, a decentering: "Act so that there is no use in a centre" (63). But various thematic focuses—if not a single center—did then develop. Whereas Stein began "Rooms" with (primarily) an interest in exploring the potential of her linguistic play, her play gradually released material from her unconscious, her cultural memory, and—much more than in *G.M.P.*—her critical intelligence. By the time she was writing "Objects" and (simultaneously) "Food," and particularly their later sections, she was engaging in a revisionary conversation with the dominant intellectual traditions of Western culture.

Let us start with the first poem of "Objects" (and therefore the

---

book was organized into its present configuration after it was written. 'Rooms,' the third section of the book, is all in the 1911, transitional style. It is essentially indistinguishable from 'Portrait of Constance Fletcher' or 'Portrait of Mable Dodge at the Villa Curonia'" (p. 76). DeKoven also argues persuasively that "Objects" and "Food"—which Stein worked on in two separate notebooks—were composed side by side rather than sequentially. "'Objects' and 'Food' . . . both begin in the transitional style [of 'Rooms' as well as earlier works such as the 'Portrait of Constance Fletcher'], then accelerate steadily through the middle style toward the extreme [and more fragmented] style of 1913" (p. 76). See DeKoven's analysis for a full account of the features of these transitional and extreme styles.

first of *Tender Buttons* in its ultimate arrangement). I turn first to this poem not because it represents in any way a meditation on sacrifice—my ultimate concern—but because it suggests something about the sort of thinking that will *evolve* in the direction of sacrificial themes. I also find it useful to start with this poem as a way of integrating my analysis of the sacrificial poems with the many poems in this work that do not take up the theme of sacrifice at all. My exploration of *Tender Buttons* tends to emphasize the last parts of "Objects" and "Food"—the two phases of sacrificial crisis—but Stein gets to these crises by way of an experiment with language, and it is on that experiment itself that she reflects in her first poem:

> A CARAFE, THAT IS A BLIND GLASS.
> A kind in glass and a cousin, a spectacle and nothing strange a single hurt color and an arrangement in a system to pointing. All this and not ordinary, not unordered in not resembling. The difference is spreading. (9)

The poem is at once an exercise in and a reflection on semantic decentering. This statement sounds paradoxical and almost is. A completely decentered, lexically random poem would have no thematic coherence at all, and hence could not "reflect on" anything. Stein's poem, instead, like all of *Tender Buttons*, fades into and out of discursive meaning. Many phrases, such as "the difference is spreading," seem coherent enough syntactically and semantically to warrant attempts at interpretation. More than that, there are words (across sentences) that belong to the same lexical universe, so that one can spend time with the poem, linking these words and seeing if they might add up to a series of thoughts "about" something. But one can also explore how Stein simultaneously destabilizes or multiplies the meanings of each of these words, so that their apparent unity or connectedness seems simply the effect of one (limiting) perspective on them, whereas another perspective—equally limiting, were one to use it exclusively—points to the spiraling off of each word into the free play of language.

For example, a number of words in the poem suggest ideas of relatedness. (I claim no special originality for the *manner* in which I am interpreting this poem; several other studies of Stein's style have explored the ways in which we can piece together, and then lose hold of, meanings in a poem like this.)[6] First, the word "kind" suggests a category or class. *Kind* can also mean "species"; the word is cognate with *kin*. This notion of familial relatedness is then echoed by the word "cousin." Things that are of the same kind are cousins to one another. We are still not told that something in particular "is" cousin to something else; we find thematically linked words but no discursive statement. The phrase "a spectacle and nothing strange" further pursues the idea of relatedness. Something (still unspecified) may be "a spectacle," an unusual thing, singled out for notice; yet in fact it is "nothing strange," not totally alien or unique. Hence, it is part of the familiar universe, bearing still some relation to other things. With "and an arrangement in a system" the idea of relatedness seems to become more emphatic; on the other hand, it is "an arrangement in a system *to pointing*," a phrase that suggests not classification of objects into perfect kinds but instead a quasi system, a mere gesturing toward or guessing at connections. The next sentence seems to echo this idea: "All this and not ordinary, not unordered in not resembling." We are still somewhere between system (or relatedness) and chaos: whatever thing these words modify is unusual, "not ordinary" or "not resembling"—not simply repeating the familiar world. Yet it is not entirely "unordered."

Thus far, the poem seems to be positing a kind of loose organization (of the world? of language? of this text itself?) that violates the notion of an entirely coherent system yet "points" suggestively to various connections. The poem could be describing its own linguistic practice; for example, I have been identifying connections between its words, but connections that fall short of shaping the poem into a single, monologic (or systematic) meaning.

As one looks further into the poem, the sense of "strange"-ness or fragmentation increases. Besides the theme of connectedness, a second thematic axis in the poem, involving eyes and sight, unifies its own cluster of words, yet bears no obvious connection to the other theme of connectedness. Issues of sight are suggested, par-

[6]See, for example, Walker, *Making of a Modernist*, pp. 134–37, an exposition that includes an analysis of the same poem I interpret here.

ticularly, by the words "blind," "glass" (in the sense of window-pane, mirror, or optical instrument), and "spectacle" (in the sense not, now, of "an unusual thing" but of a pair of eyeglasses). How are we to relate the "connection" axis to the "sight" axis? Maybe the poem, or *Tender Buttons* as a whole, is meant to initiate us in a new kind of *seeing* that exposes *connections* among things without authorizing a single system of classification.

But even if one imposes that kind of coherent meaning on the poem, some of the words thus explicated come unhinged from these unitary meanings by semantic play elsewhere. "Glass" is part of the sight axis; yet the word can also mean, quite differently, a vessel to drink out of, a connotation the word "carafe" in the title makes inevitable. So the word "glass" means (at least) two different things, and the poem is so arranged as to bring both meanings right to the surface, first by juxtaposing "glass" to "carafe," and second by juxtaposing "glass" to "spectacle." We cannot square the two lines of association; a carafe or a drinking glass has no obvious link to issues of sight. So the words "a blind glass" are a part of the joke: a carafe *is* a glass that is not linked to sight, and hence is "blind."

Similarly, the word "kind," which I have integrated into the connectedness theme, can, on the other hand, mean, adjectivally, gentle, warm-hearted—an association reinforced by "nothing strange," if we now reread those words as meaning "not at all distant or reserved." Then again, one phrase, "hurt color," fits none of these axes of meaning; it is not of a "kind" with anything else in the poem. All these last features of the poem unravel the unitary meaning I started to build. The inherent mobility of words, as well as the fragmented arrangement of this particular poem, crosscuts coherency—yet without erasing it. The poem is itself a "blind glass," something we cannot quite look through or transform into clear referentiality. On the other hand, it is "not unordered in not resembling": it does not exactly resemble the world mimetically, yet it has its own order and indeed, at times, what seems like a (referential, polemical) point. It is anything but mere surface; the longer we spend with it, the more "meaning" we find in it.

I think that if I were to turn now to the idea of indeterminacy—a move that might seem obligatory at this point—I would spoil the delicate tissue of meanings that the poem does organize. The notion of meaning that this poem seems to underwrite—and I would generalize from this poem to the rest of *Tender Buttons*—anticipates far less the poststructuralist idea of indeterminacy or undecidability than Wittgenstein's idea that meaning, even if not in a one-to-one relationship to the sign, is not entirely unanchored. According to Wittgenstein, a word can have multiple meanings, but these bear a "family likeness" to one another.[7] It is just such a notion of loosely "resembling" meanings that Stein's poem brings out (hence, just possibly, its own familial theme, with "kind" and "cousin"). "Glass," for example, can mean optical instrument or drinking vessel; yet because both meanings follow from the physical properties of glass, there is a connection. Similarly, "kind" can mean species or, alternatively, gentle; yet the two meanings are connected by their shared relation to the idea of kinship. The very quality of language as familial—as a matter of likeness or loose kinship—causes uncentering. So, to get to the last sentence of this poem—"The difference is spreading"—it is not poststructuralist *différance* so much as a kind of wobble in meaning that subtly (yet not indefinitely) diffuses itself.

Now let me suggest how all this bears on the idea Stein will develop in the course of *Tender Buttons* (and the idea that is my primary subject)—that patriarchy constitutes itself through acts of sacrifice. Univocal meaning, according to Stein, is one of the illusions and oppressions of patriarchal thinking. (As she writes in a later work, "Patriarchal Poetry is the same"[8]—the opposite, then, of "different.") And the act that ritually fixes unitary meanings in place, as we will see in due course, is sacrifice. Yet the "difference" that sacrifice represses always comes back, in the form of semantic mobility, the very difference with which this first poem (although detached so far from sacrificial themes) plays. If patriarchal poetry is the same, anti-patriarchal poetry is different. Monologic meaning is created through ritual killing, but the materiality of words can always take us past that killing.

[7]Ludwig Wittgenstein, "Blue Book," *The Blue and Brown Books* (New York: Harper and Row, 1958), p. 33.
[8]Gertrude Stein, "Patriarchal Poetry," *Yale Gertrude Stein*, p. 127.

This is to sketch out, in a compressed way, ideas that the rest of this chapter will clarify. A related idea—still to anticipate my larger argument—is that Stein sees patriarchy as dependent on a series of rigid distinctions (man-woman, culture-nature, mind-matter), classifications that form a fixed system as opposed to the mobile "system to pointing" intimated in "A Carafe." But to categorize and objectify things, and to devalue the "lower" term in each dualism (woman, nature, and matter), amounts to a sacrifice or quasi killing of the dignity, richness, and uniqueness of the thing. Yet the categories will always be susceptible to overthrow (or overflow) by the sacrificed terms. Woman and matter are always coming back to life in spite of the categories that bind and oppress them. Similarly, an anti-patriarchal or anti-sacrificial thinking is intimated in *Tender Buttons:* once we relinquish the absolute authority of our categories, we can examine and understand a thing without objectifying it. A "different" text is thus a feminist text.

Let us turn now to the sacrificial material. A number of the poems in "Objects," after this first piece, describe acts of bodily invasion, mutilation, and murder. The same poems characteristically raise issues of gender hierarchy. A question in the background of my discussion of the rest of "Objects" is thus, in what sense is sacrifice an essential feature of a patriarchal social order? What cultural work does sacrifice do? The second half of the chapter will then be about "Food," where Stein reverses the killing, pointing us beyond sacrifice and therefore beyond the social and ethical world we know.

But a point of reference for the entire chapter is a single poem (from "Food") that contains in miniature the two-part movement of *Tender Buttons* as a whole.

> VEGETABLE.
>   What is cut. What is cut by it. What is cut by it in.
>   It was a cress a crescent a cross and an unequal scream, it was upslanting, it was radiant and reasonable with little ins and red.
>   News. News capable of glees, cut in shoes, belike under pump of wide chalk, all this combing. (53)

The poem alludes to an act of violence—a cut, accompanied by a scream. There is a cross as well, suggesting a crucifixion.

"It was a cress a crescent a cross": the cress and the crescent are versions of what crucifixion kills. Crucifixion is a method of executing people, but it might also be taken to symbolize the killing of nature by culture, or the killing of nature into culture, the transformation of natural into cultural objects. The cross, in particular, is a tree that is murdered and thereby given a social use. We could take the sequence cress-crescent-cross as a chronology. There was a cress, then a crescent, then a cross. Cress turns into cross. This image makes sense visually, since a cress is a plant of the family Cruciferae, which has cross-shaped flowers. But in the transition to cross, the plant dies.

A cress is a living plant, like the vegetable referred to in the title. The next word, "crescent," connotes the moon, and signals a particular feature of the moon: the word comes from the Latin *crescere*, to grow. The moon waxes, or grows, like the cress. Cress and crescent are linked images of growth: the cyclical waxing and waning of the moon repeat in the heavens the rhythms of vegetable growth on earth.

But the cress and the crescent are then supplanted by the cross. Unlike a cress, a cross is a dead plant, a tree turned into a static artifact. When a tree was cut down to make the cross, the living plant, which grew like cress or grass, was killed into an instrument of execution, something implicated in the human or moral order rather than the natural. The "scream," the next term in the sequence, could be seen as issuing either from the dying tree or from the man who dies on it. In fact, the tree and the man are one. What happens to the cross could be taken as an analogue for what happens to Christ. Like the tree, he is born into nature but becomes a term in our legal or moral contract with God by his death.

Something like the transition from nature to culture occurs. This shift amounts to a quasi murder, a killing of the natural to make the cultural. But a second thing these words suggest is a conquest of the feminine by the masculine (whatever the gender of the victim of crucifixion). For a moon, a crescent, is replaced by a sun. The next words are "it was upslanting, it was radiant": as the cross is

erected, or slants up, there is radiance. The sun—the heavenly
body that radiates light—emerges, displacing the moon.

The sun, as in *G.M.P.*, is the insignia of the father. He has a
complement or adversary in a moon-woman. Two other poems,
separated from this by a few pages, create an opposition between
(female) moon and (male) sun. One of these, "Dinner," begins,

> Not a little fit, not a little fit sun sat in shed more mentally.
> Let us why, let us why weight, let us why winter chess, let
> us why way.
> Only a moon to soup her, only that in the sell never never
> be the cocups nice be, shatter it they lay. (55)

To confine myself for the moment to a few words here, the sun
"sat . . . mentally"—the sun is somehow mental. In this it differs
from the moon, which appears in connection with "soup," a word
suggestive of (bodily?) fluids and certainly not of the mental. The
moon, furthermore, appears near the word "her" (although gram-
matically it cannot be its antecedent). To complete the sexual polarity, "Eating," two poems later, makes the sun a male, "a grand old
man." "Eating a grand old man said roof and never never re soluble burst" (56). The final words associate the old man with the sun:
"re" is a ray; "soluble" contains the Latin *sol;* "burst" could refer to
a sunburst. (But, as I will suggest when I come back to this poem,
Stein thinks of the grand old "roof"-man as in fact "soluble": she
extinguishes him, or never-nevers him.)

This gendering of sun and moon is not new, of course, with
Stein; it forms a part of many mythological and poetic traditions.
The moon after all seems feminine; like women's bodies, it is subject to a monthly cycle. The sun, by contrast, is never "cresc-ent,"
or growing: whereas the moon expands and shrinks every month,
the sun is the same every day. Sun and man, unlike moon and
woman, seem immune to natural rhythms.

In "Vegetable," man-sun displaces woman-moon. The poem
gives an account of a killing that takes us from nature to culture,
and this transition also has the quality of a shift from female to
male. In a well-known essay, Sherry Ortner suggests a reason for
the close association in all known societies between the opposi-

tions nature/culture and female/male. Because men, who neither menstruate nor give birth, are less visibly implicated in natural cycles than women, they are permitted to be representatives of culture as women are not. Women tend to be seen as positioned uneasily between nature and culture, and hence as threatening to pollute the social with the natural. Men, by contrast, can enjoy the illusion of having transcended the body, or nature; they are permitted to think of themselves as purely social beings.[9]

Stein's sentence continues, "it was radiant *and reasonable*." Reason is a form of thinking that typically disowns connection to the body. Hence reason is paired here with the image of the masculine sun, not with the crescent, the emblem of women's implication in the cycles of nature. Just so, in the accompanying poem, it is the sun-male that "sat . . . mentally." In the last chapter I mentioned the poem "Cups," which similarly connects the male organ, the phallus, to a purely "mental" power: "A bent stick is surging and might all might is mental" (49). The mental, or the rational, is a male province.

It is difficult to imagine the opposition reason/body unaccompanied by the idea that reason is a higher thing than the body. The terms "radiant" and "reasonable" both connote approval (but an approval from which Stein will distance herself in the remainder of the poem). The sentence I have been analyzing in "Vegetable" represents the female and the natural displaced by—and subordinated to—the male and the rational. The sun is exalted over the moon, reason over the body, the cultural over the natural—in a word, the male over the female. This is a poem about the making of patriarchal categories. One could say that male supremacy is clinched in the middle of the poem.

"Cross" is the pivotal term marking the transition from what is female (cress, crescent) to what is male (radiant, reasonable). I am going to leave the remainder of the poem in suspension for a time and ask now, why does crucifixion move us from a female to a male order? How does crucifixion or sacrifice cement male dominion?

[9]Sherry Ortner, "Is Female to Male as Nature Is to Culture?" in *Woman, Culture, and Society,* ed. Michelle Zimbalist Rosaldo and Louise Lamphere (Stanford: Stanford University Press, 1974), pp. 67–87.

Patriarchy depends on the passing of privilege from father to son. Yet women are not easily shuffled out of view, for the transition from father to son depends on a mother. Sacrifice is a way of symbolically erasing women's crucial role as biological links.

This is the insight of an important article by the sociologist Nancy Jay, whose title, "Sacrifice as Remedy for Having Been Born of Woman," contains its thesis: blood sacrifice remedies or overcomes the fact that mothers, not fathers, bear children.[10] To rehearse Jay's argument for a moment before applying it to Stein, blood sacrifice (in patrilineal African societies) is essential for establishing lines of descent. In patrilineal, but not in matrilineal, societies, sacrificial ritual is prominent; and it is prominent because it constitutes kinship ties. When a group of people sacrifices together, the act proves that they are related patrilineally. It is enough to make them legal relatives. For while descent from the mother is a visible thing, "proved" by the event of birth, descent from the father must establish itself through an equally momentous event that will supersede birth, legally attaching a person to the father rather than to the mother. "The only action that is as serious as giving birth, which can act as a counterbalance to it, is killing."[11] Sacrifice is as bloody, dramatic, and irreversible as birth. Thus, while mothers can bear children, fathers can affirm their superior claims by killing.

This pattern seems useful for understanding the function of the cross and the scream in Stein's crucifixion poem. "Vegetable" traces the passage from a natural system to a legal or moral system. Crucifixion assists in the shift from the natural to the moral, from cress to what is "radiant and reasonable." For it is a sacrificial act that affirms our debt to a ("radiant and reasonable") divine Father, at the same time dissociating us from the maternal or merely natural realm whose fertility is emblematized by the moon and the grass.

"Vegetable" makes these associations in a compressed and oblique form. Other poems in *Tender Buttons* elaborate more clearly

---

[10]Nancy Jay, "Sacrifice as Remedy for Having Been Born of Woman," in *Immaculate and Powerful: The Female in Sacred Image and Social Reality*, ed. Clarissa W. Atkinson, Constance H. Buchanan, and Margaret R. Miles (Boston: Beacon Press, 1985), pp. 283–309.

[11]Jay, p. 294.

the erasure of a maternal by a paternal order. Stein never uses the word *father* in *Tender Buttons*, but the sacrificial phase of her text in "Objects" culminates in the ascendancy of a "king," a "jack," or a "nice old pole." The king-father, moreover, achieves his position of dominance through a sacrifice.

The Scene of Sacrifice in "Objects"

Whereas "Objects" as a whole has identifiable patterns, it is also filled with sound experiments, like the rest of *Tender Buttons* and like all Stein's opaque works. Frequently Stein takes up an image, a sound, or a constellation of thoughts unconnected to the sacrificial themes or to any other continuous strand of thinking elsewhere in the text. Some poems are not only thematically independent of the surrounding material but also internally so dense as to discourage interpretation (such as "Cold Climate": "A season in yellow sold extra strings makes lying places" [22]). Within poems, moreover, there are invariably words that do not contribute to any continuous idea and whose importance is either in their sheer soundplay or in their ability to dislodge other, more logically embedded words in the vicinity from unitary meanings by stimulating alternative associations. Stein constructs a text that invites the reader to find coherent themes but that also makes him or her choose a point beyond which to stop piecing things together. My readings are not meant to substitute for this experience of uncertainty and mobility. A point made in the last chapter is that the dense style has its own meanings, which in fact are closely linked to the anti-patriarchal content of these texts. These meanings are no less important as we turn to *Tender Buttons*.

Nonetheless, *Tender Buttons* is far more susceptible to interpretation than has been thought. Its ability to affect readers is due not simply to its stylistic ingenuity but also to the issues it insistently confronts, issues that reach the reader through powerful images even when they are not announced explicitly. "Objects," among all the other things it does, speaks of the sacrifice that makes a king. I trace three connected phenomena in "Objects": a murder or a cutting; an erasure of the womb, that is, an erasure of women's power as mothers; and, ultimately, the creation of a king. As in "Vegetable," a killing occurs, and sexual hierarchy is fixed in place; indeed the killing is implicated in the creation of sexual hierarchy. In these poems, furthermore, the sacrificial victim is often a woman.

The notion of sacrifice acquires a new resonance here. Often we seem to be witnessing not a crucifixion—a ritual or sacred killing—but something profane, a murder. "Vegetable" suggests that the theological symbolism of crucifixion has the effect of erasing women: the crescent, or the mother's body, is obliterated by the cross. But Stein also thinks of the erasure of women in the real world, or the claiming of their bodies by and for men, as *like* a sacrifice.

Scattered throughout "Objects," during but also before the final sacrificial crisis, are poems that seem to allude to a mutilation of the female body. In *G.M.P.*, we saw that the rule of the father stigmatizes women as dirty; they seem to stand for matter untransformed by symbolism. In that text the scapegoating led to a fantasy of disinfection: "so to clean that stinking." In *Tender Buttons*, the female body is envisioned as subject to similar control; one way to dematerialize it is through marriage, which enters a woman's body into the male economy as an object of exchange. "Objects" gives two images for such an event: the "sale" of the body or womb, and its "collapse" or impairment, so that women become sacrificial victims.

For example, the poem "Red Roses" reads, "A cool red rose and a pink cut pink, a collapse and a sold hole, a little less hot" (24). When the "rose" or "hole," the vagina (or uterus), is "sold," it is "collapse[d]"—damaged and minimized. As a poem called "Suppose an Eyes" suggests, the collapse or sale is helped along by aggressive techniques of seduction; it is dangerous to allow one's "purr" to be "rubbed" by a suitor. "Suppose a collapse in rubbed purr, in rubbed purr get. Little sales ladies little sales ladies little saddles of mutton" (27). The "sales ladies" may be either the sold (and self-selling) ladies themselves, transformed into "saddles of mutton," or a band of traitorous matchmakers. The "rubbed purr," in turn, suggests not only seduction but also the opposite—the rubbing *out* of the "purr," or women's sexual organs, in a male exchange that overrides female desire. What is rubbed out, then, is purring, or women's pleasure—just as "Red Roses" ends, "a collapse and a sold hole, a little less hot." The moment of sale coincides with a diminution of heat or desire. What then might "rubbed purr *get*" mean? To "get" the rubbed purr could mean to obtain it in marriage, or to take hold of it; if Stein indeed intends these associations, she inverts the verb and its object, and thus also creates puns on "for-get" and, just possibly, "pur-gat-ory," two references to what the rubbed-out women are subjectively experiencing. Finally, "get" means beget—the outcome of the whole procedure, in progeny.

In *G.M.P.*, the father purifies matter by converting it into symbol. In *Tender Buttons*, the transfer of women in marriage becomes a brutal instance of the same event, turning bodies into tokens in a system of exchange. This is an extension of what Stein depicts in *G.M.P.* as a burial or corseting of drives under paternal law; the sexual drives of women in particular are rubbed out by the market consciousness that turns their bodies into objects to be possessed or transferred. In "A Purse," Stein uses the purse as a figure for the womb become money (or, precisely, a money-vessel). Like the collapsed and sold hole (and like the neglected cup in "Cups"), the purse in question seems barely there. "A purse . . . was hardly seen." Yet it is good for something in a male economy:

> A PURSE.
> A purse was not green, it was not straw color, it was hardly seen and it had a use a long use and the chain, the chain was never missing, it was not misplaced, it showed that it was open, that is all that it showed. (19)

The female genitals are divested of all qualities except that of being "open," or susceptible to "use." It is as if, grotesquely, they had a "chain." (In the meantime, the next piece has an all too significant title: "A Mounted Umbrella.")

These poems in "Objects" depict the exchange, mutilation, and sexual suppression of the female body. On the other hand, let us think about "Red Roses" again. It contains an account of the erasure of sexuality, but it also has intensely sexual resonances that seem to belie this erasure. The poem, again, reads: "RED ROSES. A cool red rose and a pink cut pink, a collapse and a sold hole, a little less hot." The progression from "cool" to "pink . . . pink," to "less hot," suggests arousal and release. The "collapse" in the middle could correspondingly allude to orgasm, after which things are "a little less hot." Indeed, if the word "sold" were not present to signal an economic issue, the sexual meaning might dominate.

This is an instance of a strategy of crossed meanings which Stein perfects in *Tender Buttons*, whereby a single phrase or sentence can mean antithetical things at once. According to one possible interpretation of "Red Roses," sexuality is overridden or "collapse[d]"; according to another, it is released. Even the single word "rubbed," in "Suppose an Eyes," means "rubbed out, denied arousal," and the opposite, "aroused." The "collapse in rubbed purr," like the "collapse" mentioned in "Red Roses," could itself as easily apply to orgasm as to the erasure of sexual pleasure.

Or again, an ambiguous sentence precedes the reference to "a collapse in rubbed purr": "Go red go red, laugh white" (27). First, this sentence might allude again to the suppression of female sexuality; the "red," or the sexual body, is commanded to "go" away, and a woman is supposed to "laugh white"—titter with artificial innocence. (A few lines earlier, there is a reference to "a white dress," which "is in sign"—the wedding dress, perhaps, which imposes a code of purity [27].) But at the same time, the words could be taken to voice the very sexuality that is being whitened. "Go red" suggests "turn red," become flushed; the repetition of the phrase, without punctuation, creates a rhythmic intensity; "laugh" might signal sexual release, and therefore a move from "red" to positively "white" heat.

In all these cases, at the moment the text tells of a repression, it also tells of erotic energies that defy repression. (Since both eros and patriarchy are compulsions, their conflict is unending.) For such ambiguities, Stein relies on two strategies. First, she puns: "rubbed" can mean either "stroked" or "rubbed out"; "go red" can mean either "become red" or "redness, depart." In each instance, one meaning points to sexuality, the other to its repression. Stein's second strategy for creating ambiguities is syntactical incompletion. "Go red," because isolated from a larger syntactical context, contains insufficient information to enable us to decide whether "red" is a noun—the color red, which is being told to go away—or an adjective, in which case someone is being told to turn red. If the verb "go" had a clear subject, the ambiguity would be resolved. Instead, two competing meanings are preserved.

Another version of syntactical incompletion, which again multiplies meanings, is the elision of grammatical cues by parataxis. The line "A cool red rose and a pink cut pink, a collapse and a sold hole, a little less hot," is unified by *ands*—a minimal link, supplemented only by commas. The effect is to leave the interrelations of the serial phrases ambiguous. Subordination would clarify a single sense. As it is, the fragments could be read either as appositives—a collapsed hole *is* a sold hole, hence less hot—or as forming a sequence, from cool to hot to cool. The difference between these two interpretations is the difference, again, between the erasure of sexuality and its expression.

The crossed meanings are part of what gives *Tender Buttons* a more concentrated intelligence than *G.M.P.* The best poems of *Tender Buttons* ask to be reread many times. But the power of these particular ambiguities has something to do with their content. The drama of sacrifice is endlessly crosscut by the irruption of what is supposedly sacrificed. Paternal law is always traced over by the energies it is supposed to put under. For there is no such thing as an obliteration of drive. Even under the rule of the father, when drives give way to signs, the body covertly makes itself felt. Stein's text is constructed in such a way as to collapse into single words both the paternal taboo and its violation by the sexual body.

What these various ambiguities render thematically, they enact formally. Thematically, the paternal taboo is transgressed by sexuality; formally, it is transgressed (here and in every sentence of *Tender Buttons*) by the play of language. The very fact of ambiguity, that is, is a challenge to the mode of signification associated with the father. Symbolic language displaces attention from the fleshy feel of a word to its bodiless meaning. Yet ambiguity and punning redirect attention to the "body" of utterance. Any literary text, but particularly a difficult and ambiguous one, defies the notion of monologic meaning. In purely symbolic discourse, if such a thing existed, the words chosen would be incidental to a unitary meaning. But the more a text exploits the multiple resonances of a single

word—say, *rubbed*—the less one can image an adequate paraphrase. In order to reach the meaning of a passage, the reader
must keep crossing through the material word.

A specially polyvalent linguistic practice only emphasizes what
is true of all language. The signifier can be trivialized—and we
have seen that for Stein it is trivialized, under the father—but (like
women's sexuality) it can never be controlled absolutely. It resur-
faces as a force within language in ambiguities and wordplay, features not only of "Objects" but of all of *Tender Buttons*. The poems
of "Objects" hint thematically at the endless return of forbidden
energies, and reflect the return stylistically as well.

Many of the poems of "Objects" are not directed toward sacrificial themes. But as the text progresses, the preoccupation with
the scene of sacrifice intensifies. The last third or so of "Objects" is
filled with violent images, involving cutting, burial, and the transformation of bodies into things like leather and meat. A predator
moves in on an object; a late poem reads, "A WHITE HUNTER. A
white hunter is nearly crazy" (27). At the same time, there are
images of male dominion perfecting itself; the sacrifice is what
makes male dominion possible. The last four poems consummate
the violence in a burial and a murder.

Woman is put under in "Book" (which I quote in full):

> BOOK.
> Book was there, it was there. Book was there. Stop it, stop
> it, it was a cleaner, a wet cleaner and it was not where it was
> wet, it was not high, it was directly placed back, not back
> again, back it was returned, it was needless, it put a bank, a
> bank when, a bank care.
> Suppose a man a realistic expression of resolute reliability
> suggests pleasing itself white all white and no head does that
> mean soap. It does not so. It means kind wavers and little
> chance to beside beside rest. A plain.
> Suppose ear rings, that is one way to breed, breed that. Oh
> chance to say, oh nice old pole. Next best and nearest a pillar.
> Chest not valuable, be papered.
> Cover up cover up the two with a little piece of string and
> hope rose and green, green.
> Please a plate, put a match to the seam and really then really

then, really then it is a remark that joins many many lead
games. It is a sister and sister and a flower and a flower and a
dog and a colored sky a sky colored grey and nearly that
nearly that let. (28–29)

This poem contains no killing; instead, it gives a wry description of
the privileging of the male anatomy over the female. The phallus
commands respect; women, at least those who "breed" (or perhaps wear "ear rings"), are supposed to compliment it. "Oh chance
to say, oh nice old pole." They sometimes politely exaggerate:
"Next best and nearest a pillar." But the next sentence is, "Chest
not valuable, be papered." The female receptacle, the "chest"—or
else the "chest" in the sense of the breast—is dismissed as "not
valuable." As with the female "stains" and "linings" in the material
I discussed in the last chapter, women's bodies are here declared
not simply devoid of value but disgraceful, something to be carefully kept out of sight. "Be papered. Cover up cover up."

The cover-up is the burial of the womb or the breast, signifying
the denial that women's bodies have any special dignity or power.
Nancy Jay's anthropological theory furnishes one way of thinking
about this erasure: the passage of power from man to man depends
on the fiction that the uterus is trivial. But one can also view Stein's
poem in psychoanalytic terms. It repeats the oedipal moment in
G.M.P., when the child learned to value "tail" over "linings." So
the poem could be seen as pointing both to the global devaluation
of women's bodies and to the moment in childhood when each
individual absorbs that message about women's anatomical "inferi-
ority."

There is a countermovement in "Book," however, a last expression of "hope" in the face of violation. The sentence beginning
"Cover up" reads in full, "Cover up cover up the two with a little
piece of string and hope rose and green, green." As one thing is in
the process of being covered up, another is rising: "hope rose."
Among other things, there is hope that the female body will survive obliteration. "Hope rose" means two things—that hope arose
at the most hopeless moment and that there is a hope, a rose. The
rose may symbolize the female body itself, as in the poem "Red
Roses." If so, the flower is a locus of life that cannot be entirely

controlled by paternal law; it is a rose that "rose." It is a site of stubborn fertility: the sentence ends "and green, green." It is also a site of pleasure, so that lesbian coupling offers a particular sort of "hope": "It is a sister and sister and a flower and a flower." (In "Rooms" Stein writes, "The sister was not a mister. Was this a surprise. It was" [65].) But the note of hope will be silenced in the next poems.

The command that the chest, or the female body, "be papered" works in two ways. It refers to the papering over or denial of the female anatomy but also to the existence of a certain paper or document that will write the feminine out of existence. For a paternal script is forming, one with special emphases and erasures. The title of the poem is "Book," and the first words are, "Book was there, it was there. Book was there. Stop it, stop it, it was a cleaner, a wet cleaner." The book—the codified word of the father—is a cleaner because it factitiously washes away women's bodies, associating them with dirt. This first paragraph of "Book" conveys a particular urgency. An unexpected transition to past-tense narrative suggests that at some moment, either in history (when patriarchy began) or in one person's story (when gender hierarchy was learned), "Book was there." Alternatively, the past tense could suggest that the book "was" always there, has always been with us. The second sentence, too, communicates a certain urgency, for someone seems to be reliving the moment of fear and raising a protest: "Stop it, stop it."

The next paragraph begins, "Suppose a man a realistic expression of resolute reliability suggests pleasing itself white all white and no head does that mean soap." Although the next sentence says, "It does not so," the negation does not quite undo the suggestion that some "man" is "pleasing" himself by an act of cleaning or whitening, with "soap." This passage follows by about a page the reference, noted earlier, to whiteness as the color of falsely innocent and disembodied womanhood. The poem as a whole, then, describes the whitewashing or erasure of the feminine by the master "cleaner" or paternal book, which replaces the live energies of women with stereotypes of purity. Maybe the book suppresses women's brains as well as bodies: "and no head."

The paternal script does more damage in the next poem, one of the more chilling entries in *Tender Buttons.* "PEELED PENCIL, CHOKE. Rub her coke" (29). The verbs could be imperatives, echoing the command to "cover up" in the preceding poem: now a pencil is being ordered to "choke" someone or something. Here the murder is starting to play itself out—although simultaneously one may hear a defiant voice condemning the death-dealing pencil itself to death: peeled pencil, (go) choke.

The image of the pencil that chokes actually compresses the motifs of the preceding poem. There, the phallus—pole or pillar—was revered at the expense of the womb, and the feminine was written out of existence. Here, the phallus *is* the writing implement: the pole has become a pencil, the instrument of the father.

Its victim is a mysterious "her." The pencil evidently has a lead and an eraser, both of which are directed against "her." The words "Rub her coke" imply, first, a procedure of blackening, since they could mean something like "rub her with coke" or "make her the color of coke," black. The lead of the peeled pencil blots "her" out, making her black or bad, just as in *G.M.P.* the father stigmatized or shadowed the feminine. More than that, "rub her" is a pun on "rubber," or eraser, with the direct object "her" embedded in it. As with an earlier use of the verb *rub*—in the very similar phrase "rubbed purr"—"rub her" suggests erasure in its sense of rubbing "her" out. Stein uses personal pronouns rarely and meaningfully in *Tender Buttons;* the word *her* in this poem intimates that woman is the object of erasure.

This aggression against the person called "her" is sexualized. The image of a peeled pencil suggests an erection, and the phrase "rub her coke," since it reads "rub her [noun]," implies "rub some part of her body." "Rub her coke" also sounds like "rubber cock"; the pencil has a phallic aggression. On the other hand, there is something lighthearted about the whole image. Stein, even as she traces gruesome social facts, is able to have fun at the expense of the glorious phallus that is causing all this damage. In the previous poem, she reduced the phallus to a "nice old pole"; and here it becomes, among other things, just a "rubber cock," a sort of dildo. Her snide punning is a subversive energy that she throws back at the phallic order.

"Peeled" has one more meaning: circumcised. The phallus, as a sign of male dominance, has nothing to do with any individual's experience of his own body, except to the extent that that body differs from a woman's. Hence a man's inheritance of the phallus alienates him from his own flesh. Circumcision is the means by which some cultures mark this transformation from flesh to symbol: it is a sacrifice of flesh that turns the anatomical penis into a sign of the contract between father and son (and that therefore fits Jay's paradigm by which blood sacrifice "remedies" a child's "having been born of woman").

The circumcised or "peeled" pencil is a lifeless thing, like the *"old pole,"* and like the *"boiling* tree" in *G.M.P.* (274). For the phallus, as Stein describes it, is an artifact, a living thing tortured into a symbol, quite like the cross in "Vegetable." Stein sees gender as a social creation, not as an anatomical fact. The phallus is a symbol, an imposition by a male-dominated culture. Somewhere, there is a real male organ, robust and pleasantly physical—to which Stein is perhaps referring at the end of *Tender Buttons* with the phrase "a magnificent asparagus" (78). But patriarchal thinking buries this under the phallus. The privileged male, attached to his social identity as a bearer of phallic power, values the penis less as flesh than as symbol. Hence this moment of male dominion in "Objects" is haunted by a series of lifeless sticks—"pillar," "pole," and "pencil."

Another possibility is raised by the phrase "Rub her coke." What if it is taken to mean (what it more obviously sounds like), "rub *her* cock"? The "her" in the phrase is then hardly an erased, choked woman-victim but—by a very different reading of the same words—a live and sexual woman-with-a-surplus, whose fantasized penis, or clitoris-as-penis, her lover rubs. Similarly, a dildo (to return to the reading "rubber cock") is something women lovers can use together. Crossed gender—rather like crossed meanings—represents for Stein a way of subverting patriarchal arrangements. If gender is merely a social artifact, one way to get past it, she suggests, is through a counterartifice by which one dons the other sex. ("Lifting Belly" intimates that Stein and Toklas's sexual life included such gender play: "Please be the man. I am the man.")[12]

Similarly, in the preceding poem, "Book," after the contrast of

[12]Stein, "Lifting Belly," *Yale Gertrude Stein,* p. 51.

the exalted male pillar and the demeaned female chest, there were the words, "Cover up cover up the two with a little piece of string and hope rose and green, green." The sentence alludes to the cover-up of women's bodies, yet by an alternative reading suggests a solution to that very oppression: one can simply "cover up *the two*," in the sense of burying both gender terms, pillar and chest, thereby eluding fixed gender altogether. All it takes is the tiniest bit of a costume, "a little piece of string." Because such a vacation from gender is possible, "hope rose." Not only sexual play but also verbal play can rewrite gender: the next sentences of the same poem refer both to "a sister and sister" (two women together) and to "many many lead games," the transgressive games the author plays with her own pencil lead. In "Peeled Pencil," it is by a sort of lead game, a scribal sleight of hand, that Stein barely veils the words "her cock" within "her coke": the art of punning enables her to mix genders with impunity. A similar lead game, the deletion of a single character, gets her from "Choke" to "coke"—from (perhaps) the vaginal image of an artichoke to the male "cock." Whereas the patriarchal "Book" rigidly polarizes the male pole and the female chest, Stein's experimental pencil plays past the father's categories.

Thus even as the patriarchal violence intensifies in "Peeled Pencil," Stein sees ways of eluding it. But in the next poem, the penultimate of "Objects," the blackening continues:

> IT WAS BLACK, BLACK TOOK.
> Black ink best wheel bale brown.
> Excellent not a hull house, not a pea soup, no bill no care,
> no precise no past pearl pearl goat. (29)

The mood is somber. "It was black"—things went black—and the blackness "took" something, perhaps the same "her" who was rubbed out in the previous poem. Again the violation issues from an evil text, "black ink." The first sentence ends in a series of positive-sounding terms ("best wheel bale brown"), but is followed by what may be a list of items inked out by the paternal script. First, there is "not a hull house." It is strange to find such a topical reference in *Tender Buttons*. Hull House, a settlement house and a center for social reform, is historically linked to feminism by way of its founder Jane Addams, a leader in the woman suffrage movement. That there is "not a hull house" suggests an erasure both of women's autonomy and of a sort of maternal caring or sheltering, as well as of a particular woman's public service or career. Further, there is "not a pea soup"; the world of the mother, which in *G.M.P.* was associated with an image of "thick potato soup" (250), is obliterated. And when one puts "pea" and "hull" together, one gets a peapod: if there is "not a hull house," there is no peapod-house, no uterine space that might have provided protection from the paternal order. As in "Book," the womb, or whatever psychic state the womb might represent, is lost.

The next words, on the other hand—"no bill no care"—are ambiguous in a manner that by now should be familiar: although they might refer to an absence of caring or mothering, they could also suggest "no bill of sale, no cause for care," implying that the betrayal or sale of woman is still incomplete. But the ambiguity then passes into a uniform dreariness. With "no precise no past" the preoedipal (or, alternatively, prepatriarchal) past is crossed out entirely. "No precis[ion]" is left about it, no memory. The last words are "no past pearl pearl goat." Pearl and goat might be emblems for the mother. She is a goat, a milk giver; perhaps her body is also a "past pearl," in the sense of a buried fact or treasure. Yet a goat can also be a symbol for male lechery—an idea the next poem brings to the fore.

In this final poem, the being referred to as "her" is killed. The aggression against women culminates in a murderous rape:

> THIS IS THIS DRESS, AIDER.
> Aider, why aider why whow, whow stop touch, aider whow, aider stop the muncher, muncher munchers.
> A jack in kill her, a jack in, makes a meadowed king, makes a to let. (29)

As others have noticed, this poem is sexually charged. The repetition of "whow" and the emphasis on touch suggest excitement; "A jack in kill her" both contains the words "A jack [a man] in . . . her" and suggests the first two syllables of the word "ejaculate."

But the passage also contains the words *kill her*. It is not just about sex but also about murder.

The title sounds an alarm: "This Is This Dress, Aider," or this is distress, help me (French *m'aidez*). The distress signal could also be addressed *to* "Aider," or Ada, Stein's code name for Alice Toklas.[13] Perhaps Alice is appealed to as an "aider," an ally against the aggressor at this crucial moment. Or "aider" could be a last plea to whoever might be listening: "aid *her*," the feminine presence that is being sacrificed. If one reads "aider," on the other hand, as "ate her," and connects it with "stop the muncher" and "A jack in kill her," it seems that one is witnessing the killing of "her" and her consumption as food. This looks like a scene of sacrifice and communion.

If so, a woman—or, simply, woman—has become the sacrificial victim, occupying the place of Christ in the crucifixion poem. "Suppose an Eyes," five poems earlier, makes the comparison of women to mutton: "Little sales ladies little sales ladies little saddles of mutton" (27). As we will see, "mutton" is also a word Stein uses for the Eucharist. But here it is women who are the mutton, the lambs subjected to munching.

The idea of munching destabilizes the poem's affect; to kill a woman is terrible, but to munch her is less serious. Similarly, the repeated word "whow" suggests a feeling of happy surprise. Once again, Stein's sense of play prevents her from giving in to a uniform sense of horror. This poem in which the climactic murder happens is also one of the most ornately punning poems in *Tender Buttons*. By another wild, distancing joke, Stein writes this scene as a telegram: "THIS IS THIS DRESS, *AIDER*"—that is, the French *m'aidez*, or "mayday," an SOS call. Then, the word "stop," as in a telegram, stands as punctuation: "Aider, . . . whow *stop* touch, aider whow, aider *stop* the muncher, muncher munchers."[14] I have been emphasizing Stein's use of language as a medium for veiled messages and (alternatively) as an instrument of subversion through the "spread-

---

[13]Stein had written her portrait of Toklas, called "Ada," between 1908 and 1910. See Bridgman, p. 93.

[14]I owe this interpretation of the words *aider* and *stop* to a suggestion from Lauren Berlant.

ing" of "difference," but throughout *Tender Buttons* one senses as well her appreciation for language as sheer fun.

The emotional meaning of the scene of munching is further complicated by the possibility that Stein herself could be the muncher, enjoying "Ada" or Alice; this poem in fact has most often been interpreted as a sexual scene involving Stein and Toklas.[15] In that case, Stein is identifying not just with the woman in distress but also with the person who distresses her. (Similarly, the "peeled pencil" just before could be not just the patriarchal implement but also Stein's own subversive writing implement, itself a substitute phallus or "rubber cock.") For all Stein's insight into the workings of patriarchy, she resists an easy polarization of a bad male world and a female utopia. As happens again in "Food," she sees that her own consciousness is implicated in sacrifice.

The poem ends, "A jack in kill her, a jack in, makes a meadowed king, makes a to let." The person identified as "jack" rapes and murders "her." That is how I understand "A jack in kill her": a jack, who is in her, kills her. This image of rape-murder compresses all the motifs I have been observing: the co-opting of women's sexuality, the enforcement of male supremacy, and killing.

This phrase marks the moment of sacrifice. Then, eerily, the sentence goes on to obscure the sacrifice itself. The phrase "A jack in kill her" is straightforward both about the murder and about its victim. Yet it is followed by "a jack in," which deletes both the "killing" and its object, "her." The next phrase, "makes a meadowed king," describes perfect male dominion with no precise sense of who is dominated; this king simply, and pleasantly it seems, rules over grass. (Perhaps he is "meadowed" in the even milder sense of being put out to pasture.) Yet embedded in the sentence as a whole is the notion that it was the murder of a woman that made him a king: "a jack in kill her . . . *makes* a meadowed king." The sentence chronicles a murder of "her," the creation of a king, and a repression of the murder.

The creation of a king has another meaning, in the context of

---

[15]See particularly the rich interpretations by Stimpson ("Gertrude Stein and the Transposition of Gender," pp. 14–15) and Schmitz ("Gertrude Stein as Post-Modernist," p. 126).

what could be an oedipal drama. "A jack in kill her, . . . makes a . . . king" could mean, "a jack kills her; this makes a king." The jack—the queen's inferior in a deck of cards—kills "her" and becomes, himself, the king. The son, that is, inherits the status of the father by slaying the mother or overcoming his dependence on her. It is a sign of the immense compression of this poem that other phrases, already considered, fit this narrative of achieved manhood. The movement from "stop the muncher," in the first sentence, to "a jack in . . . her" in the second, could mark the end of an oral phase—"stop the [mouth]"—and the inauguration of a genital phase. The breast is abandoned to make way for phallic sexuality. (Hence perhaps the use of the past participle in "meadowed," a word that ends with *wed*.) But if so, Stein (unlike Freud) does not see this phallic orientation in positive teleological terms, for the other meanings of the poem connect adult male sexuality with appropriation and rape.

"Objects" then concludes, with the phrase "makes a to let." The reference could be to a ritual bloodletting, finally sacralizing the murder that has been happening all along. Alternatively, the victim known formerly as "her" becomes a mere object of sale or rental, a space "to let." She is also, plausibly, "a toi-let," a debased vessel for male desire. She is passive to violation, "letting" it happen. "To let" also means "empty"; the woman is expunged, declared a vacancy. The final words are mild and pleasant; the human victim, formerly an object of anxiety, has been transformed into a meadow or a blank space.

The sacrifice that creates sexual hierarchy magically makes itself invisible. Thereupon sexual hierarchy is not perceived *as* a sacrifice or a violation at all. It is naturalized; it becomes part of the landscape.

What Stein has done in these poems is to make sacrifice visible, to expose it as sacrifice. First she shows how a particular sacrifice, the crucifixion, has the effect of cementing the dominion of men over women. The crucifixion, a drama of killing required by a paternal God, obliterates the drama of birth, the province of the mother-moon and of human mothers. Second, Stein has suggested how in daily social relations, women are violated in ways that amount to mutilation or sacrifice. They are subjected to sexual aggression and sold in marriage. They become objects of male consumption; they are "munched" alive, as if they were mutton.

Yet one can do more than merely make sacrifice visible. Sacrifice is in fact reversible. The first part of *Tender Buttons* exposes the various sacrifices at the heart of gender hierarchy, but the second part offers a route past them. In "Food," Stein "hang[s] hanging" (47), or kills sacrifice itself.

"Roastbeef" and the Remainder

The answer to sacrifice is what I would like to call an ethics of the remainder. Sacrifice leaves a remainder; after a crucifixion, something is left over that refuses to die. We have seen what sacrifice attempts to make disappear: woman, matter, and natural process. But these things are still there—inevitably so—as the ground upon which mind and culture support themselves. The redemptive moment comes when we decide to see and love the things that sacrifice tells us are not there.

In "Objects," acts of killing and mutilation are disrupted by a trace of life that resists extinction, a "hope rose." The next section, "Food," is devoted to retrieving this source of life, transforming it into a remembered body. A sacrifice undergirds social and linguistic codes, but beyond sacrifice, an archaic form of life goes on in spite of social formations, and threatens them. Within the psyche, the threat (or hope) comes from drives, repressed but never exterminated, and from forbidden memories of the pre-oedipal mother. Within culture, what is never quite controlled by codes is "raw," or unsymbolic, matter. And finally, women's sexuality is something that can be sold but never possessed. Simply to respect the autonomy of these things is to begin to situate oneself outside patriarchal culture.

A sentence that could stand as a motto for the "Food" section is, "I spy" (52). Here Stein demonstrates a way of seeing through patriarchal structures. Like the rest of *Tender Buttons*, this section is a promiscuous mix of sophisticated thoughts and homely images. "Food" is about food—its preparation and consumption. Yet Stein's use of the discourse of the kitchen is witty, even sly. Beside the sophisticated and brain-cracking poems, the list of contents

that opens "Food" has an absurd innocence: "ROASTBEEF; MUT-
TON; BREAKFAST; SUGAR; CRANBERRIES; MILK; EGGS; AP-
PLE; [the incongruous] TAILS; LUNCH"; and so forth (32). This
menu may disarm readers. The feminism of the text lurks within
the stereotypically feminine business of the kitchen.

"Roastbeef," the unusually long first poem, chronicles the fate of
a piece of meat. After the thorough munching of matter in "Objects," something is still raw and untouched, although for the moment we locate it just in time to see it get roasted again. In the end,
the poem replays in miniature the cycle of sacrifice just completed
in "This Is This Dress, Aider." Yet the rest of "Food" will involve a
new cycle, one that will partially reverse sacrifice and challenge the
psychic and social formations that sacrifice supports.

"Roastbeef" opens with the words, "In the inside there is sleeping" (33). After rape-murder, there is still an inside to things, a
locus of sleeping life. "Objects" ended with the creation of static
meanings by the peeled pencil, or phallus. The "book," the paternal code, imposed categories, erasing some things and exalting
others. "Roastbeef" exposes what always exceeds such categories:
matter in flux. Just now I am describing the effects of the two
juxtaposed passages rather than, necessarily, Stein's intention in
juxtaposing them. For Stein kept two separate cahiers for "Objects" and "Food" and, as I have noted, probably worked on both
sections simultaneously.[16] Thus, as she wrote the last poems of
"Objects," she may not have been looking immediately forward to
the already-composed "Roastbeef" at the beginning of "Food."

The beefsteak is slowly transforming itself from flesh into food.
It has a mysterious center, "tender and changing" (34). In *G.M.P.*,
matter-made-symbol was pictured as matter cooked through,
"boiled" past change by paternal codes. But the present beefsteak,
still half-raw, is in process and eludes simplification. The following
phrases, which I take to be about the inside and the outside of the
meat, recall the confusion of categories in the mind of a young boy
in *G.M.P.*: "tender and changing and external and central and
surrounded and singular and simple and the same and the surface . . . and the red and the same and the centre and the yellow

[16]See DeKoven, p. 76.

and the tender and the better, and altogether" (34). The last word is a summary: all things mingle here.

The passage describes raw thinking as well as raw meat. It summons up the undifferentiated mental process of the preoedipal stage, anterior to the paternal codes that polarize concepts like surface and center, or the same and the changing. Judged from the perspective of the just concluded "Objects," this material is regressive: in spite of the patriarchal script, preoedipal thinking goes on. It has just been asleep.

Sensations described in this section belong to the presymbolic stage dominated by the mother. "There is no use at all in smell, in taste, in teeth, in toast, in anything" (35): archaic oral drives are present. That "there is no use" suggests that instrumental thinking, victorious in "Objects" in the form of a market consciousness, has relaxed. Read together, the words "there is no use . . . in teeth" mean also perhaps that the mouth now serves not as an instrument for symbolic communication but as an autonomous source of pleasure. Drive has leaked back into vocalization: "if there is singing then there is the resumption" (33).

Stylistically, Stein signals the resumption of singing—the reassertion of pleasure in language—by a paragraph that, though no more nonsensical than many others in *Tender Buttons*, is uniquely musical: "Lovely snipe and tender turn, excellent vapor and slender butter, all the splinter and the trunk, all the poisonous darkening drunk, all the joy in weak success, all the joyful tenderness, all the section and the tea, all the stouter symmetry" (35). The qualities of language repressed during the Oedipus complex are in force here. What keeps the sentence going is the sheer pleasure in repetition—in rhyme and rhythm. Like the simplest poem imaginable, the sentence falls into tetrameter "lines" which (after the first two) rhyme. Even their first feet echo one another: six consecutive lines are introduced by the phrase "all the." The syntax, too, repeats itself, with minor variations. "Roastbeef" thus suggests the triumph of the mouth (and the ear) over the symbol—a motif forecast by the title of the section, "Food." By returning to "taste" and "teeth," "Roastbeef" resurrects the realm of body and matter that the phallic order at the end of "Objects" had partially buried.

G.M.P. ended with a rediscovery of "much raw sampling." Just so, "Roastbeef" locates a raw place the father has not touched. It is a place of seeding—something like the womb. As "Roastbeef" continues, the poem passes from a description of a slowly changing piece of beef into an evocation of the site of slow change in a woman's body: "Room to comb chickens and feathers and ripe purple, room to curve single plates . . . , all room has no shadow" (35). The words "room," "curve," and "ripe purple" suggest a round, red, fertile space. This room has "no shadow": Stein retains the iconography of *G.M.P.* To rediscover the womb is to escape from the paternal shadow that obscures the womb by figuring it as an absence.

Matter is always in flux; so is mother. The transition from raw to cooked is a piece of magic transcending paternal categories; and so is the ripeness of mothers. To take pleasure in women's fertility is to step outside the sacrificial order that transfers privilege from father to son by co-opting the mother's role in reproduction, reducing the womb to a "sold hole" (24). A child does not perceive (or later remember) the preoedipal mother *as* a womb. But the same oedipal structure that causes a child to repress the early maternal bond leads within culture to a trivialization of women's fertility. "Roastbeef" "regresses" past the Oedipus complex, both by calling up features of preoedipal thought and by figuring the womb not as something impure or invisible, or as property, but as a site of mysterious transformation.

To see past the Oedipus complex is to see past sacrifice. The last poem of "Objects" signaled sacrificial action with a pun on "distress": "This Is This Dress" (29). Yet in "Roastbeef," which comes just afterward (though we must remember that it was almost certainly *composed* before), "when there is turning there is no distress" (34). When there is process—when things are "turning" into other things—there is no sacrifice. "Turning," or process—in the mutations of matter, in the gestation of babies, and in the motility of drive—is what the phallic order, cemented by the Oedipus complex, suppresses or sacrifices but never extinguishes. "Roastbeef" plunges into "the change the dirt" (33). Change *is* dirt, tabooed by the father. Yet we may take pleasure in it all the same. "Not to change dirt means that there is no beefsteak" (33): not to change dirty matter into symbol means that one has not (yet) made a "beefsteak" or a cooked meal.

Soon, however, the catastrophe happens again.

> Please be the beef, please beef, pleasure is not wailing. Please beef, please be carved clear, please be a case of consideration.
> Search a neglect. A sale, any greatness is a stall and there is no memory, there is no clear collection.
> A satin sight, what is a trick, no trick is mountainous and the color, all the rush is in the blood.
> Bargaining for a little, bargaining for a touch, a liberty, an estrangement, a characteristic turkey. (37)

A request is issued that the beef "be carved." (The command takes a mystifying form: some unidentified scapegoat is asked to *be* the beef, and then to "be carved.") Thereupon, there is a "rush" of "blood."

The features of the oedipal, or sacrificial, break are collapsed into these sentences. "Carved" or sliced beef has no inside; the place of secret change has been invaded. An object "carved clear" falls into distinct sections—a figure for the imposition of stable categories. Things are for "sale" again: the contractual world of the father is back in place. In fact, sex is for sale, as in the instance of women turned "sales ladies": there is "bargaining for a touch." (Perhaps women, then, were the addressees of the command, "be the beef.") Or maybe bargaining is being substituted "for a touch": a market mentality replaces the immediacy of the body.

At the same time, a repression occurs: "there is no memory, there is no clear collection [recollection?]." These words recall those used for the oedipal repression in "Objects": "no precise no past" (29). Again, the figure that looms over the moment of repression is the phallus:

> Please spice, please no name, place a whole weight, sink into a standard rising, raise a circle, choose a right around, make the resonance accounted and gather green any collar.
> To bury a slender chicken, to raise an old feather, to surround a garland and to bake a pole splinter. (37–38)

The paternal insignia that in *G.M.P.* took the form of a "boiling tree" here is a baked tree: "bake a pole splinter." Stein's imagery is so consistent, even in its peculiarities, as to lead me to suspect a private symbolism knowingly repeated from one text to the next.

Like the old pole of "Objects," the pole in "Roastbeef" erects itself over a covered-up body. "To bury a slender chicken, to raise an old feather": as a chicken goes down, a feather goes up. The old feather may be another version of the phallus-pole, for a feather is the hollow, sticklike part of the bird. This weightless thing is exalted to prominence while the body, the chicken itself, is put underground. An *old* feather moreover is a dead feather—perhaps a quill, a reincarnation of the peeled pencil of "Objects." Or indeed one could hear in "old feather" a reference to the quill-wielder himself, the old father.

The symbolic order (fixed in place by the paternal quill) erects itself at the cost of a repression of drive, of matter—or simply of body, which is the "chicken" that gets buried. Simultaneously, the phallus becomes what the same passage refers to as "a standard rising"; it is applied as the "standard" of sexual difference, defining men as presence and women as absence. What "sink[s] into" or beneath this "standard" is then the womb, devalued or made invisible; the chicken (female, full of eggs) is the mother, buried again as she was in the guise of a chest at the end of "Objects."

The final paragraph of "Roastbeef" then replays the murder scenario of "Objects," and names it sacrifice:

> There is coagulation in cold and there is none in prudence. Something is preserved and the evening is long and the colder spring has sudden shadows in a sun. All the stain is tender and lilacs really lilacs are disturbed. Why is the perfect reëstablishment practiced and prized, why is it composed. The result the pure result is juice and size and baking and exhibition and nonchalance and sacrifice and volume and a section in division and the surrounding recognition and horticulture and no murmur. This is a result. There is no superposition and circumstance, there is hardness and a reason and the rest and remainder. There is no delight and no mathematics. (39)

The magical transformation is over. The beef has been cooked, carved, and now abandoned to "coagulation" on the platter. The animal's body is perfectly "cold" and dead. Process too is dead; coagulation replaces the "turning" of the earlier section. As happens often in *Tender Buttons*, Stein gives the scene an unsettled affect: "sacrifice" is terrible, but the image of "coagulation" is both amusing and disgusting. She is having a laugh at the paternal order, even as she describes its horrors.

The "sudden shadows in a sun" attest to the presence of the paternal code, which subjects a confused perceptual field to polarities of black and white—as in the similar sentence in *G.M.P.*, "all the shade is in the sun" (256). Furthermore, "there is hardness and a reason." Reason, the form of thought speciously severed from the body, *is* mental "hardness." Its fixed categories are the consequence of a repression. The "sun" (the father, but also the light of reason) shines only at the expense of consigning something to the shadows: drive, unconscious process, and changing matter.

Yet those things are still there, as "the rest and remainder." A few vocabularies are superimposed: that of cooking; that of sacrifice; and that of mathematics. A math problem has reached completion, leaving "the pure result." "There is no delight and no mathematics" any longer, because mathematics—with its functions of addition, division, and so forth—has yielded its "result" and hence ceased as delightful process.[17] Nonetheless, "there is" still the "remainder," something left over after the final calculations—everything that in *G.M.P.* Stein called "left over bundles." Process never quite succumbs to code. From the remainder, the forces that reverse sacrifice will come.

"The result . . . is . . . exhibition and nonchalance and sacrifice and volume and a section in division and the surrounding recognition and horticulture and no murmur." The sacrifice occurs; then, as in "Objects," it is erased. The paternal "volume," or book, subjects things to a dominating code, a "surrounding recognition." The word "volume" might also refer to the loud noise of the sacrifice. Yet the sacrifice is thereupon silenced; the volume goes down. Suddenly there is "no murmur"—no complaint, no whisper of what has happened. "No murmur" could also signal a repression

---

[17]For this interpretation of "mathematics," I am indebted to a seminar paper by Nancy Jacobson.

of the aural to make way for a quasi-visual mode of thought. This sentence associates sacrifice with "exhibition." Sight is the one sense that does not depend on bodily contact with its object; to approach the world, then, in a detached, hyperrational way is to approach it as if through sight, as against smell, taste, hearing, or touch.

The sacrifice of body no sooner happens than it is suppressed. As in "Objects," which ended with a meadow, killing is now masked as mere "horticulture." This is (as I interpret these poems) the last instance of perfected sacrifice in *Tender Buttons*. From this point, the "remainder"—drives, matter, and body—will leak back in.

By merely regressing to the archaic forms of thought that in "Objects" were seen put under, "Roastbeef" sets the scene for a repetition of the sacrifice. Regression, in fact, will not move us beyond the cycle of sacrifice. "Spying" will.

The Return of the Mother's Body

Some time ago I left "Vegetable," the crucifixion poem, suspended in midsentence. The poem appears not in the earlier, sacrificial part of *Tender Buttons* but in the present section, "Food," where sacrifice is reversed. "Vegetable" does begin with crucifixion, but then takes a peculiar turn. Here is the sentence in the middle of which I paused: "It was a cress a crescent a cross and an unequal scream, it was upslanting, it was radiant and reasonable with little ins and red" (53). These words, as I have suggested, rehearse the crucifixion, the killing that erases matter and exalts autonomous reason. Yet the sentence goes on to end with that odd tag: "with little ins and red."

The cross has a little inside; it has red in it. (Or, perhaps, Christ's wounds are little red inner places.) The crucifixion may be a sign of our radiant and reasonable contract with the Father, but a particular sort of reader can appropriate the image and turn it inside out. If the wood has "little ins," it has an interior, which is red. It has a body. More than that, it has a womb.

For the words "little ins and red" are part of Stein's symbolism for the female body. In "Shoes" (from "Objects"), she uses similar phrases to describe admiring or touching Alice Toklas's body: "A shallow hole rose on red, a shallow hole in and in this makes ale less [Alice]. It shows shine" (26). Alice's body is a red rose, which can be entered: one can go "in." So also, the words "shoes" and "shows" punningly refer to Alice's *chose*, French slang for vagina.

What the sentence about the cross ultimately does, with its phrase "little ins and red," is to suggest that one can approach the cross in the way one approaches another person's body. The cross has a red place, which we can go into. So reinterpreted, the cross symbolizes not mastery or bodiless reason but our ability to encounter the world through touch. In a word, the symbol of the cross is greater than its sacrificial meaning.

Stein is initiating us in a creative rereading—a different thing from regression. She does not jettison the symbols she inherits from the Western fathers and from their governing text, the Bible (which in fact her earlier poem about the "Book" may have been referring to). Instead, she decodes the text, unlocking the feminine and material powers it still preserves.

Her notion that the cross, or Christ on the cross, contains a womb may sound unusual to some readers, but this response to the cross has a long history. Crucifixion, like any powerful theological image, is overdetermined and can be read and responded to in a variety of ways. The crucifixion does have sacrificial meanings—involving a contract that demands a death in payment for humanity's sins—but it also has countersacrificial possibilities. Here are two uses of crucifixion, from different sources, which bring out the competing facets of the image. The first, as an example of what might be termed sacrificial thinking, is Saint Paul's exhortation to the Galatians (5:16, 24): "Walk by the Spirit, and do not gratify the desires of the flesh. . . . those who belong to Jesus Christ have crucified the flesh with its passions and desires." As in Stein's sacrificial poems, crucifixion marks the break (here, of spirit) from the body. Paul uses crucifixion as an image and a model for our repression of the flesh.

But the following is a different reading of the crucifixion, which gives the image the opposite of a sacrificial or body-suppressing meaning and anticipates Stein's cross with its "little ins and red." It is from a meditation by the Monk of Farne, one of the fourteenth-century clerics whose writings Carolyn Bynum analyzes in *Jesus as Mother*. Like a number of Bynum's subjects, he thinks of himself as loving the crucified Christ as a baby loves its mother's body. "Christ our Lord," he writes, "opens his side to give us suck; and though it is blood he offers us to suck we believe that it is health-giving and sweeter than honey and the honey-comb. Do not wean me, good Jesus, from the breasts of thy consolation."[18] The wound in Christ's side becomes a breast, and the faithful are the suckling infants.

The writer makes no sharp division between bodily and spiritual desires; he freely compares his desire for Christ to a child's desire for the mother's breast. Christ turns into a taste, a bodily tang. Julian of Norwich uses the same imagery: "Jesus, our true Mother, feeds us not with milk but with himself, opening his side to us."[19] Like Stein after her, she even thinks of entering the wound-breast, almost making it a womb-breast: "Our tender Mother Jesus simply leads us into his blessed breast through his open side" (170). For there is such a thing as a spiritual longing for a mother's body, as well as for a father's law, and the image of the crucifixion can be so interpreted as to answer this alternative need.

In Stein's sentence, a second thing happens, a different thing. The phallus is given a body. The cross becomes something more than a dead tree; it has an inside, with red: it contains life. When the living organ is turned into a symbol of men's superiority to women, it is disembodied, or killed, and becomes itself an instrument of killing, a pencil that chokes. Stein sees the cross as an instance of this "old pole," sign of paternal dominion. But at the end of her sentence, the pole is given "little ins and red": it has an inside, blood, and a body. The phallus itself is de-crucified.

Stein thinks of herself not simply as reading the image of the cross but (unlike the Monk of Farne and Julian of Norwich) as subversively rereading it, perhaps because in her view the dominant tendency within Christianity, in spite of alternative strains, has been to exalt spirit over body, matter, and mother. As this

[18]"Meditations," quoted in Carolyn Bynum, *Jesus as Mother: Studies in the Spirituality of the High Middle Ages* (Berkeley: University of California Press, 1982), p. 152.

[19]Julian of Norwich, *Revelations of Divine Love*, trans. Clifton Wolters (New York: Penguin, 1966), p. 168, hereafter cited in the text.

poem concludes, we find Stein reflecting on the significance of the rediscovered body or mother in the cross. "News. News capable of glees, cut in shoes, belike under pump of wide chalk, all this combing." The tree brings us news, for the restored meaning of the tree *is* the good news, the gospel: that is what is meant by "news capable of glees." Stein has revised the meaning of *gospel:* the good news is not quite that Christ came to die for us but that mother and matter outlive that killing. This tree gives not eternal life, as part of a bargain, but an experience in the present moment that is at once sensual and spiritual. Stein's deviation from the theology of redemption will be clear in some other poems, as she questions the entire notion of transcendence.

Also glee-giving is the very possibility of revisionary reading. That is how I understand the words, "under pump of wide chalk, all this combing."[20] The gospel's deep meaning is "under" the "chalk," beneath the surface of the written word. We slip "under" the manifest meaning ourselves, as we comb the text for latent meanings. That is the textual combing the poem has just performed; these last words are Stein's way of saying, what I just did, what I just discovered, was fun.

Combing could also be a code word for sexual touching, an image for running a hand along a lover's body; similarly, it could suggest orgasm, or "coming." In other words, the phrase "all this combing" punningly refers both to the subversive fun of textual probing and to the transgressive fun of an erotic life with another woman. The spirituality and the sexuality of the poem are of a piece. Both revisionary reading and loving a woman lead to a single discovery, that the female body survives sacrifice. In this part of *Tender Buttons* generally, a body—an archetypal mother's or a real lover's—emerges to subvert the male script that tried to reduce women's anatomy to an absence, or something to be used, or something to be ashamed of.

"Cut in shoes": a synonym for textual combing is "cutting in," piercing through the surface of the paternal script. The first sentences of the poem used the same word: "What is cut. What is cut

[20]In the more widely available edition of *Tender Buttons* in *Selected Writings,* "pump" is misprinted as "plump."

by it. What is cut by it in." Those sentences prepare for the movement of the poem as a whole, from the plain cut of sacrifice to the
cutting-in, or subversive reading, that undoes sacrifice. The phrase
"cut in shoes" links creative misreading and lesbian eroticism
again, for it suggests (using the same pun as the poem "Shoes"
does), "cut into [that is, place something in] the *chose*." (Alternatively, the "cut" is also itself a reference to the vagina.) Finally,
the chalk is "wide": "under pump of wide chalk, all this combing."
The chalk, or the received text, is not immaterial. The right sort of
reading gives it a body. The poem "pump[s]" life into a biblical
image or, alternatively, turns the image itself into an irrigating
pump. *Pump* is also a colloquialism for "heart"; the chalk or text,
like the cross, now gets a pulse, a heartbeat. The life that fills the
pump-text, moreover, is masculine and feminine at the same time,
since a "pump of wide chalk," in the (alternative) sense of a pump
that emits chalky fluid, could equally well be breast and penis.

Stein reveals the cross to be a container of life and also a lively
symbol. As presented in this poem, the symbol of the cross eludes
rational control; "it was" many things, some of them contradictory.
The polyvalence of the symbol is its life. The poem teases meanings out of the cross not by logical exegesis but by a series of
compressed, mysterious images. Something is in the tree—"little
ins and red"—but the meaning of that phrase is mobile. Or—what
amounts to the same thing—the symbol of the cross is brought
back to life by a poetic language that stimulates process in the
reader's mind. I am tempted to reread the phrase "cut in shoes" as
a pun for "cut and choose." Active readers cut into the paternal
text and choose meanings—just as Stein provokes her reader to cut
into her own text and to choose meanings for its difficult, concentrated sentences. A sentence from "Rooms" might similarly allude
to interpretive "choice" or reading-as-translation: "translate more
than translate the authority, show the choice" (76).

"Vegetable," like much of *Tender Buttons*, seems to me profoundly gnostic—not in its metaphysics (quite the contrary) but in
its hermeneutics. Gnosticism was a historical movement associated
with a repudiation of matter, but gnosticism is also a temperament,
which has much in common with Stein's intellectual turns in *Tender
Buttons*. A gnostic thinks of received doctrine, or the biblical text,

as distorting but secretly containing the truth. Readers who are party to the secret know how to read the text subversively to get back its spiritual meaning. Stein rereads a received image, seeing that it conceals but contains a saving wisdom. The phallus contains a mother, if we know how to get her back from the symbol.

This feminist gnosticism—yet let us call it "hermeticism" instead, so as not to confuse it with historical gnosticism, which after all had an opposite metaphysics—is the most surprising thing I have uncovered in Stein. It is original, often witty, and unlike anything else in its era. In some ways Stein's spirituality is similar to that of H.D., whose iconography and ethics are similarly directed toward a "flowering," or reembodying, "of the rod."[21] But H.D.'s poetry, with its more straightforward mode of expression, does not force the reader into the position of a hermetic reader as Stein's poetry does. Just as Stein spies secrets buried in the patriarchal texts, she buries her own anti-patriarchal secrets in a text just pliant enough to invite us to try to retrieve her meanings. And since each reader of this polysemous text will recover different meanings, each interpretation amounts to a creative and individual act, a revision.

Stein's feminist rereadings resemble those of Mary Daly in our decade. "The Tree of Life," Daly writes, "has been replaced by the necrophilic symbol of a dead body hanging on dead wood. The Godfather insatiably demands more sacrifices, and the fundamental sacrifices of sadospiritual religion are female." According to Daly, we can nonetheless still get the tree-woman back from the cross: "The Sacred Tree . . . is the Goddess. . . . This Cosmic Tree, the living Source of radiant energy/be-ing, is the deep Background of the christian cross, the dead wood rack to which a dying body is fastened with nails."[22]

Like Daly, Stein finds the woman in the "background" of the cross. Many of the poems in "Food" rest on a revision of a biblical or liturgical image: cross, fish, serpent, the mass. The poet's mind takes a "left hop," a sinister leap (55). The outlawed knowledge that she offers locates the body, or the woman, concealed in the

[21]See H.D., "The Flowering of the Rod," Trilogy, in Collected Poems, 1912–1944, ed. Louis L. Martz (New York: New Directions, 1944), pp. 575–612.
[22]Daly, Gyn/Ecology, pp. 17–18, 79.

symbols of the fathers. Read transgressively, these symbols illuminate the mysteries of blood, body, and matter. These poems envision patriarchal symbols as secretly containing a body and, along
with that, a saving insight. Read aright, the received word instructs
us in a "new mercy," an ethics of tenderness to replace that of
mastery (53). The sacred symbols, although their meaning has historically been deformed to serve a sacrificial order, still contain the
power to destabilize sacrifice by bringing us into fleshly communion with living things.

The word *excreate*, which Stein coins in this section of *Tender
Buttons*, suggests how radical she perceives her revision of tradition to be. Unlike the medieval mystics who honored the feminine
aspects of God, Stein believes that in order to recover the lost
feminine principle one must challenge an entire misogynistic tradition. Hence in her recovery of the mother she uses words suggestive of reversal, deviation, and unmaking. "Orange In" is the
poem in which she invents the word *excreate*:

> ORANGE IN.
> Go lack go lack use to her.
> Cocoa and clear soup and oranges and oat-meal.
> Whist bottom whist close, whist clothes, woodling.
> Cocoa and clear soup and oranges and oat-meal.
> Pain soup, suppose it is question, suppose it is butter, real is,
> real is only, only excreate, only excreate a no since.
> A no, a no since, a no since when, a no since when since, a
> no since when since a no since when since, a no since, a no
> since when since, a no since, a no, a no since a no since, a no
> since, a no since. (58)

"*Go* lack go lack use *to her*." As Stein writes three poems later, in
"A Centre in a Table," "re letter and read her" (58). As we "go to
her" or (there) "read her"—recovering an "orange in" or a maternal orig-in—we must re-letter, learn to spell in a new way. But in
order to remake, one must unmake, ex-create, or dismantle the
existing order. "Pain soup, suppose it is question": Stein, in re-
suscitating "her," questions paternal law and thus issues "a no" to
the fathers. She "excreate[s] a no since," creates innocence by ex-

creating, perhaps in the sense of undoing the sacrificial crime that buried the body.

Here, as in "Vegetable," Stein grounds the spiritual in the bodily. "Real is only, only excreate, only excreate a no since": Stein's artistic creation is continuous with excretion, coming (as if) from the body. Also, *"real* is only, only excreate." There is no objective reality, which we neutrally survey; instead, we all differently make the real for ourselves, in a way that is somehow continuous with our intestinal or embodied experience. Stein's awareness of the connection between lowly anatomical functions and higher experiences is of a piece with her hermetic act of looking into the background of the text of the fathers; behind the screen of patriarchal thinking, there is a body, one's own. She subversively reinterprets the theological term *innocence,* to mean a return to an excremental source.

I have made comparisons to medieval mysticism and to gnosticism, but for a source of Stein's revisionary theology we must look to the intellectual context of her early adulthood. I suspect that a stimulus for Stein's woman-centered spirituality was the feminist theology of the late nineteenth century, in particular the *Woman's Bible* of Elizabeth Cady Stanton. If so, we are seeing another instance of delayed influence, just as at a previous moment in her career Stein suddenly brought William James's psychological theories into her fiction, twelve years after having studied those theories in college.

The year in which Stanton's book would have been an unavoidable part of Stein's intellectual milieu was 1897, when Stein moved to Baltimore to begin her medical studies at Johns Hopkins. An important event for American feminism in the previous year—and an event that must still have figured into the conversations of the intellectually and politically sophisticated women medical students at Johns Hopkins—was the twenty-eighth annual Woman Suffrage Convention, held in Washington, D.C.[23] There, Stanton's *Woman's Bible,* published in 1895, had been an object of major controversy. The convention delegates, fearing that any association of

[23]Mary A. Hill, *Charlotte Perkins Gilman: The Making of a Radical Feminist, 1860–1896* (Philadelphia: Temple University Press, 1980), p. 260.

their cause with the *Woman's Bible* (whose author was of course a major figure in the suffrage struggle) would alienate potential supporters, passed a formal resolution disavowing any connection to the *Woman's Bible*, but only after heated debates in which Charlotte Perkins Stetson (later Gilman), among others, "spoke forcefully in support of Stanton's book."[24]

A reason that I believe Stein is likely to have been aware of the *Woman's Bible* and its fortunes is that just after arriving at medical school she became quite interested in the ideas of Charlotte Perkins Stetson. In 1898 Stein gave before a group of Baltimore women a speech called "The Value of College Education for Women," whose theses about the economic bases of women's oppression were derived directly from "a book of Mrs. Stetsons [*sic*] recently published"—that is, from *Women and Economics* by Charlotte Perkins Stetson.[25] Stein's speech, like its source, makes economic rather than theological arguments about the origins of women's oppression; Stetson herself was not to write her feminist religious tract, *His Religion and Hers* (in some ways comparable to the *Woman's Bible*), for another twenty-five years.[26] Yet Stein's heavy reliance on Stetson's ideas for her speech suggests at least that she was aware of current developments in feminist thinking; and her evident admiration for Stetson's work leads me to wonder whether she was aware of Stetson's larger intellectual life and commitments, including her enthusiasm for the controversial *Woman's Bible*.

I am thinking tentatively in terms of an influence because Stanton's *Woman's Bible*, quite like *Tender Buttons* some seventeen years after it, looks through the biblical text to recover images of a divine female presence. Here for example are Stanton's thoughts on the account in *Genesis* (1:26–28) of the creation of Adam and Eve ("And God said, Let us make man in our own image, after our likeness. . . . So God created man in his *own* image, in the image of God created he him; male and female created he them"):

> Here is the sacred historian's first account of the advent of woman; a simultaneous creation of both sexes, in the image of God. It is evident

[24]Hill, p. 263, and see generally pp. 262–63.
[25]Bridgman, p. 36; Stein, "The Value of College Education for Women," YCAL, p. 3.
[26]See Hill, p. 263.

from the language that there was consultation in the Godhead, and that the masculine and feminine elements were equally represented. Scott in his commentaries says, "this consultation of the Gods is the origin of the doctrine of the trinity." But instead of three male personages, as generally represented, a Heavenly Father, Mother, and Son would seem more rational.[27]

Stanton reinterprets the creation account to emphasize the parity of Eve with Adam. More than that, she sees the deity as a composite of paternal and maternal elements: the idea of the Trinity, in fact, although it has traditionally yielded "three male personages," can be reread so as to include a divine mother, the Holy Spirit, obscured by misogynistic traditions that have neutered or masculinized her but still available to those who know how to read the text aright. (This idea of Stanton's is not historically unique; it is anticipated by the gnostic *Apocryphon of John,* which, as Elaine Pagels writes, "concludes that the feminine 'Person' conjoined with the Father and Son must be the Mother.")[28]

Let us turn to a poem in *Tender Buttons* called "Chicken," which reads, "Alas a dirty word, alas a dirty third alas a dirty third, alas a dirty bird" (54). A bird who traditionally is a third is the Holy Spirit, the last person of the Trinity. Yet Stein's bird is also "alas": a lass (and perhaps, at the same time, Alice again). Hence she is a chicken, a female bird, rather than a genderless dove. (The constellation bird-third-alas reappears in *Four Saints in Three Acts,* a repetition that cannot be accidental: "Pigeons on the grass alas"; "He [Saint Ignatius?] had heard of a third and he asked about it it was a magpie in the sky."[29] I am thus with those who see some sort of "Trinitarian significance"[30] in the bird[s] in *Four Saints,* even though Stein's magpie and her pigeons are in some respects antithetical beings.)

[27]Elizabeth Cady Stanton, *The Original Feminist Attack on the Bible (The Woman's Bible)* (New York: Arno Press, 1974), p. 14, hereafter cited in the text. The Scott to whom Stanton refers is Thomas Scott, English clergyman and biblical commentator, whose four-volume commentary on the Bible appeared 1788–1792.

[28]Elaine Pagels, *The Gnostic Gospels* (New York: Random House, 1979), p. 62.

[29]Gertrude Stein, *Four Saints in Three Acts,* in *Operas and Plays* (Paris: Plain Edition, 1932), p. 36.

[30]See Bridgman's discussion of this view (from which he mildly dissents), p. 183.

Patriarchal thinking, Stein's poem suggests, has demoted the bird-mother to third rank in the Trinity and masked her gender. The genderlessness of the Holy Spirit means that mother (perhaps) has become "a dirty word."[31] Yet the dove, though marginalized, still marks the mother's place; we can always turn her back into a hen, a lass.

It is odd that Stein became so interested in Christian themes and symbols, having been herself Jewish. She wrote *Tender Buttons* while traveling in Spain with Toklas, and perhaps the powerful images of Catholic worship there affected her, intersecting now with her feminism in such a way as to revive her earlier awareness of feminist Christian thinking from the Johns Hopkins years. Her notebooks suggest, further, that there had been a period in her more recent life when she had been drawn to the Christian Science of her sister-in-law Sally Stein:

> Three stages [of her own development], early just being of the earth, then ethical . . . —then experience in Spain when got the awful depression of repetition in history, then realising that I was not a pragmatist . . . then realise, that aesthetic has become the whole of me, not so sweet as I was or virtuous, *and then through christian science realising gullible through a certain fear like Mike* [her brother, Sally's husband] but au fond like the Jew in Auctioneer [?] but I did see him. (NB 14.7, emphasis added)

Whatever Stein's circuit "through christian science" had involved, and however intensely or faintly Sally's religion had impressed her, it sounds as if her religious feeling at the time had been rather joyless ("through a certain fear"). In *Two*, however, which Stein wrote after this notebook entry and before *Tender Buttons*, she drew an admiring portrait of Sally, which used a Christian vocabulary ecstatically:

> She with anticipating praying, she with augmenting dispersion, she is the one having a connection that expressing is the thing that rising again has risen, and rising is rising and will be having come to be risen. . . . She is the anticipation of expression having immaculate

[31] I thank William Veeder for this interpretation.

conception. She is the anticipation of crossing. She is the anticipation of regeneration. . . . She is the rising having been arisen. She is the convocation of anticipation and acceptance. She is the lamb and the lion. She is the leaven of reverberation. She is the complication of receiving, she is the articulation of forgetting, she is the expression of indication, she is the augmentation of condensing, she is the inroad of releasing.[32]

Around the figure of an archetypal "she," Stein clusters words associated with Mary ("immaculate conception") but also with Christ ("regeneration," "arisen"). The unnamed "she" of *Two*, through whom these divine powers course, is the prototype for the mother-in-the-cross and the bird-lass of *Tender Buttons*.

Mother/Father

Stanton's *Woman's Bible* may have served as an inspiration for Stein's revisionary thinking in *Tender Buttons*. Yet the sheer gusto of Stein's "excreation," or her subversive dirty-thinking, sets her text apart from Stanton's. The very word *excreate*—to spend a last moment on it—leads me to wonder whether, like some of Stein's earlier texts, *Tender Buttons* has anal meanings and motivations. Although the poems of *Tender Buttons* are often consciously erotic, their eroticism seems to be located not so much in the pleasures of the anus as in those of the mouth (the muncher) and the genitals (the *chose*). But there are occasional bawdy references to excremental processes, as in "A BROWN. A brown which is not liquid not more so is relaxed and yet there is a change, a news is pressing" (25). The phrase "A brown which is not liquid" suggests, of course, a brown solid, one that "is relaxed" in the sense of being produced by muscular relaxation. "There is a change," in the sense that the intestines have changed food into waste, or that what was inside the body is now outside. So, "a news is pressing": a-nus is pressing, or (thereafter) a scrap of news-paper presses against the body, undergoing its own surprising change from reading matter into material for the sewer.

So much is clear if one takes this poem as an isolated unit. One

[32]Stein, *Two*, pp. 107–8.

might pair it with a passage in "Rooms" about observing and using a toilet: "looking into this place and seeing a chair did that mean relief, it did, it certainly did not cause constipation" (72). Still, I wish to spend a moment asking whether the excretory image, from one or two poems, can tell us something about Stein's practice in *Tender Buttons* as a whole. She coins the word *excreate*: is her entire act of artistic creation linked to excretion? Just so, "a news is pressing": is the pressing or urgent news that she herself offers in the text as a whole analogous, in some way, to the operations of a-news, or anus? And finally, is there any link between all this and the "*news* capable of glees," her act of spiritual discovery?

The poem "A Brown" tells of "a change." Excremental processes are interesting (to children and, normally unconsciously, to adults) not just for their pleasurable physical component but also for the sense of omnipotence that follows from the activity of digestive change, as if one imagined one could magically change everything to excrement. Janine Chasseguet-Smirgel, in an essay I alluded to earlier, identifies such a fantasy of digestive omnipotence as belonging to "a 'perverse core' latent within each one of us," which can become manifest in certain works of art.[33] Chasseguet-Smirgel describes the excremental fantasy thus: "I think this recurring theme [in Sade] of the *changing of forms*—of man's ability not to annihilate things but to dissolve and metamorphose them—after breaking down the molecules, means that *all things* must revert to chaos, the original chaos that may be identified with excrement" (295). These words describe what Sade's heroes do with their bodies, but they could also be used to describe what *Tender Buttons* does with language. Words, as Stein uses them in *Tender Buttons*, are not fixed, determined, and exterior to their user. Instead, they are subject to appropriation, incorporation, and change. A punning, ambiguous literary practice makes words mobile, "dissolv-[ing] and metamorphos[ing]" them, as if the text could digestively transmute everyday language into something else.

To use a local example, Stein's pun "a news" reorganizes the syllable *news*, changing it, surprisingly, into part of the word "anus." The syllable becomes semisolid; its meaning is halfway to

---

[33]Chasseguet-Smirgel, "Perversion and the Universal Law," p. 293.

turning into something else, as if in the process of passing through the digestive tract. Chasseguet-Smirgel writes of "man's ability . . . to dissolve and metamorphose [things]—after breaking down the molecules." The other pun I have recently noticed in *Tender Buttons*, "excreate," performs its own semantic metamorphosis: as a neologism, it disintegrates two words from the standard lexicon—excrete and create—and uses their "molecules" to piece together a new word. It exemplifies the gut-speak to which it refers.

I have been describing "Food" as thinking past the mind-body dualism, turning the cross, for example, from a static symbol into a body one can enter and touch. The linguistic practice that corresponds to the embodied thinking of poems like "Vegetable" and "Orange In"—and Stein's linguistic practice throughout *Tender Buttons*—is an "excreatory" wordplay that uses language for thinking but at the same time for quasi-bodily gratification, by tearing words from their normal contexts and subjecting them to digestive change in what amounts to a textual body-cauldron. Stein's spirituality is anchored in the most mundane and commonly devalued bodily processes. Medieval mystics wrote of tasting Christ's body; Stein, quite unusually (although along a similar spiritual axis), imagines herself excreating innocence, or excreting a strange new paradise.

But if she sometimes alludes to her practice as excremental, she more often pictures it as oriented toward a lost mother. (On the other hand, these two ideas are themselves connected, as alternative ways of thinking of a return to pre-phallic origins.) A woman's body is what sacrifice makes invisible. As sacrificial thinking is unsettled in "Food" as a whole, a woman's body is located, recovered, and touched. "Food" is filled with images of finding a mother's body. Many poems have titles that suggest fertility or nurturing—titles like "Milk," "Eggs," and "Chicken." One of two poems called "Milk" reads as follows: "Climb up in sight climb in the whole utter needles and a guess a whole guess is hanging. Hanging hanging" (47). The piece envisions a climb into the udder, or the mother's breast. The title, "Milk," and the references to something "hanging" help to make us hear "utter" as "udder." By another pun, we hear "climb in the hole," or the womb. And it is just possible that the final words, "hanging hanging," are meant to suggest "killing killing." Stein hangs hanging, does away with sacrifice, by recovering the udder that sacrifice erased.

At the same time, the return to the udder has its own "dirty" meaning, for it amounts to a violation of the incest prohibition and a subversion of the phallic order that earlier sustained itself by tabooing the mother's body. Yet "udder" is spelled "utter." The poem does not describe an unmediated return to the breast. We recover the udder by *utterance*, by putting words together in particular ways. For as adults we can find the preoedipal mother only in and through the symbolic.[34] The poem, therefore, combines images suggestive of the archaic urge to suckle, such as milk and udder, with references to speech and intellect—"utter," "guess," "in sight" (insight). This piece refers to a form of thought that synthesizes primitive and advanced mental functions. The phrase "utter needles" suggests a kind of speech that is physically felt; utterance takes on a quality of oral aggression. Such speech is palpable; it has the feel of needles in the mouth. Yet it retains an attachment to the intellectual and the symbolic, to utterance. The act of uttering needles hangs between the presymbolic—the mental phase in which words are materially felt—and the symbolic.

The revival of the material dimension of speech amounts to a recovery of the mother within language. "Milk" conveys the idea of an udder-speech, a mother tongue. The presymbolic is the udder of language because it forms a link to the preoedipal mother. It also itself resembles an udder or a womb; it is a pocket of bodily richness within language, normally obscured by the signifying function of words. In "Cups," which appears in "Food" as well, Stein uses (as will be recalled) an imagery of the presymbolic as a womb, "a stir and a behave"—astir and a beehive (49).

In these poems from *Tender Buttons*, a new spirituality has been added to the linguistic-familial perspective of *G.M.P.*, a text that traced the daughter-poet's recovery of the "left over bundles" of maternal or presymbolic language. That same scenario plays itself out here, but with an added dimension, so that not only linguistic

---

[34]See, generally, Kristeva's discussion of "the introduction of jouissance into and through language" in *Revolution in Poetic Language*, pp. 72–85.

jouissance but also hermetic reading represents a point of access to the lost mother. Both hermeticism and wordplay, moreover, open up choice and mobility in language. Verbal "hanging," either in the hermetic or in the psychoanalytic-linguistic sense, hangs hanging. Polyvalence, directed toward either of these two ends, undoes the earlier murder of mother and of body. In fact, the very choice Stein's words always give us between unlocking their possible messages (the hermetic option) and enjoying their material qualities (the option of *jouissance*) makes our reading process mobile in a way that it would not be if the text were either of these things singly, either a coded work with fixed correspondences between sign and "message" or, at the opposite extreme, simply an exploration of the properties of the linguistic medium.

"Milk," then, intimates a liberated, postsacrificial thinking, one that hangs hanging. The same words, however—"hanging. Hanging hanging"—might be taken to mean simply: "killing. Killing, killing." While one possible reading shows sacrifice undone, another shows sacrifice just repeating itself. The point can be generalized: "Food" describes sacrifice giving way to revival, yet the section is punctuated by allusions to killing. In "Objects," the story of the victory of the father was crosscut by a return of the presymbolic drives associated with the mother. Here, in turn, when the mother finally comes back into view, her figure is traversed by the old hanging.

A nearby phrase has the same ambiguity: "silence the noon and murder flies" (46). The noon is the time of the father-sun's dominion; to "silence the noon" would be to overcome the father. When one silences him, "murder flies": the paternal sacrifice disappears. On the other hand, "murder flies," if one takes "murder" instead as the verb, means "kill insects." So interpreted, the phrase suggests that murder has hardly ceased. Another piece is as ambiguous: "CHICKEN. Stick stick call then, stick stick sticking, sticking with a chicken. Sticking in a extra succession, sticking in" (54). Is this poem about "sticking with" a chicken—remaining faithful, perhaps, to the chicken-mother who was buried in "Roastbeef"? Or is it about "sticking" a chicken, piercing and killing her once again? Stein so layers the poem that neither interpretation can stabilize.

These pieces describe a state of mind poised between the symbolic and the body, and hence between killing and revival. Stein, although honoring the body, is still herself implicated in the symbolic order, by virtue of being a poet using words carefully. Her artistic practice depends on a symbolic use of words. *Tender Buttons* does not "regress" to a purely bodily speech; it is not nonsense, in the sense of nonsignificant syllables. Nonsense, or sheer word-music, would not be susceptible to interpretation. The poetry of *Tender Buttons*, instead, is delicately suspended between texture and meaning.[35] Because it does not cease to combine words in meaningful ways, it is still implicated in sacrifice.

Thus, despite a strong maternal identification, Stein retains an attachment to the phallus, symbol of paternal rule and, one might almost say, symbol of the symbolic. In "Food," even though this is the section in which paternal *dominion* ends, the newly unearthed maternal dimension of mental life does not overwhelm the paternal/symbolic; instead, it starts an oscillation.

A pair of poems identically titled "Orange" claims the mother as an ideal "type" but finally retains an alliance with the father as well. The first of the poems metaphorically associates orange with mother. "ORANGE. Why is a feel oyster an egg stir. Why is it orange centre" (57). The words "oyster" and "stir" recall the passages in "Cups" that compare the female body to an oyster and associate its interior with "a stir" (49). The image of the orange now acquires the same associations, for an orange is another round thing with a hidden, soft, seed-filled interior. The womb-orange is an "egg stir," a place of hatching. "Egg stir" also puns on "extra," making the association again between the womb and the extra, or the presymbolic surplus in language (as in the sentence, "Any extra way is the way of speaking").[36]

But the second "Orange" poem positions itself ambiguously with respect to this orange-mother. It reads, "ORANGE. A type oh oh new new not no not knealer knealer of old show beefsteak, neither neither" (57). The first words (breathlessly) exalt the mother-orange as "A type oh oh new," a new type or model to replace the phallus

[35]Cf. Schmitz, *Of Huck*, p. 178.
[36]Stein, "Scenes," *GP* 121.

that dominated the sacrificial phase. The father for his part seems to be disclaimed: "no not knealer knealer of old show beefsteak." "Old . . . beefsteak" is an image (as in "Roastbeef") for matter made lifeless, cooked or thoroughly symbolized by the paternal order. "Old *show* beefsteak" also stands as the opposite of *"feel oyster"* in the companion poem; the father is associated with an optical, detached mode of perception, which stands against the tactile and sensuous. More pointedly, "old show beefsteak" sounds like another disparaging epithet for the phallus itself, along the lines of "nice old pole"—that "old" thing, which has always to "show" itself about. The poem, then, says no to the beefsteak in all its aspects. "No not *knealer knealer* of old show beefsteak" could mean: no, one must not kneel before the father—and in the manuscript, Stein originally wrote "knee" for "knealer."[37]

Orange-mother seems to be utterly favored over beefsteak-father; yet two final words succinctly undo the opposition: "neither neither." The poem says, sequentially: orange, yes; beefsteak, no; yet—really—neither. The speaker finally embraces neither mother nor father as the one ideal type. The doubled phrase, "neither neither," has the same effect as the earlier "hanging hanging"; it suggests vacillation. It also suggests a slippage between the categories of mother and father—that is, a breakdown of the gender polarity altogether. The new orientation Stein develops is neither male nor female, but some new thing. As Catharine Stimpson has noted of Stein's images of gender in *Tender Buttons* generally, "Stein wishes to evade the trap of placing anything or anybody in a class, such as 'The Feminine' or 'The Masculine,' that values the set over the individual member, or that arranges sets in binary opposition to each other."[38]

Even though Stein does build up an association of the presymbolic with the mother, and of the symbolic with the father, the kind of thinking she considers genuinely "new" sets the two modes of thought into play with each other. In this poetry, presymbolic *jouissance*, instead of producing nonsense, makes itself felt as a rupture within symbolic language. Similarly, hermetic reading does not

---

[37]In YCAL.
[38]Stimpson, "Gertrude Stein and the Transposition of Gender," p. 15.

dismiss but "cuts" into the paternal text, subversively unfolding it.

So while these poems point toward a countersacrificial possibility, they retain connections to the "paternal" and sacrificial functions. Stein—and I would distinguish her from a contemporary like D. H. Lawrence, who in "The Man Who Died" imagines that a person can simply step off the cross—is re-knowing, in these poems, something that the Christian iconography on which she draws already "knows," namely, that there is no such thing as slipping past the sacrificial order and still remaining human. Stein partially unfixes sacrificial thinking and challenges its traditional misogyny; yet she sees that to the extent that one makes meanings at all, one is implicated in sacrifice. This is why images such as crucifixion interest Stein in the first place; they have historically served to underwrite oppressive dualisms, and yet they tell us something fundamental about ourselves. Where, then, does this leave *Tender Buttons* as a work of ethical imagination? What does it mean to think past sacrifice and still see oneself as a sacrificer?

Merciful Thinking

In its ethical aspect, *Tender Buttons* points to a replacement of repressive, purely sacrificial consciousness with a form of thought that knows its ties to the body. This wisdom, which bridges mind and matter, resists description from the perspectives of psychoanalysis and linguistics. It is part of the dimension of *Tender Buttons* that must be called spiritual.

Let us return to the poem "Milk": "Climb up in sight climb in the whole utter needles and a guess a whole guess is hanging. Hanging hanging" (47). The poem recommends an ascent—a climb *up*, to "in sight." This insight differs from "hardness and a reason," the state of mind proclaimed at the moment of sacrifice in "Roastbeef." Reason is hard because it dominates by imposing fixed categories from without, extremes of sun and shadow. The words *"in* sight" suggest by contrast a perception charged with inwardness. The phrase implies either an act of introspection or an intuitive fusion with a perceptual object. In either case, knowledge issues from sensitivity rather than from mastery.

Insight knows its own partiality. Instead of claiming authority, it limits itself to "a guess." Such thinking is like a climb in the udder because of its knowing dependency; it has something in common with drinking milk from a source outside the self. It is "hanging," or dependent, both on the autonomous object and on the perceiving subject's own mysterious "in"-sides.

The reason of the earlier, sacrificial scenes is, or seems, self-created. Pencil, book, and quill—raised and weightless—give the illusion of a realm of pure text or mind detached from matter. Yet the body is still present, even if screened; beneath quill or book, one always finds, as its support, a buried chicken or a chest. In "Food" we witness the collapse of the illusion of autonomous reason. "Milk" recovers the continuity between mind and matter; the in-sight it describes is a knowledge that begins with a "climb" back into the body.

The poems of "Food" mend the mind-body split and suggest what kind of thinking might follow from such a repair.

> DINNER.
> Not a little fit, not a little fit sun sat in shed more mentally.
> Let us why, let us why weight, let us why winter chess, let us why way.
> Only a moon to soup her, only that in the sell never never be the cocups nice be, shatter it they lay.
> Egg ear nuts, look a bout. Shoulder. Let it strange, sold in bell next herds.
> It was a time when in the acres in late there was a wheel that shot a burst of land and needless are niggers and a sample sample set of old eaten butterflies with spoons, all of it to be are fled and measure make it, make it, yet all the one in that we see where shall not it set with a left and more so, yes there add when the longer not it shall the best in the way when all be with when shall not for there with see and chest how for another excellent and excellent and easy easy excellent and easy express e c, all to be nice all to be no so. All to be no so no so. All to be not a white old chat churner. Not to be any example of an edible apple in. (55)

This poem begins with a clear polarity (noted earlier), between sun-mental and moon-her. But the second sentence interjects: "let us why way," let us question this arrangement or the orthodox way.[39] "Look a bout": look about, come to your senses, listen with your "Egg ear," eag-erly. When you do, you perceive alternative possibilities; so, the last paragraph goes on to reject the very polarization of sun-man and moon-woman. "All to be no so no so"— that is, it should all be not so. There should exist neither "a white old chat churner" (the sun-man, a bodiless being who produces chat) nor Eve, the "example of an edible apple in." The white old chat churner—perhaps in the sense of the patriarch or the male authority—in order to enjoy the illusion that he is pure mind, must project body onto woman, then degrade her, as Eve, although, like "jack" the killer, he still penetrates her sexually, churns her *chat* (by another French pun). But if it all were not so, if this situation were changed, autonomous reason could not sustain itself. Chatting and body would be united. There would cease to be a dirty, taboo region or a buried woman. The sacrifice of the female term would end.

I have not said anything about the very long middle sentence of the poem ("It was a time . . . "), which is an example of the word-play before which my interpretation halts. In the previous chapter, I suggested how I would analyze such material stylistically. Now, partly to suggest how I would go on speaking about this or any other poem in *Tender Buttons* once my thematic reading has exhausted itself, I wish to pause over the sentence.

I notice, among other things, a play with the written medium. The word "excellent" (whatever prompts it in the first place) initiates the string, "and excellent and easy easy excellent and easy express e c." Stein is thinking about the silent, superfluous characters in "excellent," which she spells "xcellent" in the manuscript.[40] One could also spell it "x-ellent" (she reflects) and convey one's meaning, omitting the initial *e* and the *c*. Yet rather than keep these characters silent, she then brings them out as "e c," and punningly turns them into "easy"—as if to suggest that the word "easy" is buried within "excellent," as its inessential, suppressed, and leftover signification. "Express e c," she writes; in other words, she

---

[39]In the *Selected Writings*, "way" is misprinted as "why."
[40]In YCAL. Stein's manuscripts often substitute *x* for the prefix *ex*.

will express the previously silent characters—an example of the ethics of the remainder as applied to the medium of the written word. On the other hand, I have just given myself the opportunity to connect all this to my thematic reading, for Stein's textual practice of revaluing the silenced letter is analogous to her intellectual practice of revaluing a silenced woman, an "edible apple." Yet there are many other parts of the sentence that I cannot connect to my interpretation at all—including the phrase "and needless are niggers," which anyone thinking about this poem must simply register as a fragment of bigotry with no context that would enable the reader to explain it (away).

"Mutton" is a poem that mends the mind-body split by way of a return to the crucifixion themes, this time in the context of the Eucharist. The poem reads in part (this time I elide a long middle section):

> MUTTON.
> A letter which can wither, a learning which can suffer and an outrage which is simultaneous is principal.
> Student, students are merciful and recognised they chew something.
> . . . A cake, a real salve made of mutton and liquor, a specially retained rinsing and an established cork and blazing, this which resignation influences and restrains, restrains more altogether. A sign is the specimen spoken.
> A meal in mutton, mutton, why is lamb cheaper, it is cheaper because so little is more. Lecture, lecture and repeat instruction. (39–41)

The cake, or salve "made of mutton and liquor," could be the Eucharist. (Mutton and liquor are versions of body and blood; and mutton is the appropriate meat, for Christ is the lamb.) The communion is given sacrificial overtones; the first sentence contains the words "suffer" and "an outrage." For the Eucharist in one of its aspects is a renewal or repetition of Christ's passion; a common synonym for the Eucharist is the Sacrifice.

In its role as sacrifice, the Eucharist is "a letter which can wither"; it is a term in the letter of the law that is fulfilled by Christ's death. The letter that withers is another version of the "book," or the "peeled pencil" that chokes; these lines are again about a sacrificial text that withers, or puts down the body. Hence, "a learning which can suffer."

But the second sentence takes the Eucharist beyond its purely sacrificial meaning. "Students are merciful and recognised they chew something." The first sentence depicted a principal, perhaps a school principal; he taught or enforced the sacrificial or suffering meaning of the Eucharist. Just so, at the end of the poem, there is the command, "Lecture, lecture and repeat instruction." But in the meantime his students—the communicants, perhaps—"are merciful and recognised they chew something." They know that they are eating food.

They know, that is, that they have mouths and physical desires. Like the Monk of Farne, to whom Christ tasted sweeter than honey, Stein's "students" fuse the spiritual with the bodily. Moreover, they are merciful, for they know they are chewing *something;* that is, they are eating a body but do not repress the fact. To the extent that they raise themselves above the body by sacrificing, they also, through communion, put that body back in their mouths, introject it, and remind themselves that they depend on the body and are themselves flesh. Stein suggests that whereas the "principal," culturally dominant meaning of the Eucharist has emphasized its sacrificial nature, the rite of communion is so structured as to enable the humble students—perhaps simply the laity—to experience an embodied spirituality.

The students are merciful: a word for the ethics of the remainder is *mercy.* In "Way Lay Vegetable," Stein writes, "Suppose it is ex [simply "x" in the manuscript][41] a cake suppose it is new mercy" (53). Again, while the crucifixion represents the moment of sacrifice, the ritual of communion, wherein we make a "cake" out of "x" or Christ, readmits the not-to-be-suppressed body. The reference to "a new mercy" alludes to the orthodox view of Christ as ushering in a new forgiveness (and in fact the phrase as a whole seems quite orthodox, if removed from the context of *Tender Buttons*); but the revisionary edge of the other poems, particularly those in which Stein challenges ideas of transcendence, leads me to

[41]In YCAL.

wonder whether the mercy she emphasizes is not that of the communicants themselves. In "Mutton," and perhaps also here in "Way Lay Vegetable," Stein uses the word *mercy* to suggest a few things: humility before matter; denial of the fiction of transcendence; and a kind of thinking that does not suppress the fact of the desiring body, which is always taking in and expelling bits of the material universe. Even while using symbolic language or enjoying our identities as social beings, we must always recognize that we "chew something."

Tender Buttons, with its anti-transcendental thinking, represents an intellectually dazzling revision of the struggle with the father(s) in *The Making of Americans* and *G.M.P.* In those works, Stein fashioned her own freedom by making "dead" her father, or the bourgeois fathers; yet she retained a sense of a paternal debt or alliance. Here, she envisions a new theological type that is both father and mother but really "neither neither," and that therefore involves dispelling the tradition of the purely male and disembodied "white old chat churner"—both God the Father, as conventionally understood, and the hoary human patriarchs who handed down a theology that devalued woman and matter. She sees more deeply now past the patriarchal foreground, defining herself not just against her father Daniel Stein, against the nineteenth-century fathers as in *The Making of Americans,* or against a linear-paternal discourse as in *G.M.P.* These are still her objects, but more profoundly she is assaulting the dualisms of the dominant strain in Western onto-theology.

The "king" who established his ascendancy in "Objects" is now dethroned; more than that, he is eaten, just as in "Objects" he himself munched women and matter. In a vengeful parody of communion, Stein thinks of eating the king:

> EATING.
>   Eat ting, eating a grand old man said roof and never never re soluble burst, not a near ring not a bewildered neck, not really any such bay.
>   Is it so a noise to be is it a least remain to rest, is it a so old say to be, is it a leading are been. Is it so, is it so, is it so, is it so is it so is it so.

Eel us eel us with no no pea no pea cool, no pea cool cooler, no pea cooler with a land a land cost in, with a land cost in stretches. (56)

I mentioned this poem earlier, in connection with the association of the sun with maleness; it appears toward the end of "Food." Stein writes of "eating a grand old man"—this, within a page of her reference to God the "white old chat churner." The man could be taken as the subject of the verb "said," in which case the meaning would be, "While eating, a grand old man said, 'roof. . . .'" But especially in context, the sentence suggests just as strongly that someone else is "eating a grand old man."

I interpret the sentence as follows: "Eat ting [eat the king?], eating a grand old man said roof": someone is eating the grand old man, the "said roof" or "aforementioned heavenly person," perhaps the same sun who, two poems earlier, "sat in shed more mentally." "Never never" is like the no that Stein has elsewhere issued to the father; and here, the no reappears: "Eel us eel us with no no pea no pea cool." "Eel us with no" is another version of the hermetic imperative: "with no" to the orthodox wisdom, let us "eel us," or snake ourselves, becoming wise like the serpent who was originally our ally against paternal dominion. (Hence, "no pea cooler": our "no" is deviant, pe-culiar.) Perhaps Stein is also du-plicating the idea one finds in some branches of historical gnosti-cism, that the snake was our benign tutor who was then dis-credited by the patriarchs as evil—a view echoed by Stanton's *Woman Bible:* "[The tempter] roused in the woman that intense thirst for knowledge, that the simple pleasures of picking flowers and talking with Adam did not satisfy"; "It was a serpent super-naturally endowed, a seraphim . . . who talked with Eve" (25, 26). Along with the eel or snake, Stein has another ally, "eel-us," Alice. As in *The Making of Americans* and *G.M.P.*, at the moment when she deposes the "grand old man" it is important to have her friend beside her.

The last sentence of this poem is, "George is a mass" (56). George—the generic guy, like "jack," the murderer in "Objects"— is consumed, in a mock communion. The words "re soluble burst," in the first line, punningly tell the whole story: the ray-sol-sunburst is in fact soluble, through a subversive intellectual alchemy; we can make him burst. This fantasy is aggressively anti-paternal, although the deity whom Stein is assaulting seems a sham God, a male projection, whom she elsewhere replaces with a "neither neither" being of mixed gender (or rather de-essentializes altogether, replacing a male *or* female "being" with a process).

In *Tender Buttons,* Stein's contest with the fathers has taken her in a new direction. Now for the first time, she feels free to enter into dialogue with another text, the Bible, and thereby with a dominant strain in the Western cultural tradition. In *The Making of Americans,* she dissolves the nineteenth-century novel in the acid bath of her unconscious; here, she becomes what Harold Bloom calls a strong poet, not dissolving but correcting the text she inherits, turning it alchemically into something better. With Bloom's strong poets, Stein thinks of her intellectual-spiritual process as a swerve—a "left hop" (55), a "bent way" (43).[42]

In "Cream," she writes of the necessity of making an "eddy," a deviation from the current:

> CREAM.
> In a plank, in a play sole, in a heated red left tree there is shut in specs with salt be where. This makes an eddy. Necessary. (54)

Hidden inside a piece of wood—"in a plank," "in a . . . tree"— "there is shut in specs." Maybe the wood is the cross once again, and the "sole" the fish, or Christ. In that case, the cross and the body on it again contain "shut in specs"—a concealed, spec-ulative meaning, or a pair of hermetic spectacles we might learn to use. The tree is "heated red left"—a phrase that points in many directions at once. The "heated . . . tree" sounds like another instance of the "boiling tree" or baking "pole splinter," the disembodied phallus. Yet that interpretation cuts against some of the meanings of "red": in "Vegetable," the cross, with its "little ins and *red*," was coming alive again (53). The "heated red" tree, then, suggests both the phallus and its antithesis, the wood reviving, turning red with

[42]For Bloom's definition of the *clinamen,* or swerve, see *The Anxiety of Influence: A Theory of Poetry* (New York: Oxford University Press, 1973), p. 14.

a living warmth. It is, at the same time, "left": the tree is the remainder, the thing left behind after the crucifixion. (The father-son-cross triad deforms what was once a father-son-mother triad? The mother is still "left" there, in the tree, for us to find with our "specs"?)

The concealment of the wisdom inside the tree (preserved, per-haps, "with salt") makes "an eddy" necessary. In order to get back the full meaning of the symbol, we must deviate from the current of orthodoxy. Hence the tree is a "left tree" also in the sense of containing a swerving, left-leaning knowledge. As we make our eddy, Stein warns, "be where": beware of the explosive secrets you are about to uncover; or beware of the patriarchs, and make sure to eddy out of their sight.

Stein eddies out of our sight much of the time, half concealing her own powerful insights. A belief that underlies the readings in this chapter is that Stein's text itself contains a wisdom, which she provokes us to try to decipher. When she writes "I spy," she makes us want to see what she sees. She writes in the same place, "pit on in within," which sounds like an invitation to keep searching for the pit within, the hidden kernel in the text (52).

I have been thinking of *Tender Buttons* in terms both of a psycho-analytic-linguistic vocabulary of recovered *jouissance* and of a her-metic vocabulary of recovered wisdom. Stein's own thinking ran in both directions: she sounds rather like Julia Kristeva at one moment and like Mary Daly at another. But the two vocabularies compete with each other. An opaque sentence, viewed from a Kristevan perspective, is a piece of music or primary process that lets drive back into the linguistic surface; such a sentence is an experience for the reader, not primarily a communication. But from a hermetic perspective, the same sentence is a message to be deciphered.

The debate about whether or not it is acceptable to call Stein's writing coded has raged for some time, and will be with us as long as readers apply themselves to these texts. Some critics have iden-tified discursive meanings, but others have pointed to the impor-tance of Stein's stylistic experiment, which unsettles the monologic understanding of language wherein each sign has one (latent or manifest) meaning assigned to it. The two axes of language that these different critical perspectives emphasize are opposed. Yet I am certain that Stein wanted to give her reader both kinds of pleasure—both the release that comes from hearing words become mobile and the sense of power that comes from "spying" along with her and sharing her secrets. If *Tender Buttons* is Stein's most powerful work, that is because it activates multiple powers in us.

Conclusion:
Modernism and Sacrifice

This book has traced the series of intellectual leaps—or unmoorings—by which Gertrude Stein evolved into one of the most original authors of this century. As she transformed *Q.E.D.* into "Melanctha," Stein created an ethical polyphony where before there had been a rigid attachment to bourgeois values. She allowed her sympathies to divide themselves between Jeff Campbell, whose original in *Q.E.D.* had been a character based on herself, and the "wandering" Melanctha, the character who in a previous incarnation in *Q.E.D.* had stood for everything threatening to social stability and moral coherence. Melanctha transgresses her father's rules and lives at the margins socially; yet she knows things that Jeff Campbell, the fine middle-class doctor, needs to learn. At the same time, Stein experimented in this story with a wandering style that duplicated within language the heroine's disturbance of Jeff Campbell's orthodoxy.

But at this stage Stein could not shake off the thought that to wander outside a father's orbit is to court disaster. Her heroine dies transgressing. In *The Making of Americans,* Stein slowly reoriented herself, finally risking a break with all paternal authority. In that novel, she found a way to put to rest the inhibiting specter of her own father, and began to imagine herself comfortably exploring the cultural margins, accompanied by a particular "some one" who accepted her and her "crazy" book (485). Correspondingly, she developed an experimental style based on a primitive, normally repressed dimension of consciousness called loving repeating, so

253

that her linear plot virtually succumbed to the erotic movement at its own margins. Formally as well as socially, she was breaking out of the linear and paternally identified story she had initially thought she had to tell about herself, which had run: "We need only realise our parents, remember our grandparents and know ourselves and our history is complete" (3). It is as if a new version of Melanctha's "wandering" had been turned against the paternal regulations that had earlier made transgression, of any sort, tantamount to death.

I hope I have also shown that Stein's private risk-taking was inseparable from her aesthetic daring. Stein, writing *The Making of Americans* in 1908–1911, had no *Ulysses* for a precedent. Her experiment with the play of irrational process in narrative was much bolder in 1911 than it would have been in the twenties or thirties; it amounts to a discovery. More than that, her novel contains a uniquely theoretical series of reflections on its own process. Stein uncovers a drive-to-repeat that she sees as an essential, if normally repressed, aspect of people's experience of language. Her thoughts about the hidden erotic dimension of everyday life parallel Freud's theories in the same generation, while they illuminate the aspect of pleasure in language in such a way as to anticipate more recent, post-Freudian theories of textual "pleasure," such as those of Roland Barthes and Julia Kristeva.

In *G.M.P.*, a year after *The Making of Americans*, Stein pictured herself as escaping from the "fathers" into a zone of specifically female resistance and bonding. Again one can think retrospectively about "Melanctha" and notice there what seems a preliminary and muffled allusion to alternative possibilities, in the heroine's special closeness to women at such critical moments in their embodied lives as parturition and death. But whereas in that story the heroine's bonds with women are alternately deformed and shattered by male presences, Stein later envisions a zone of female privacy that daughters in flight from the father can inhabit together. She is able to imagine female ties that are immune to male interruption. Once again, it is as if a scene of defeat at the margins of "Melanctha" were reversed—almost as if Rose Johnson were to stay in Melanctha's house after giving birth there, or as if Jane Harden, the dissipated lesbian whom Melanctha leaves behind in the course of her heterosexual journey, were to be reimagined as a solid friend positioned at the end of the journey.

I see a connection between Stein's rejection, in texts like *G.M.P.*, of the conventional heterosexual plot and her abandonment of prose narrative altogether (and of any other recognizable genre). In other words, her emotional experiment in this period led to—or in fact followed from—an artistic experiment that propelled her even farther past her contemporaries than *The Making of Americans* had. The only text before the Second World War that seems to proceed from a similar faith in the richness of "raw" consciousness is *Finnegans Wake*, some twenty years later.

At the same time, *G.M.P.* turns what in *The Making of Americans* had been an assault on the figure of the bourgeois patriarch into a more searching critique of patriarchal thinking. Stein here sees herself as revaluing everything that patriarchal categories devalue: woman, matter, and the matter-within-language, or the "left over bundles" of presymbolic pleasure (276). Her new style amounts to an unsettling of everything patriarchal hierarchies seem to fix in place. Because she is violating the intellectual rules, her image of what she is about as an artist is not just erotic, as it was when she spoke in *The Making of Americans* in terms of loving repeating, but "outrageous" (278). If patriarchy is itself an outrage, it cannot be dismantled or even seriously questioned without a comparable violence to our ordinary forms of thought.

Thus what I have called modernism at some moments in this book, I have called feminism at others. Experimental modernism, by exploring the pleasures of the material word, challenges the polarity of mind and matter that traditionally has devalued women, and thus can prepare the way for a feminist insight. But again, with the possible exception of Joyce, who in *Ulysses* reflects on the irruption of his own experimental language with the extraordinary sentence "Digs up near the Mater,"[1] no other modernist thought as

[1]James Joyce, *Ulysses* (New York: Modern Library, 1934), p. 425. The most obvious meaning of the sentence is "House up near the Mater Misericordiae Hospital," a reference to where the Blooms live; but this heavily punning sentence also points to the recurring motif in *Ulysses* of the buried and dug-up mother, this time at the moment in the "Oxen of the Sun" chapter when English prose, having gone through its various literary-historical permutations, breaks into a modern(ist) fragmentation.

deeply as Stein did about the implications of formal experimentation for a new intellectual orientation that might recover a lost, and
somehow feminine, aspect of language or experience.

What makes *Tender Buttons* different from these others is the
further questioning that enables Stein to "spy" into the sacrificial
origins of patriarchal culture. I have described *Tender Buttons* as an
experiment in countersacrificial thinking. What I want to reflect on
now is the prescience of that experiment. *Tender Buttons*, which
exposes the sacrificial enterprise of male culture and envisions a
means of subversion, anticipates an important strand of later
modernism.

Tender Buttons was one of the first imaginative works to echo (or
independently to duplicate) an anthropological insight that received various theoretical articulations in the early modern period,
namely, that cultures ground themselves through acts of ritual
killing. In 1898, Henri Hubert and Marcel Mauss published their
seminal "Essai sur la nature et la fonction du sacrifice," which
described sacrifice as the essential rite in certain ancient religions,
the rite by which groups grounded themselves in the divine. In
1913 (a year after Stein composed *Tender Buttons*), Freud proposed
in *Totem and Taboo* that the act initiating social organization and
moral constraints was the murder of a father by a band of brothers,
who later commemorated their crime by ritually sacrificing totem
animals.[2] And as early as 1887, Nietzsche had posited (differently)
that the fear-inducing spectacle of "blood, torture, and sacrifices"
was the original means by which groups "burned" social imperatives into their minds:

> Man could never do without blood, torture, and sacrifices when he
> felt the need to create a memory for himself; the most dreadful sacri-
> fices and pledges (sacrifices of the first-born among them), the most
> repulsive mutilations (castration, for example), the cruelest rites of all
> the religious cults (and all religions are at the deepest level systems of
> cruelties)—all this has its origin in the instinct that realized that pain
> is the most powerful aid to mnemonics.[3]

[2]Freud, *Totem and Taboo: Some Points of Agreement between the Mental Lives of Savages
and Neurotics, SE* 13:1–162.

[3]Friedrich Nietzsche, *On the Genealogy of Morals*, ed. Walter Kaufmann, trans.
Walter Kaufmann and R. J. Hollingdale (New York: Random House, 1967), p. 61,
hereafter cited in the text.

Nor, according to Nietzsche, is humanity at its present stage of civilization removed from the machinery of sacrifice, which has simply been internalized: "Might one not add that, fundamentally, this world has never since lost a certain odor of blood and torture? (Not even good old Kant: the categorical imperative smells of cruelty.)" (65).

Nietzsche denaturalizes such concepts as the "soul" and "reason," claiming that these entities, far from being autonomous of our animal or instinctual natures, are by-products of a sort of internal torture that deforms the instinctual self: "Ah, reason, seriousness, mastery over the affects, the whole somber thing called reflection, all these prerogatives and showpieces of man: how dearly they have been bought! how much blood and cruelty lie at the bottom of all 'good things'!" (62).

In *Tender Buttons*, Gertrude Stein experiments with a similar vision of the slanting-up of reason from a crucifixion and a "scream." "It was a cress a crescent a cross and an unequal scream, it was upslanting, it was radiant and reasonable" (53). Time and again, *Tender Buttons* sees through the opposition of the rational and the material, showing that the supposedly higher faculties are projections caused by the murder of a body. Where there is reason, as "Roastbeef" shows, there is also a buried corpse.

This notion—that sacrifice supports a mind-body dualism—itself contains the kernel of a feminist idea. For there is a sense in which woman is the term that sacrifice buries (whatever the gender of the sacrificial victim). The reason-body opposition created by sacrifice characteristically identifies the higher functions as male and the merely physical as female. Although Nietzsche, who is no feminist, does not think about the gendered quality of sacrificial thinking, Freud comes close to identifying the implications of sacrificial ritual for gender hierarchy. He sees the totemic sacrifice as cementing the pact of a band of brothers, whose sisters and mothers are not agents but objects of the pact, simply bodies that the brothers agree to renounce sexually as the cost of their peaceful social organization.[4] On the other hand, this arrangement seems perfectly natural and acceptable to Freud. He conceives of culture as an agreement among men and does not expend thought on

[4]See *Totem and Taboo*, SE 13:143–44.

women's highly ambiguous role as simultaneously members and objects of the social group he describes.

Stein not only denaturalizes the sacrificial dualism but also exposes its gendered quality, as some feminists in our own era—notably Nancy Jay and Mary Daly—have done. The killing that keeps repeating itself in *Tender Buttons* prompts the "upslanting" of a phallic pillar over such feminine terms as a "chicken," a "chest," or simply a "her" (38, 28, 29). Hence, Stein in some sense perceived the way in which sacrificial ritual can interact with forms of social oppression, as the theorists of sacrifice in her own day did not. I think she has this in common with certain other important modern novelists and poets.

Freud, Nietzsche, and Hubert and Mauss wrote for generations for whom the notion of culture as anchored in anything transcendent was seriously threatened. Their works speculate about the means by which cultures give themselves the illusion of a transcendent ground. Each of their theories contains an account of how sacrifice "creates" the divinity who will then authorize the group. The modern novelists and poets inherited the intellectual universe these theorists helped to create, and some began to think in similar terms about the sacrificial origins of culture. But they saw the absence of a cultural ground as a stimulus for emancipatory thinking. Sacrifice, for some modernists—besides Gertrude Stein, I think of Woolf, Faulkner, Joyce, H.D., and Lawrence—is not just a peculiar fact of human social existence but a dangerous fact, for a group that thinks of its social arrangements as divinely authorized immunizes itself to critique. And conversely, these authors believe that in order seriously to challenge existing social formations one must expose their sacrificial underpinnings.

Hence Woolf, in *The Waves*, shows how a communion mythology is used by a group (the six main characters, but also British imperialist culture) to support its exploitation of India and, at home, its enforcement of rigidly defined gender roles. *Ulysses* shows how the mentality of ritual scapegoating operates in the practice of anti-Semitism. Faulkner's *Light in August* exposes (yet not knowingly enough to avoid replicating) the sacrificial script supporting southern American racism, a script that factitiously turns blacks into "crosses" upon which whites are crucified. H.D., in *Trilogy*, associates the myth of crucifixion with a culture—the West in mid–twentieth century—that values militarism over what she perceives as a feminine life principle. D. H. Lawrence, in "The Man Who Died," similarly associates crucifixion with a devaluation of the feminine, although his sexism leaks back into his text as he elaborates just what the feminine "is."

If one shows how a particular ethos sacrificially makes itself, one can then start to imagine its unmaking. While social scientists in the early modern period were speculating that cultures constitute themselves through acts of sacrifice, their near contemporaries in the literary arts used this idea not only for critique but also for utopian gestures toward some sort of post-sacrificial existence. A subject for a different book would be the often self-critical and self-dismantling nature of these gestures.

This is all to suggest that *Tender Buttons*, both in its understanding of patriarchal relations as dependent on sacrifice and in its exploration of post-sacrificial forms of thought, represents a very early instance of what would become an important intellectual strand within modernism. Still, I wish to distinguish *Tender Buttons* from these later texts, because of its early appearance and because of its uniquely radical linguistic experiment. H.D., or Lawrence, may imagine looking behind the cross to recover (or "un-freeze")[5] a lost goddess, but they do not uncook language in quite the way Stein does.

In the present era, we are still living in the intellectual universe of the modernists, in which Cartesian dualisms are an object at once of attention and of skepticism. I hope I have suggested in the foregoing chapters that the breakdown of dualisms need not involve the breakdown of ethical meanings. Gertrude Stein, like some of her contemporaries, attempted a post-sacrificial thinking that denaturalizes various patriarchal dualisms. Yet I believe that her great experiment in countersacrificial thinking, *Tender Buttons*, orients us ethically, rather than disorients us in the play of language. Perhaps the experiments of the major modernists can offer us models for a theoretical language that avoids oppressive dualisms while leaving us a vocabulary for moral, political, and spiritual insight.

[5]See H.D., *Trilogy*, in *Collected Poems*, pp. 561, 559.

Bibliography

Abel, Elizabeth, ed. *Writing and Sexual Difference*. Chicago: University of Chicago Press, 1982.

Abraham, Karl. *Selected Papers on Psycho-Analysis*. Trans. Douglas Bryan and Alix Strachey. London: Hogarth Press, 1948.

Barthes, Roland. *The Pleasure of the Text*. Trans. Richard Miller. New York: Farrar, Straus, and Giroux, 1975.

Benstock, Shari. *Women of the Left Bank: Paris, 1900–1940*. Austin: University of Texas Press, 1986.

Blankley, Elyse. "Return to Mytilène: Renée Vivien and the City of Women." In *Women Writers and the City: Essays in Feminist Literary Criticism*. Ed. Susan Merrill Squier. Knoxville: University of Tennessee Press, 1984, pp. 45–67.

Bloom, Harold. *The Anxiety of Influence: A Theory of Poetry*. New York: Oxford University Press, 1973.

Bloom, Lynn Z. "Gertrude Is Alice Is Everybody: Innovation and Point of View in Gertrude Stein's Autobiographies." *Twentieth-Century Literature* 24 (1978): 81–93.

Boswell, John. *Christianity, Social Tolerance, and Homosexuality: Gay People in Western Europe from the Beginning of the Christian Era to the Fourteenth Century*. Chicago: University of Chicago Press, 1980.

Bridgman, Richard. *Gertrude Stein in Pieces*. New York: Oxford University Press, 1970.

Bynum, Caroline. *Jesus as Mother: Studies in the Spirituality of the High Middle Ages*. Berkeley: University of California Press, 1982.

Chasseguet-Smirgel, Janine. "Perversion and the Universal Law." *International Review of Psycho-Analysis* 10 (1983): 293–301.

Chessman, Harriet. *The Public Is Invited to Dance: Representation, the Body, and Dialogue in Gertrude Stein*. Stanford: Stanford University Press, 1989.

Cixous, Hélène, and Catherine Clément. *The Newly Born Woman*. Trans.

Betsy Wing. Theory and History of Literature Series, 4. Minneapolis: University of Minnesota Press, 1986.

Conley, Verena Andermatt. *Hélène Cixous: Writing the Feminine*. Lincoln: University of Nebraska Press, 1984.

Daly, Mary. *Gyn/Ecology: The Metaethics of Radical Feminism*. Boston: Beacon Press, 1978.

DeKoven, Marianne. *A Different Language: Gertrude Stein's Experimental Writing*. Madison: University of Wisconsin Press, 1983.

Deutsch, Helene. "On Female Homosexuality." *Psychoanalytic Quarterly* 1 (1932): 484–510.

Dubnick, Randa. *The Structure of Obscurity: Gertrude Stein, Language, and Cubism*. Urbana: University of Illinois Press, 1984.

Dydo, Ulla E. "Must Horses Drink; or, 'Any Language Is Funny if You Don't Understand It.' " *Tulsa Studies in Women's Literature* 4 (1985): 272–80.

Fifer, Elizabeth. "Is Flesh Advisable? The Interior Theater of Gertrude Stein." *Signs* 4 (1979): 472–83.

Freud, Sigmund. *Sexuality and the Psychology of Love*. Ed. Philip Rieff. New York: Macmillan, 1963.

——. *Standard Edition of the Complete Psychological Works of Sigmund Freud*. Ed. James Strachey. London: Hogarth Press, 1953–74.

——. *Totem and Taboo: Some Points of Agreement between the Mental Lives of Savages and Neurotics*. Trans. James Strachey. New York: Norton, 1950.

Gallup, Donald, ed. *The Flowers of Friendship: Letters Written to Gertrude Stein*. New York: Knopf, 1953.

Gilbert, Sandra M., and Susan Gubar. *The Madwoman in the Attic: The Woman Writer and the Nineteenth-Century Literary Imagination*. New Haven: Yale University Press, 1979.

H.D. *Trilogy. Collected Poems, 1912–1944*. Ed. Louis L. Martz. New York: New Directions, 1944, 505–612.

Haas, Robert Bartlett, ed. *A Primer for the Gradual Understanding of Gertrude Stein*. Los Angeles: Black Sparrow Press, 1971.

Hadas, Pamela. "Spreading the Difference: One Way to Read Gertrude Stein's *Tender Buttons*." *Twentieth-Century Literature* 24 (1978): 57–75.

Hill, Mary A. *Charlotte Perkins Gilman: The Making of a Radical Feminist, 1860–1896*. Philadelphia: Temple University Press, 1980.

Hoffman, Michael J. *The Development of Abstractionism in the Writings of Gertrude Stein*. Philadelphia: University of Pennsylvania Press, 1965.

——. "Gertrude Stein and William James." *Personalist* 47 (1966): 226–33.

——, ed. *Critical Essays on Gertrude Stein*. Boston: G. K. Hall, 1986.

Irigaray, Luce. *Speculum of the Other Woman*. Trans. Gillian C. Gill. Ithaca: Cornell University Press, 1985.

Irwin, John. *Doubling and Incest/Repetition and Revenge: A Speculative Reading of Faulkner*. Baltimore: Johns Hopkins University Press, 1975.

James, William. *Essays in Philosophy*. In *Works of William James*. Ed. Frederick

Burkhardt, Fredson Bowers, and Ignas Skrupskelis. Cambridge: Harvard University Press, 1978.

——. *The Letters of William James*. Ed. Henry James. 2 vols. Boston: Atlantic Monthly Press, 1920.

——. *Psychology: The Briefer Course*. Ed. Gordon Allport. New York: Harper and Row, 1961.

——. *A William James Reader*. ed. Gay Wilson Allen. Boston: Houghton Mifflin, 1971.

Jay, Nancy. "Sacrifice as Remedy for Having Been Born of Woman." In *Immaculate and Powerful: The Female in Sacred Image and Social Reality*. Ed. Clarissa W. Atkinson, Constance H. Buchanan, and Margaret R. Miles. Harvard Women's Studies in Religion. Boston: Beacon Press, 1985, 283–309.

Joyce, James. *Ulysses*. New York: Modern Library, 1934.

Julian of Norwich. *Revelations of Divine Love*. Trans. Clifton Wolters. New York: Penguin, 1966.

Katz, Leon. "The First Making of *The Making of Americans*," Ph.D. diss. Columbia University, 1963.

Kristeva, Julia. *Desire in Language: A Semiotic Approach to Literature and Art*. Ed. Leon S. Roudiez. Trans. Thomas Gora, Alice Jardine, and Leon S. Roudiez. New York: Columbia University Press, 1980.

——. *Revolution in Poetic Language*. Trans. Margaret Waller. New York: Columbia University Press, 1984.

Levinson, Ronald. "Gertrude Stein, William James, and Grammar." *American Journal of Psychology* 54 (1941): 124–28.

Marcus, Jane, ed. *New Feminist Essays on Virginia Woolf*. Lincoln: University of Nebraska Press, 1981.

Mellow, James R. *Charmed Circle: Gertrude Stein and Company*. New York: Avon, 1974.

Miller, Rosalind S. *Gertrude Stein: Form and Intelligibility*. New York: Exposition Press, 1949.

Nietzsche, Friedrich. *On the Genealogy of Morals*. Ed. Walter Kaufmann. Trans. Walter Kaufmann and R. J. Hollingdale. New York: Random House, 1967.

Noy, Pinchas. "A Revision of the Psychoanalytic Theory of the Primary Process." *International Journal of Psycho-Analysis* 50 (1969): 155–78.

Ortner, Sherry. "Is Female to Male as Nature Is to Culture?" In *Woman, Culture, and Society*. Ed. Michelle Zimbalist Rosaldo and Louise Lamphere. Stanford: Stanford University Press, 1974.

Pagels, Elaine. *The Gnostic Gospels*. New York: Random House, 1979.

Peller, Lili E. "Comments on Libidinal Organizations and Child Development." *Journal of the American Psychoanalytic Association* 13 (1965): 732–47.

Perloff, Marjorie. *The Poetics of Indeterminacy*. Princeton: Princeton University Press, 1981.

Perry, Ralph Barton. *In the Spirit of William James*. New Haven: Yale University Press, 1938.

————. *The Thought and Character of William James.* 2 vols. Boston: Little, Brown, 1935.

Porte, Joel. "Gertrude Stein and the Rhythms of Life." *New Boston Review* 1 (June 1975): 16–18.

Rich, Adrienne. *The Dream of a Common Language: Poems 1974–1977.* New York: Norton, 1978.

Rubin, Gayle. "The Traffic in Women: Notes on the 'Political Economy' of Sex." In *Toward an Anthropology of Women.* Ed. Rayna R. Reiter. New York: Monthly Review Press, 1975, pp. 157–210.

Schmitz, Neil. *Of Huck and Alice: Humorous Writing in American Literature.* Minneapolis: University of Minnesota Press, 1983.

Shengold, Leonard. "Defensive Anality and Anal Narcissism." *International Journal of Psycho-Analysis* 66 (1985): 47–73.

Shiff, Richard. "Seeing Cézanne." *Critical Inquiry* 4 (1978): 769–808.

Simon, Linda, ed. *Gertrude Stein: A Composite Portrait.* New York: Avon, 1974.

Stein, Gertrude. *The Autobiography of Alice B. Toklas.* New York: Harcourt, Brace, 1933.

————. *Everybody's Autobiography.* New York: Random House, 1937.

————. *Fernhurst, Q.E.D., and Other Early Writings by Gertrude Stein.* New York: Liveright, 1971.

————. *The Geographical History of America.* New York: Random House, 1936.

————. *Geography and Plays.* Boston: Four Seas, 1922.

————. *Last Operas and Plays.* Ed. Carl Van Vechten. New York: Rinehart, 1949.

————. *Lectures in America.* New York: Random House, 1935.

————. *The Making of Americans: Being a History of a Family's Progress.* Paris: Contact Editions, 1925.

————. *Matisse Picasso and Gertrude Stein with Two Shorter Stories.* Barton, Vt.: Something Else Press, 1972.

————. *Operas and Plays.* Paris: Plain Edition, 1932.

————. *Selected Writings of Gertrude Stein.* Ed. Carl Van Vechten. New York: Random House, 1945.

————. *Tender Buttons.* New York: Claire Marie, 1914.

————. *Three Lives.* New York: Random House, 1936.

————. *Two: Gertrude Stein and Her Brother and Other Early Portraits (1908–12).* Yale Edition of the Unpublished Writings of Gertrude Stein. New Haven: Yale University Press, 1951.

————. *Wars I Have Seen.* New York: Random House, 1945.

————. *The Yale Gertrude Stein.* Selections with introduction by Richard Kostelanetz. New Haven: Yale University Press, 1980.

Stein, Leo. *Journey into the Self: Being the Letters, Papers and Journals of Leo Stein.* Ed. Edmund Fuller. New York: Crown, 1950.

Steiner, Wendy. *Exact Resemblance to Exact Resemblance: The Literary Portraiture of Gertrude Stein.* New Haven: Yale University Press, 1978.

Stewart, Allegra. *Gertrude Stein and the Present.* Cambridge: Harvard University Press, 1967.

Stimpson, Catharine R. "Gertrice/Altrude: Stein, Toklas, and the Paradox of the Happy Marriage." In *Mothering the Mind: Twelve Studies of Writers and Their Silent Partners.* Ed. Ruth Perry and Martine Watson Brownley. New York: Holmes and Meier, 1984, pp. 122–39.

_____. "Gertrude Stein and the Transposition of Gender." In *The Poetics of Gender.* Ed. Nancy K. Miller. New York: Columbia University Press, 1986, pp. 1–18.

_____. "The Mind, the Body, and Gertrude Stein." *Critical Inquiry* 3 (1977): 489–506.

Toklas, Alice. *What Is Remembered.* San Francisco: North Point Press, 1985.

Walker, Jayne. *The Making of a Modernist: Gertrude Stein from "Three Lives" to "Tender Buttons."* Amherst: University of Massachusetts Press, 1984.

Wittgenstein, Ludwig. *The Blue and Brown Books.* New York: Harper and Row, 1958.

Woolf, Virginia. *To the Lighthouse.* New York: Harcourt, Brace, and World, 1927.

_____. *A Writer's Diary.* Ed. Leonard Woolf. London: Hogarth Press, 1969.

Wright, Doris. "Woman as Eros-Rose in Gertrude Stein's *Tender Buttons* and Contemporaneous Portraits." *Transactions of the Wisconsin Academy of Sciences, Arts, and Letters* 74 (1986): 34–40.

Index

Library of Congress Cataloging-in-Publication Data

Ruddick, Lisa Cole, 1954–
    Reading Gertrude Stein : body, text, gnosis / Lisa Ruddick.
        p.   cm. — (Reading women writing)
    Includes bibliographical references (p.).
    ISBN 0-8014-2364-3 (alk. paper)
    1. Stein, Gertrude, 1874–1946—Criticism and interpretation.
I. Title.   II. Series.
PS3537.T323Z8213   1990
818'.5209—dc20

89-46133